KAGEKI SHOJO!!

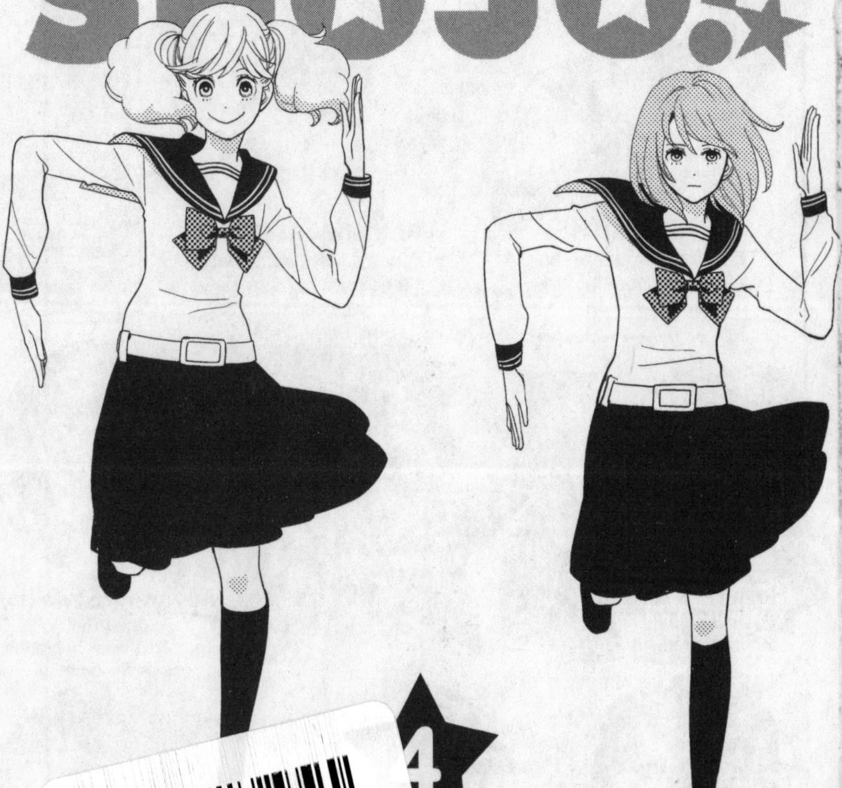

4

story & art by

Kumiko Saiki

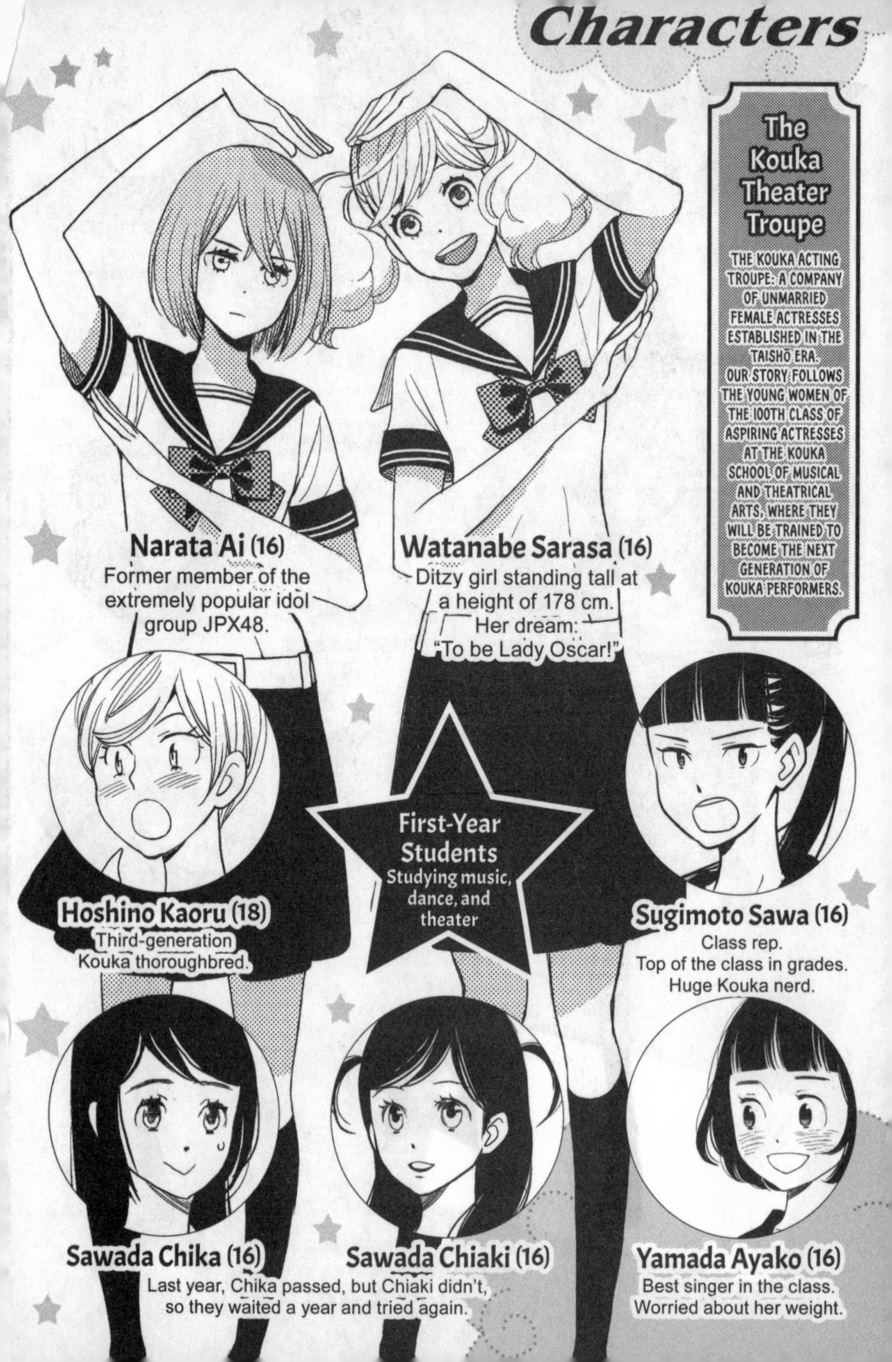

Characters
The Kouka Theater Troupe
THE KOUKA ACTING TROUPE: A COMPANY OF UNMARRIED FEMALE ACTRESSES ESTABLISHED IN THE TAISHO ERA. OUR STORY FOLLOWS THE YOUNG WOMEN OF THE 100TH CLASS OF ASPIRING ACTRESSES AT THE KOUKA SCHOOL OF MUSICAL AND THEATRICAL ARTS, WHERE THEY WILL BE TRAINED TO BECOME THE NEXT GENERATION OF KOUKA PERFORMERS.
Watanabe Sarasa (16)
Ditzy girl standing tall at a height of 178 cm. Her dream: "To be Lady Oscar!"
Narata Ai (16)
Former member of the extremely popular idol group JPX48.
First-Year Students
Studying music, dance, and theater
Sugimoto Sawa (16)
Class rep. Top of the class in grades. Huge Kouka nerd.
Hoshino Kaoru (18)
Third-generation Kouka thoroughbred.
Yamada Ayako (16)
Best singer in the class. Worried about her weight.
Sawada Chiaki (16)
Sawada Chika (16)
Last year, Chika passed, but Chiaki didn't, so they waited a year and tried again.

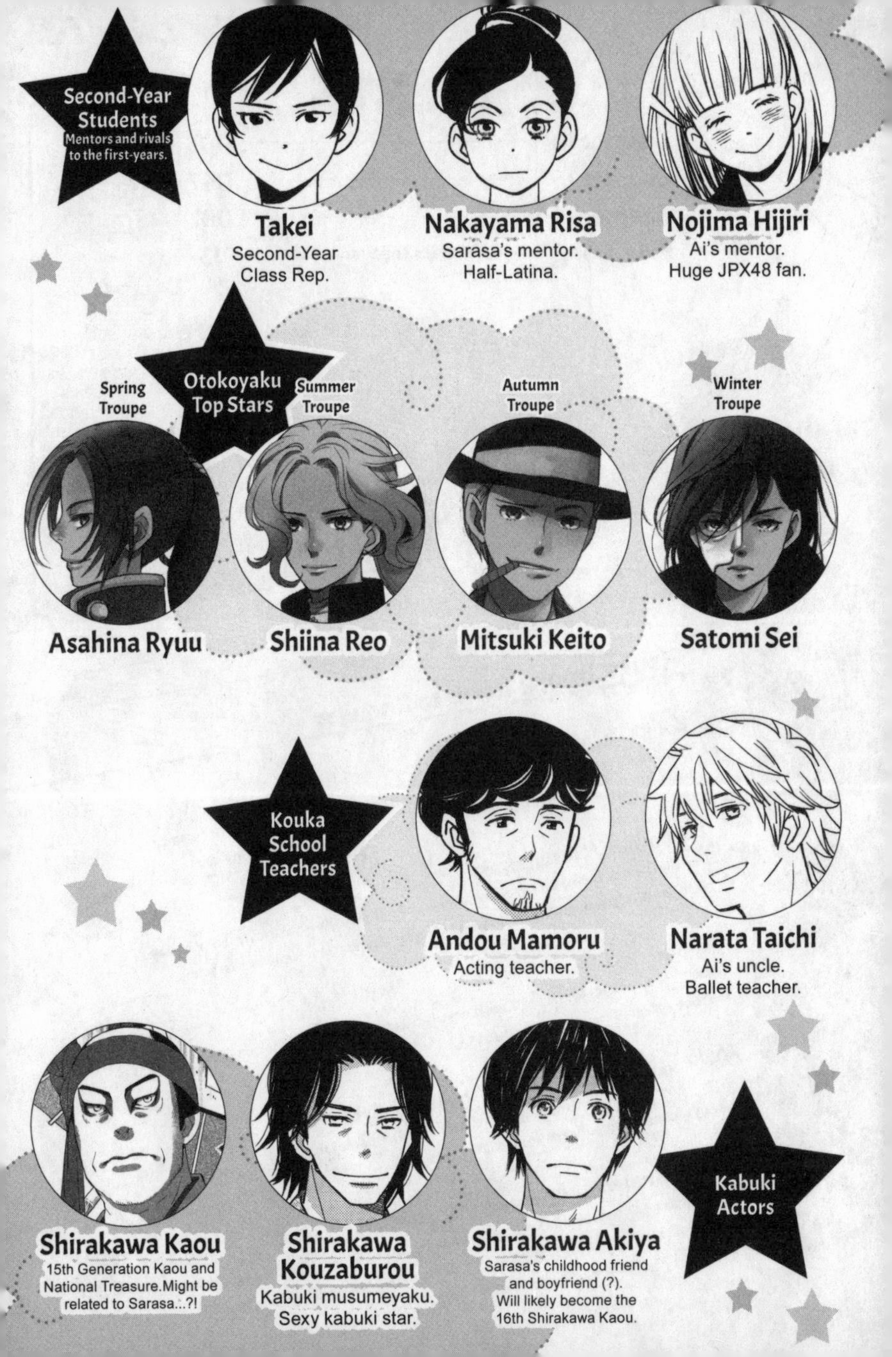
Second-Year Students
Mentors and rivals to the first-years.
Takei
Second-Year Class Rep.
Nakayama Risa
Sarasa's mentor. Half-Latina.
Nojima Hijiri
Ai's mentor. Huge JPX48 fan.
Otokoyaku Top Stars
Spring Troupe
Asahina Ryuu
Summer Troupe
Shiina Reo
Autumn Troupe
Mitsuki Keito
Winter Troupe
Satomi Sei
Kouka School Teachers
Andou Mamoru
Acting teacher.
Narata Taichi
Ai's uncle. Ballet teacher.
Kabuki Actors
Shirakawa Kaou
15th Generation Kaou and National Treasure.Might be related to Sarasa...?!
Shirakawa Kouzaburou
Kabuki musumeyaku. Sexy kabuki star.
Shirakawa Akiya
Sarasa's childhood friend and boyfriend (?). Will likely become the 16th Shirakawa Kaou.

CONTENTS

No.

Date

Kouka Troupe Terms to Know! ★

Kouka Theater Troupe
Founded a hundred years ago as a theater troupe comprised of young, unmarried women.
Split into four troupes (Spring/Summer/Autumn/Winter). Main theater is in Kobe.

Otokoyaku / Musumeyaku
Designated roles for the gender of characters actresses play. Otokoyaku actresses play male or
masculine characters, while musumeyaku actresses play female or feminine characters.

Top Star
The actress who heads her troupe. Each troupe has an otokoyaku top star and musumeyaku top star.
Top stars appear in every major production.

Kouka School of Musical and Theatrical Arts
Two-year prep school where the next stars of the Kouka Troupe are forged.
Girls can apply anytime between 9th and 12th grade!

First-Year Students vs. Second-Year Students
While first-year students primarily focus on their studies, second-year students are tasked both
with their studies and mentoring the first-year students, as well as managing their cleaning
schedule and helping them with lifestyle adjustments.

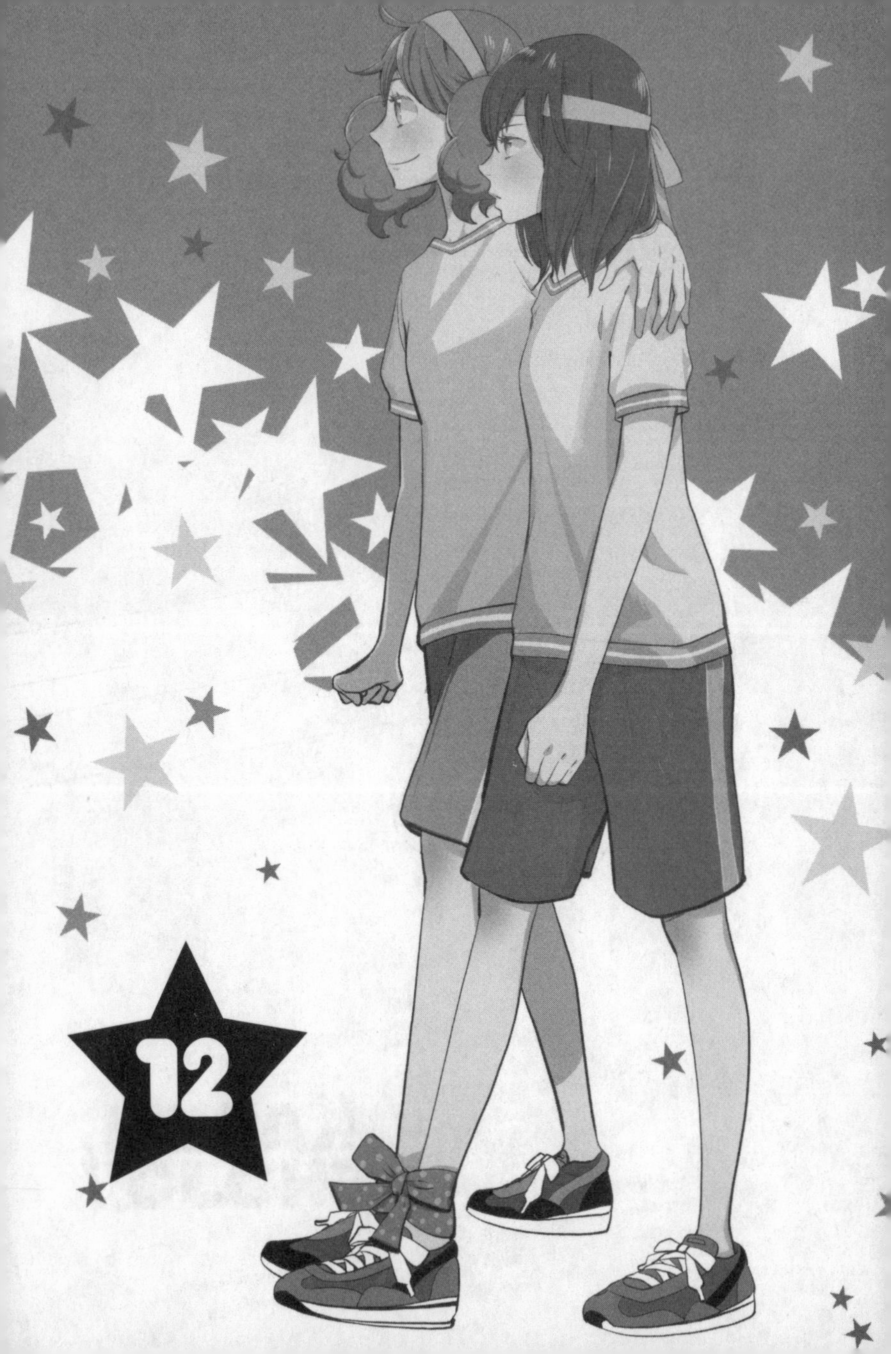
12

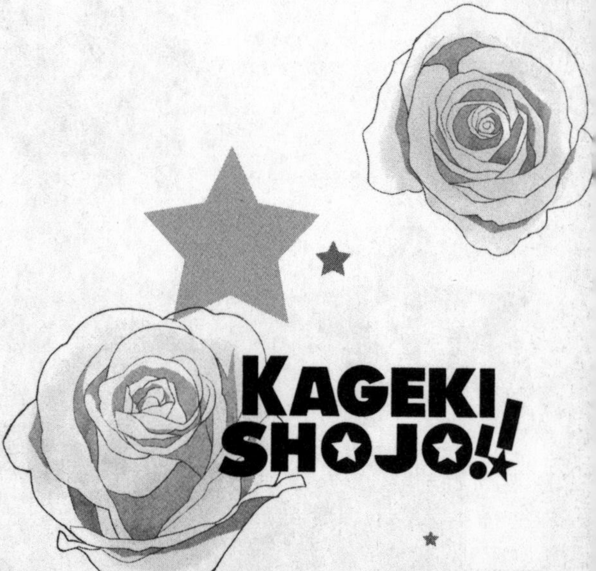
KAGEKI SHOJO!!

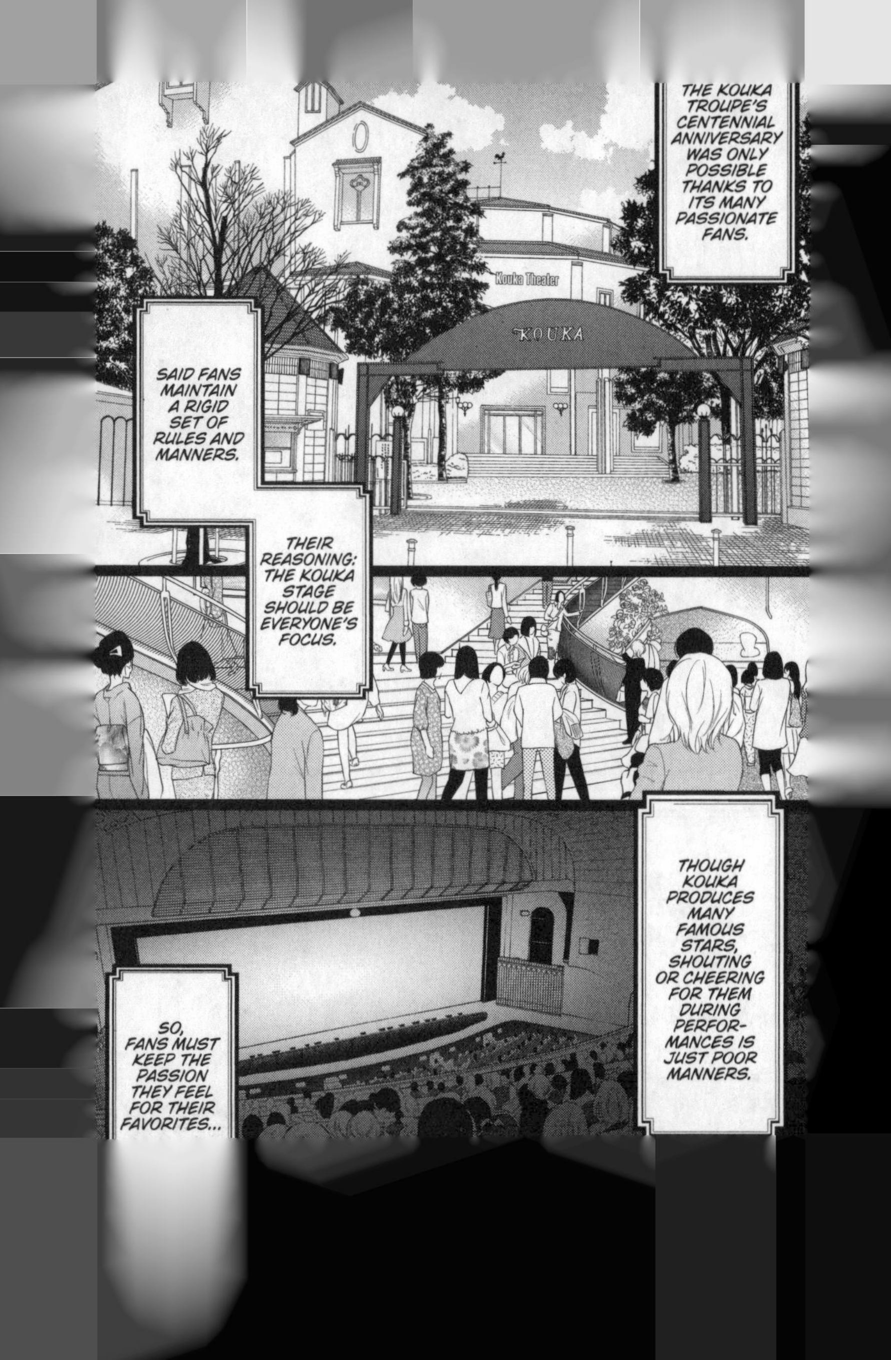
THE KOUKA TROUPE'S CENTENNIAL ANNIVERSARY WAS ONLY POSSIBLE THANKS TO ITS MANY PASSIONATE FANS.
Kouka Theater
KOUKA
SAID FANS MAINTAIN A RIGID SET OF RULES AND MANNERS.
THEIR REASONING: THE KOUKA STAGE SHOULD BE EVERYONE'S FOCUS.
THOUGH KOUKA PRODUCES MANY FAMOUS STARS, SHOUTING OR CHEERING FOR THEM DURING PERFOR-MANCES IS JUST POOR MANNERS.
SO, FANS MUST KEEP THE PASSION THEY FEEL FOR THEIR FAVORITES...

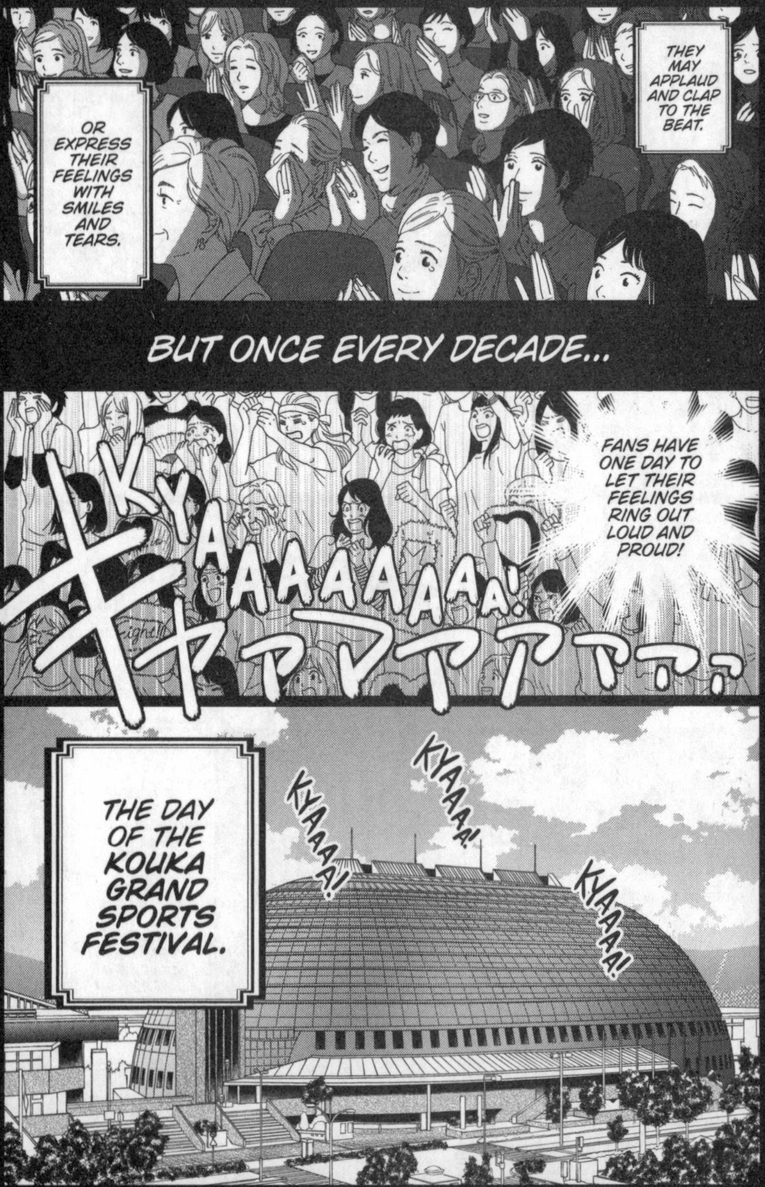
THEY MAY APPLAUD AND CLAP TO THE BEAT.
OR EXPRESS THEIR FEELINGS WITH SMILES AND TEARS.
BUT ONCE EVERY DECADE...
FANS HAVE ONE DAY TO LET THEIR FEELINGS RING OUT LOUD AND PROUD!
KYAAAAAAAAA!
キャアアアアァ
KYAAAAA!
KYAAAA!
KYAAAA!
THE DAY OF THE KOUKA GRAND SPORTS FESTIVAL.

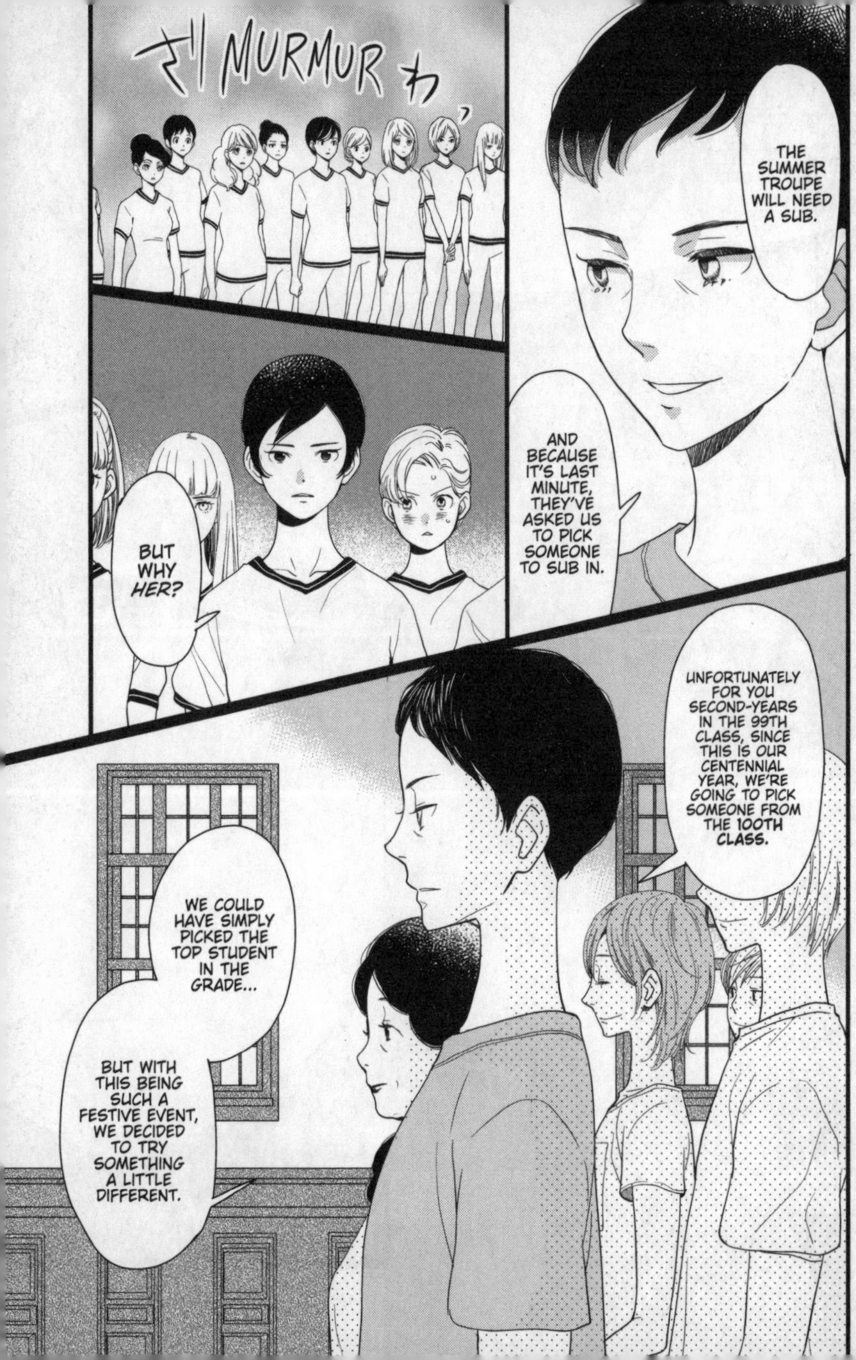
THE SUMMER TROUPE WILL NEED A SUB.
AND BECAUSE IT'S LAST MINUTE, THEY'VE ASKED US TO PICK SOMEONE TO SUB IN.
ざ MURMUR わ
BUT WHY *HER?*
UNFORTUNATELY FOR YOU SECOND-YEARS IN THE 99TH CLASS, SINCE THIS IS OUR CENTENNIAL YEAR, WE'RE GOING TO PICK SOMEONE FROM THE 100TH CLASS.
WE COULD HAVE SIMPLY PICKED THE TOP STUDENT IN THE GRADE...
BUT WITH THIS BEING SUCH A FESTIVE EVENT, WE DECIDED TO TRY SOMETHING A LITTLE DIFFERENT.

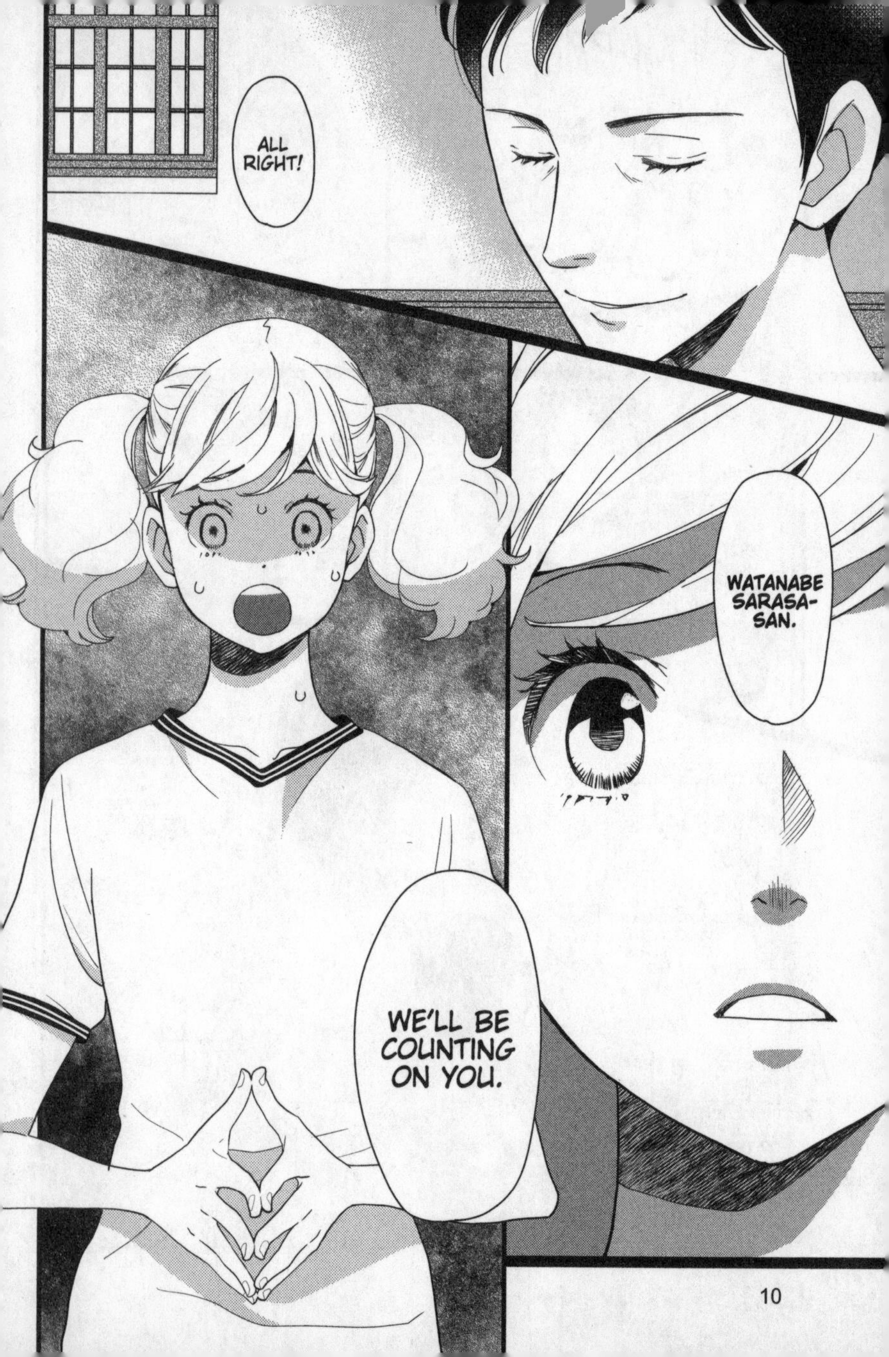
ALL RIGHT!
WATANABE SARASA-SAN.
WE'LL BE COUNTING ON YOU.

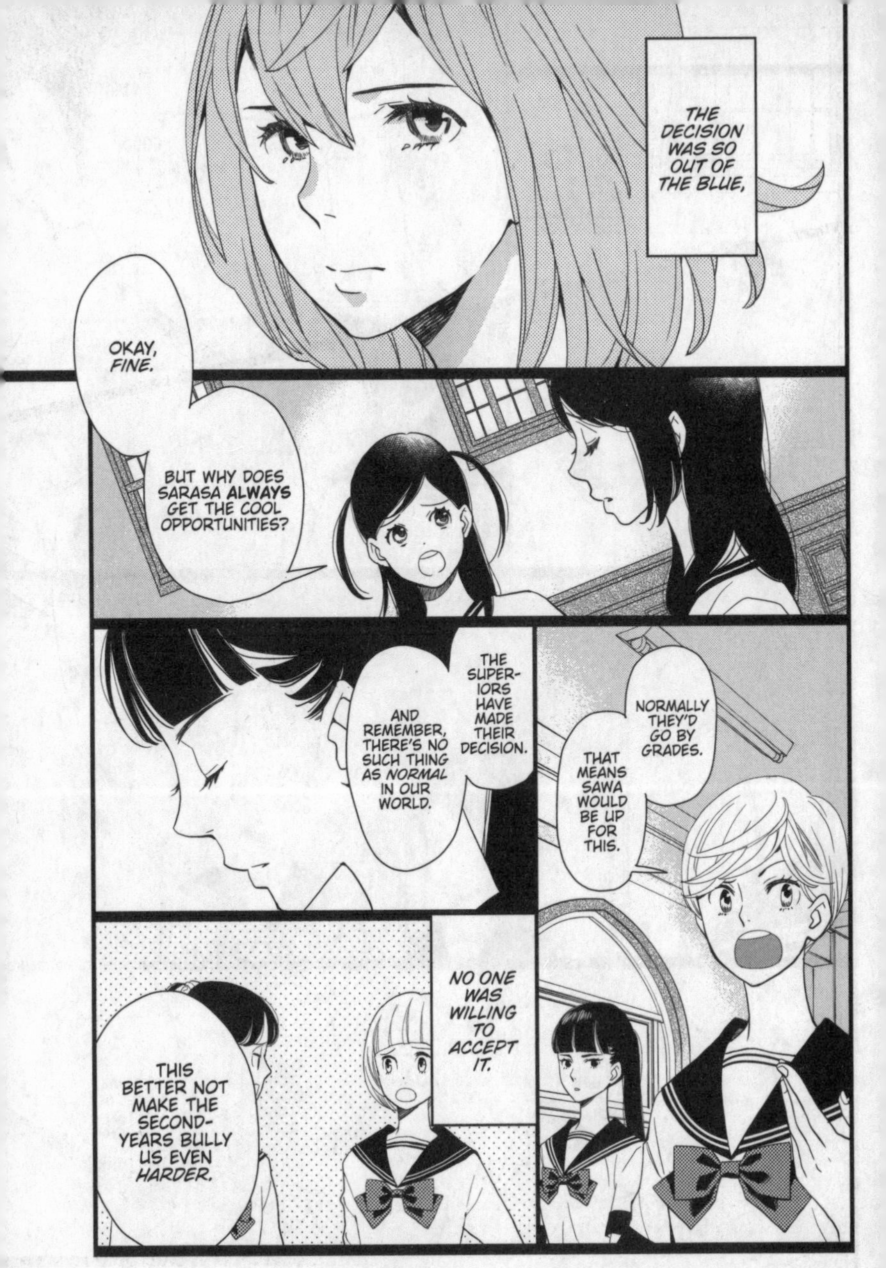
THE DECISION WAS SO OUT OF THE BLUE,
OKAY, FINE.
BUT WHY DOES SARASA ALWAYS GET THE COOL OPPORTUNITIES?
NORMALLY THEY'D GO BY GRADES.
THAT MEANS SAWA WOULD BE UP FOR THIS.
THE SUPERIORS HAVE MADE THEIR DECISION.
AND REMEMBER, THERE'S NO SUCH THING AS NORMAL IN OUR WORLD.
NO ONE WAS WILLING TO ACCEPT IT.
THIS BETTER NOT MAKE THE SECOND-YEARS BULLY US EVEN HARDER.

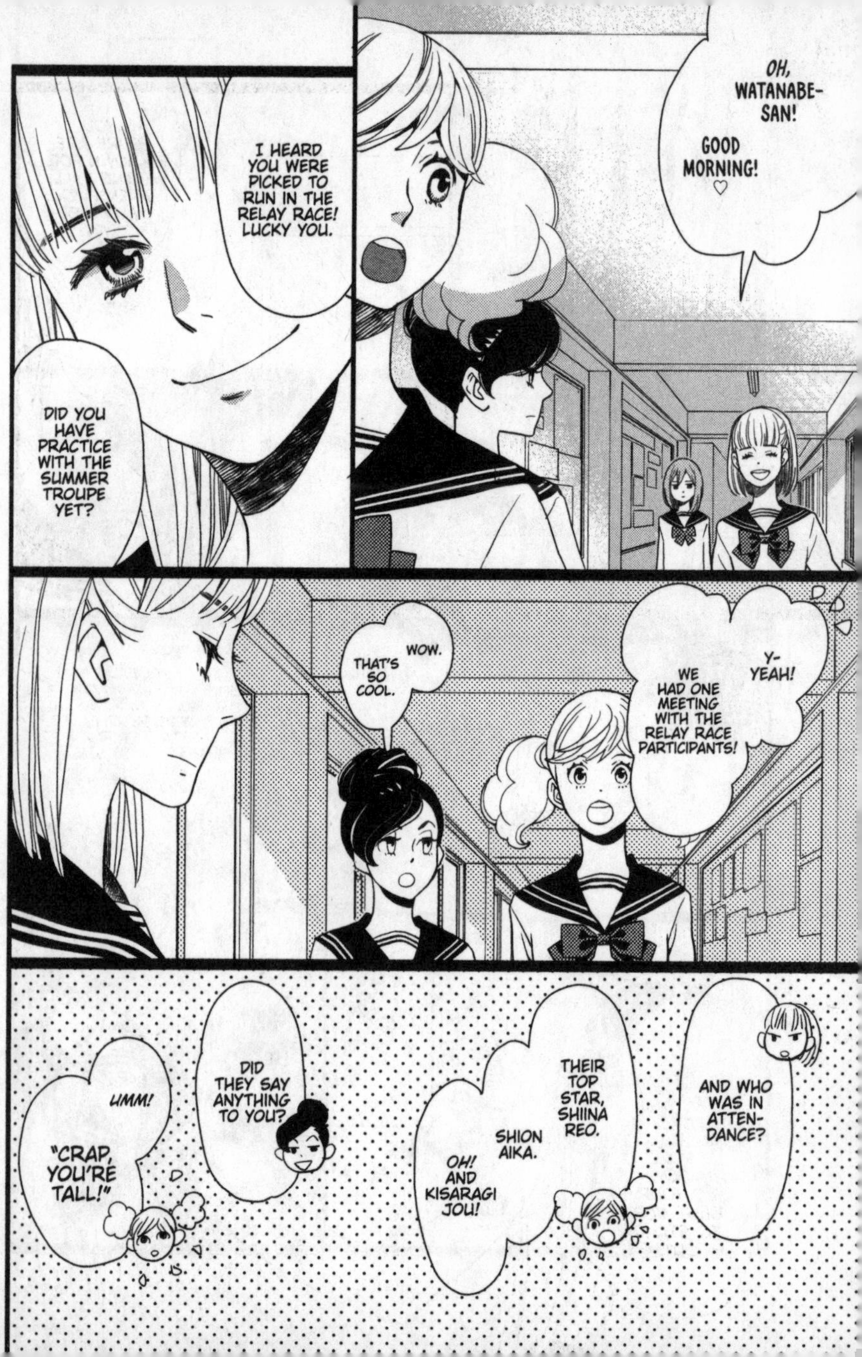
OH, WATANABE-SAN!
GOOD MORNING! ♡
I HEARD YOU WERE PICKED TO RUN IN THE RELAY RACE! LUCKY YOU.
DID YOU HAVE PRACTICE WITH THE SUMMER TROUPE YET?
Y-YEAH!
WE HAD ONE MEETING WITH THE RELAY RACE PARTICIPANTS!
WOW.
THAT'S SO COOL.
AND WHO WAS IN ATTEN-DANCE?
THEIR TOP STAR, SHIINA REO.
SHION AIKA.
OH! AND KISARAGI JOU!
DID THEY SAY ANYTHING TO YOU?
UMM!
"CRAP, YOU'RE TALL!"

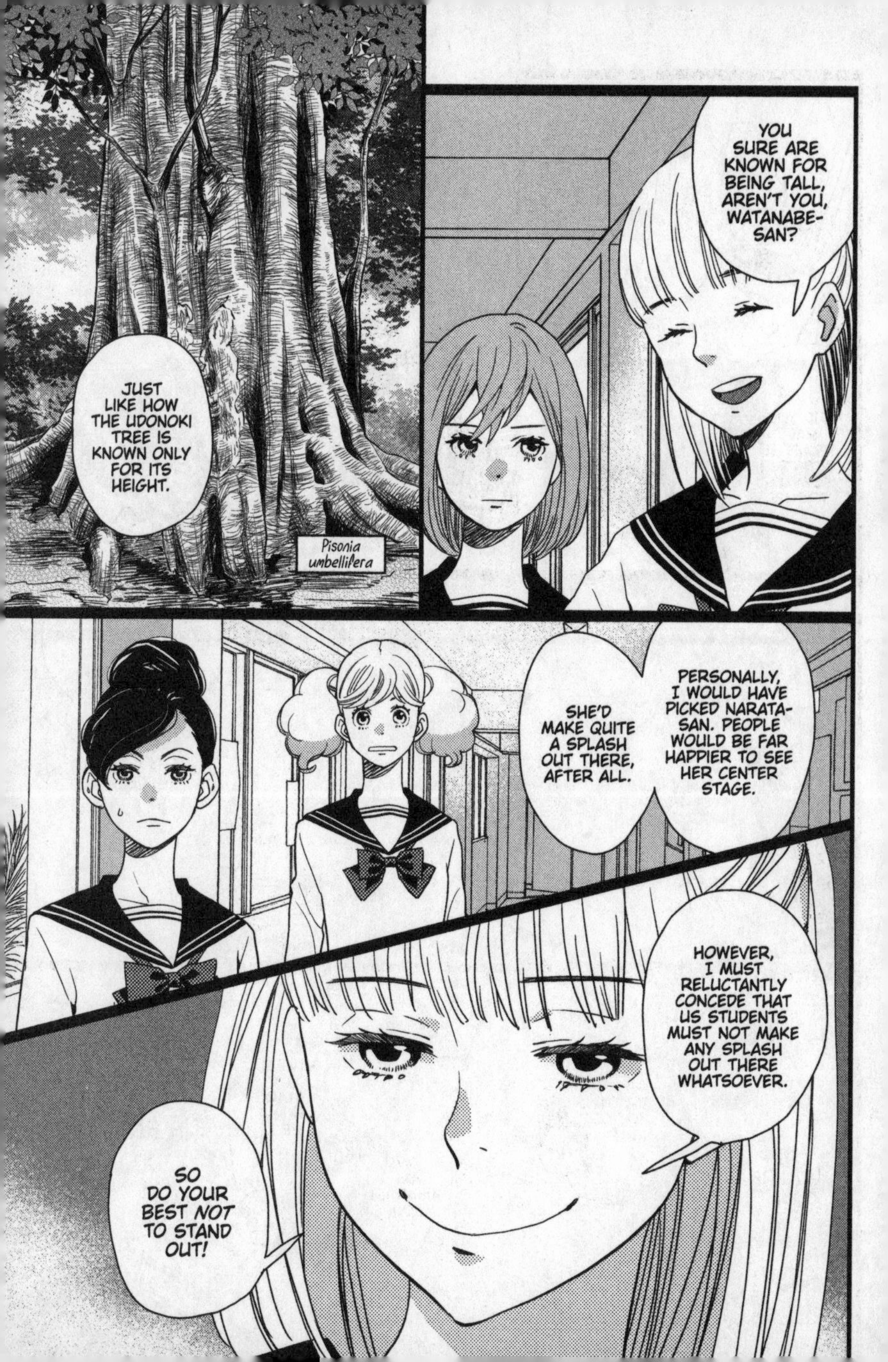
YOU SURE ARE KNOWN FOR BEING TALL, AREN'T YOU, WATANABE-SAN?
JUST LIKE HOW THE UDONOKI TREE IS KNOWN ONLY FOR ITS HEIGHT.
Pisonia umbellifera
PERSONALLY, I WOULD HAVE PICKED NARATA-SAN. PEOPLE WOULD BE FAR HAPPIER TO SEE HER CENTER STAGE.
SHE'D MAKE QUITE A SPLASH OUT THERE, AFTER ALL.
HOWEVER, I MUST RELUCTANTLY CONCEDE THAT US STUDENTS MUST NOT MAKE ANY SPLASH OUT THERE WHATSOEVER.
SO DO YOUR BEST *NOT* TO STAND OUT!

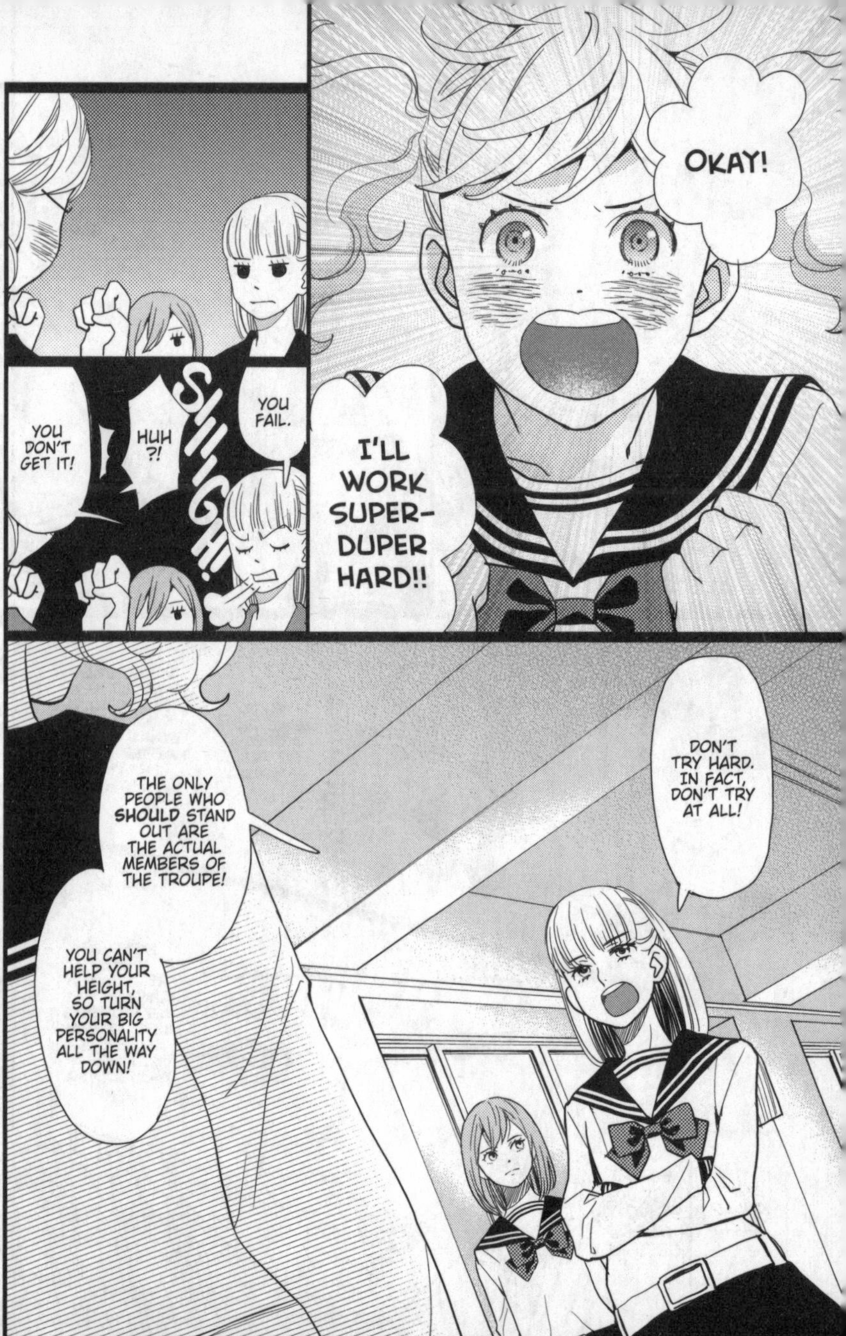
OKAY!
I'LL WORK SUPER-DUPER HARD!!
YOU FAIL.
SIIIGH!
HUH ?!
YOU DON'T GET IT!
DON'T TRY HARD. IN FACT, DON'T TRY AT ALL!
THE ONLY PEOPLE WHO **SHOULD** STAND OUT ARE THE ACTUAL MEMBERS OF THE TROUPE!
YOU CAN'T HELP YOUR HEIGHT, SO TURN YOUR BIG PERSONALITY ALL THE WAY DOWN!

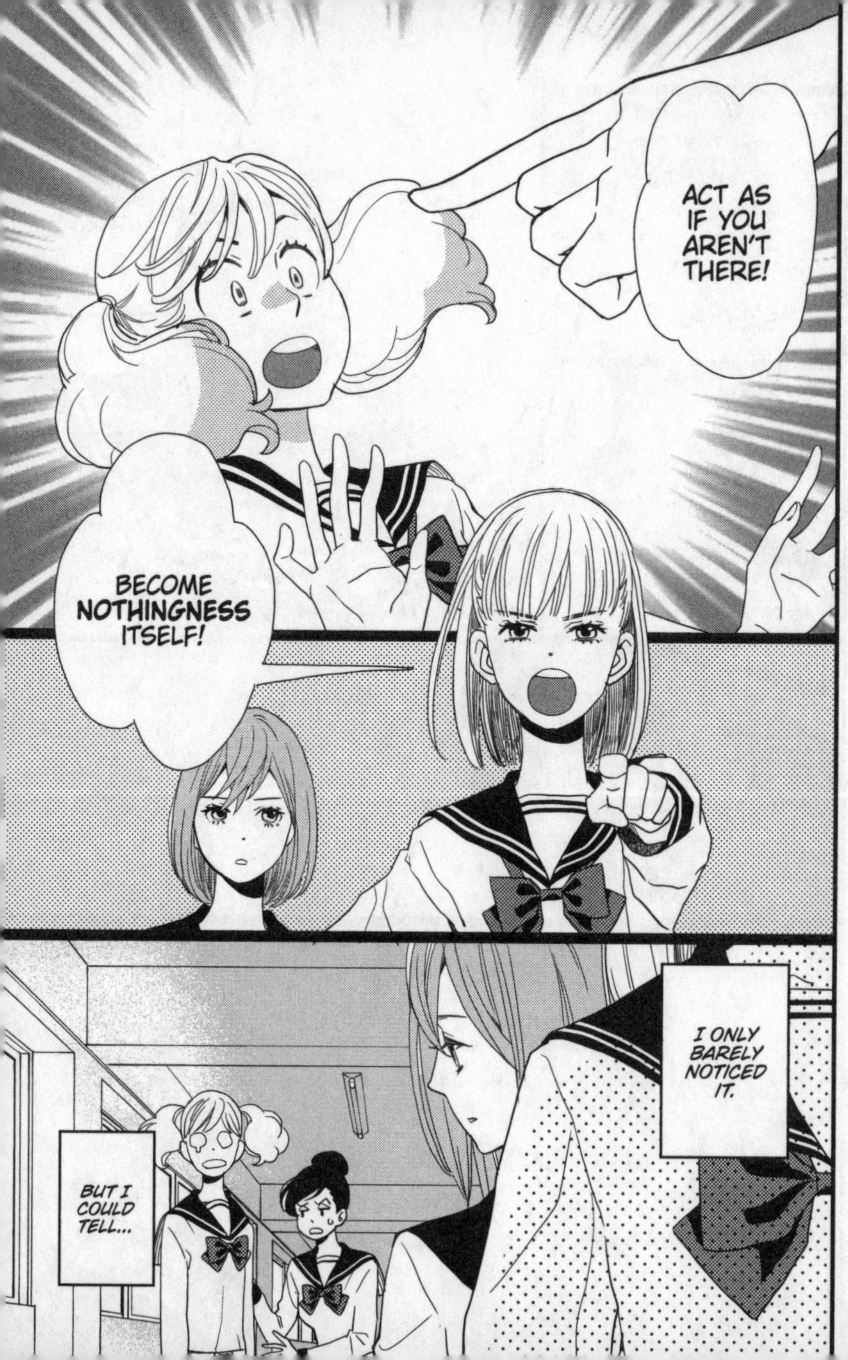
ACT AS IF YOU AREN'T THERE!
BECOME NOTHINGNESS ITSELF!
I ONLY BARELY NOTICED IT.
BUT I COULD TELL...

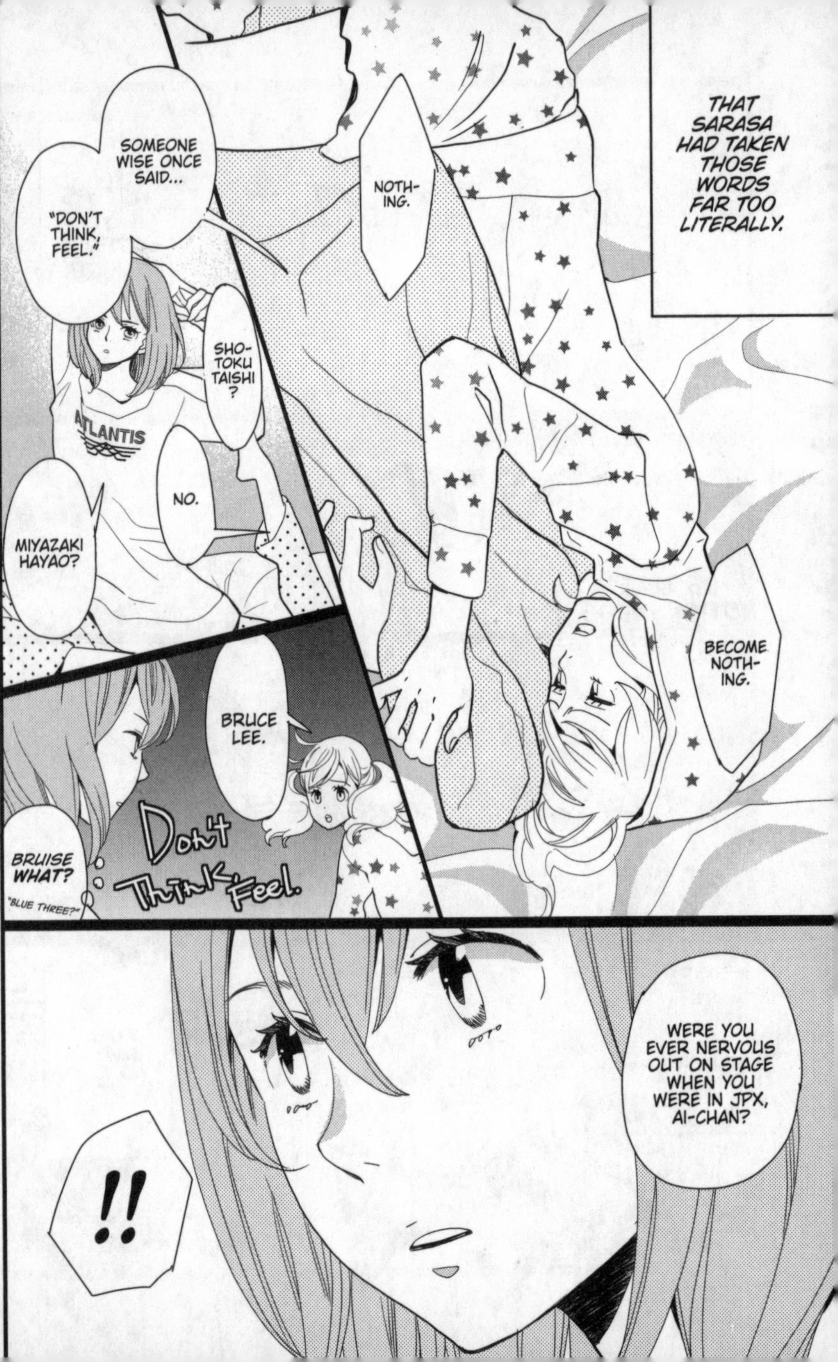
THAT SARASA HAD TAKEN THOSE WORDS FAR TOO LITERALLY.
NOTH-ING.
BECOME NOTH-ING.
SOMEONE WISE ONCE SAID...
"DON'T THINK, FEEL."
SHO-TOKU TAISHI?
NO.
MIYAZAKI HAYAO?
BRUCE LEE.
Don't Think, Feel.
BRUISE WHAT?
"BLUE THREE?"
WERE YOU EVER NERVOUS OUT ON STAGE WHEN YOU WERE IN JPX, AI-CHAN?
!!

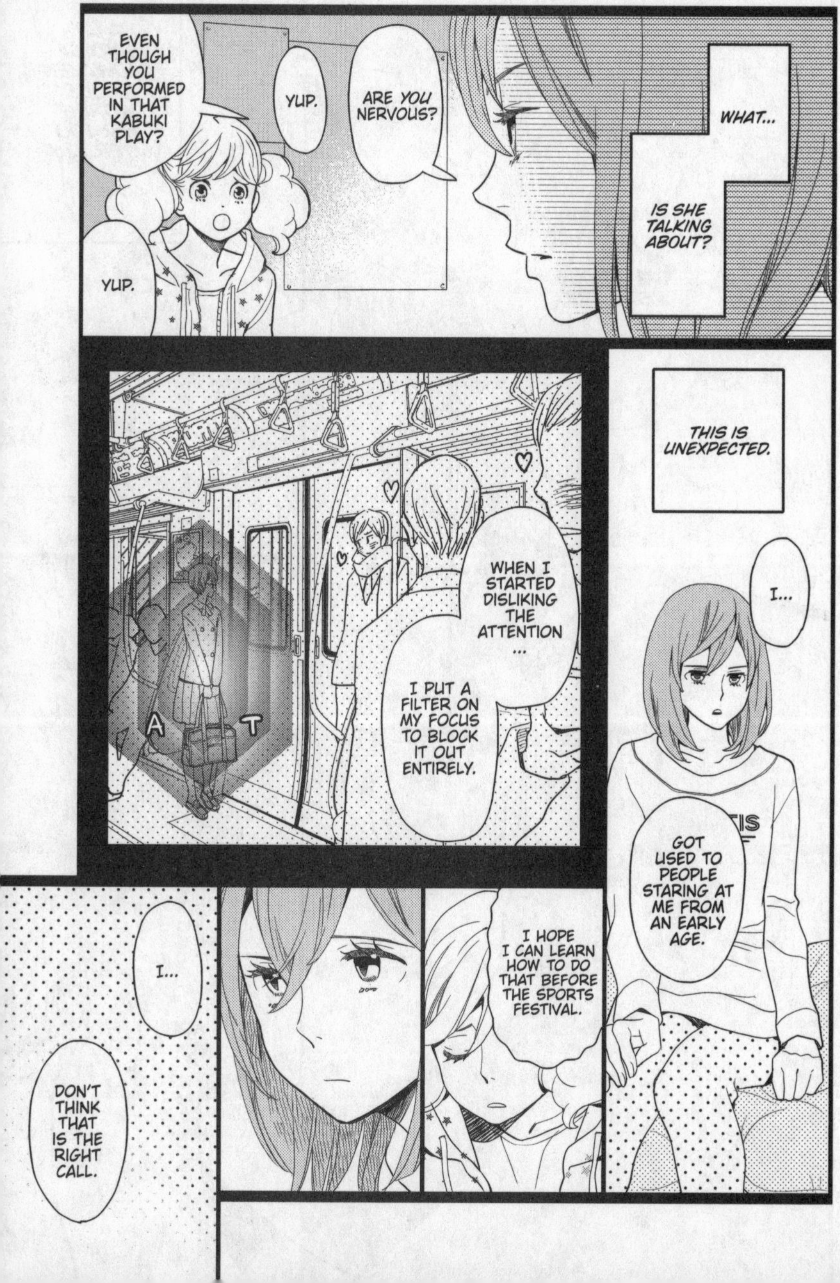
WHAT...
IS SHE TALKING ABOUT?
ARE YOU NERVOUS?
YUP.
EVEN THOUGH YOU PERFORMED IN THAT KABUKI PLAY?
YUP.
THIS IS UNEXPECTED.
I...
GOT USED TO PEOPLE STARING AT ME FROM AN EARLY AGE.
WHEN I STARTED DISLIKING THE ATTENTION ...
I PUT A FILTER ON MY FOCUS TO BLOCK IT OUT ENTIRELY.
I HOPE I CAN LEARN HOW TO DO THAT BEFORE THE SPORTS FESTIVAL.
I...
DON'T THINK THAT IS THE RIGHT CALL.

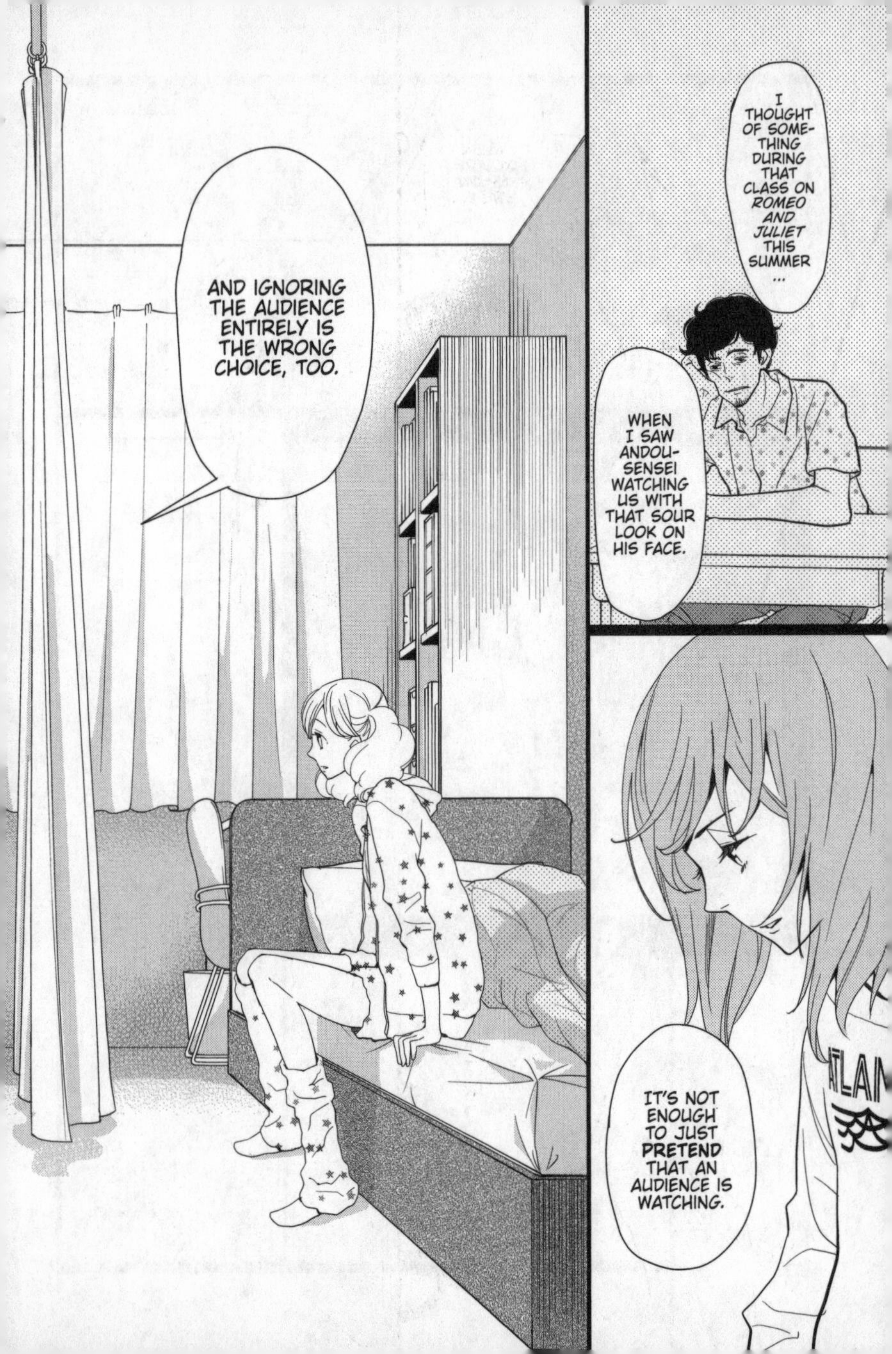
I THOUGHT OF SOMETHING DURING THAT CLASS ON *ROMEO AND JULIET* THIS SUMMER...
WHEN I SAW ANDOU-SENSEI WATCHING US WITH THAT SOUR LOOK ON HIS FACE.
IT'S NOT ENOUGH TO JUST **PRETEND** THAT AN AUDIENCE IS WATCHING.
AND IGNORING THE AUDIENCE ENTIRELY IS THE WRONG CHOICE, TOO.

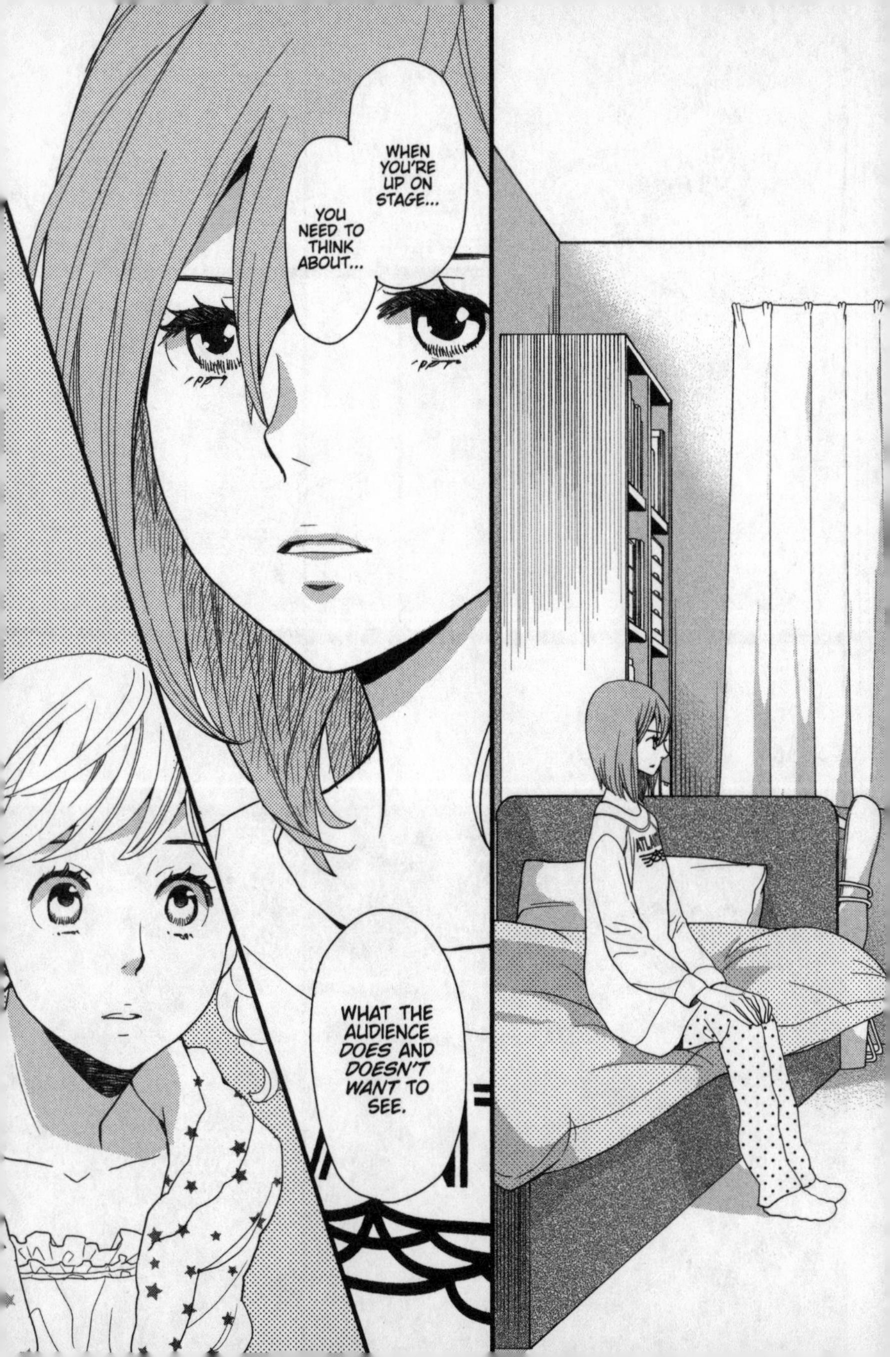
WHEN YOU'RE UP ON STAGE...
YOU NEED TO THINK ABOUT...
WHAT THE AUDIENCE *DOES* AND *DOESN'T* WANT TO SEE.

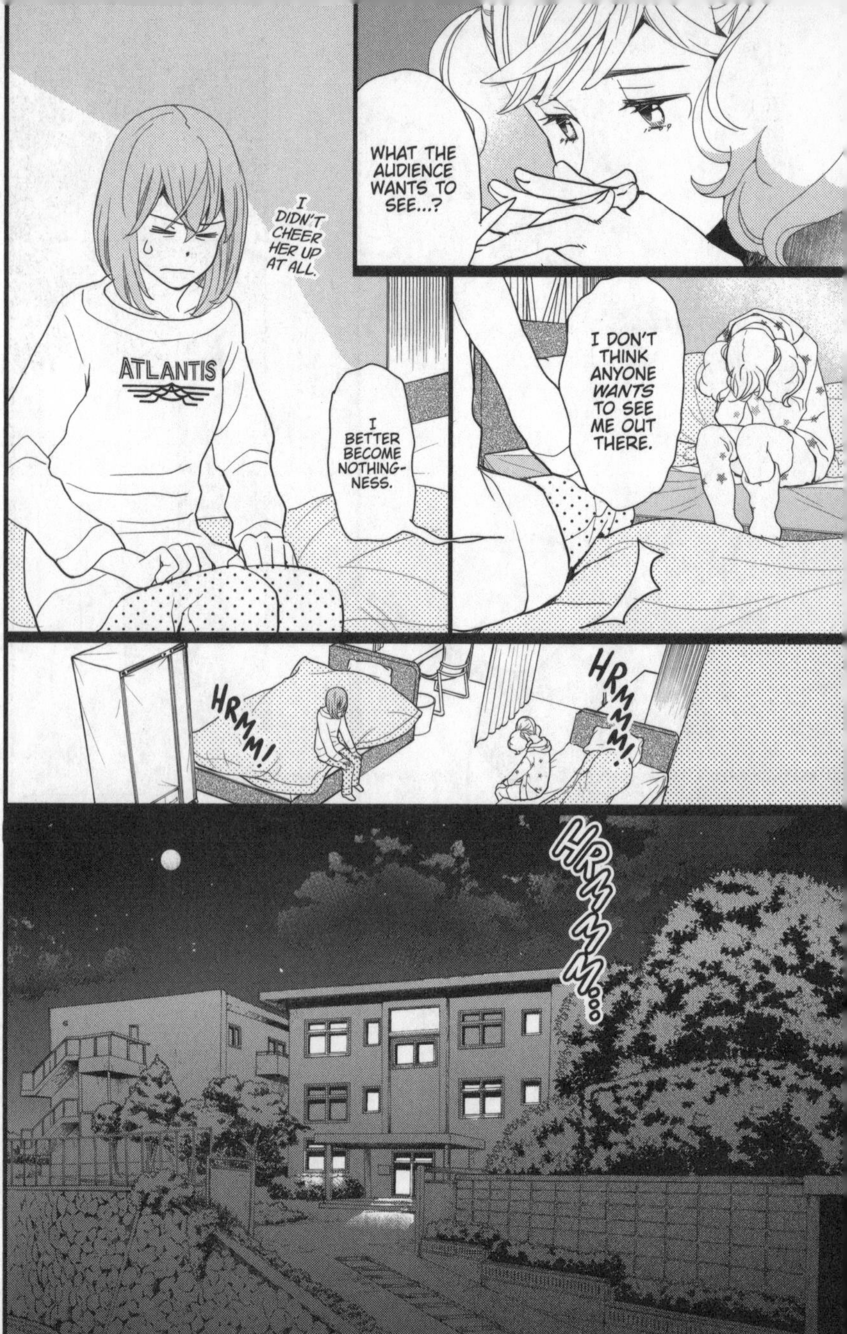
WHAT THE AUDIENCE WANTS TO SEE...?
I DON'T THINK ANYONE WANTS TO SEE ME OUT THERE.
I BETTER BECOME NOTHINGNESS.
I DIDN'T CHEER HER UP AT ALL.
ATLANTIS
HRMMM!
HRMM!
HRMMMM...

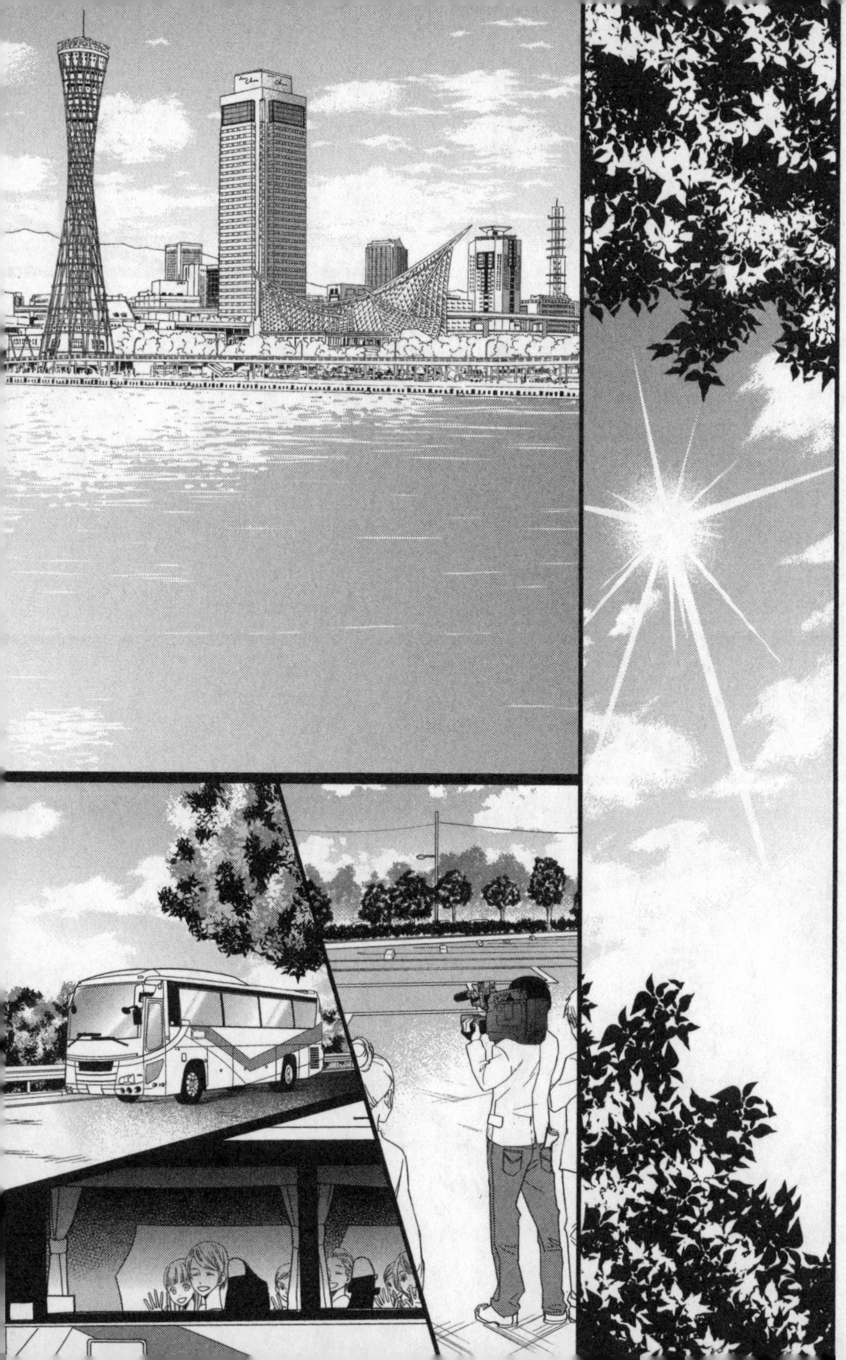

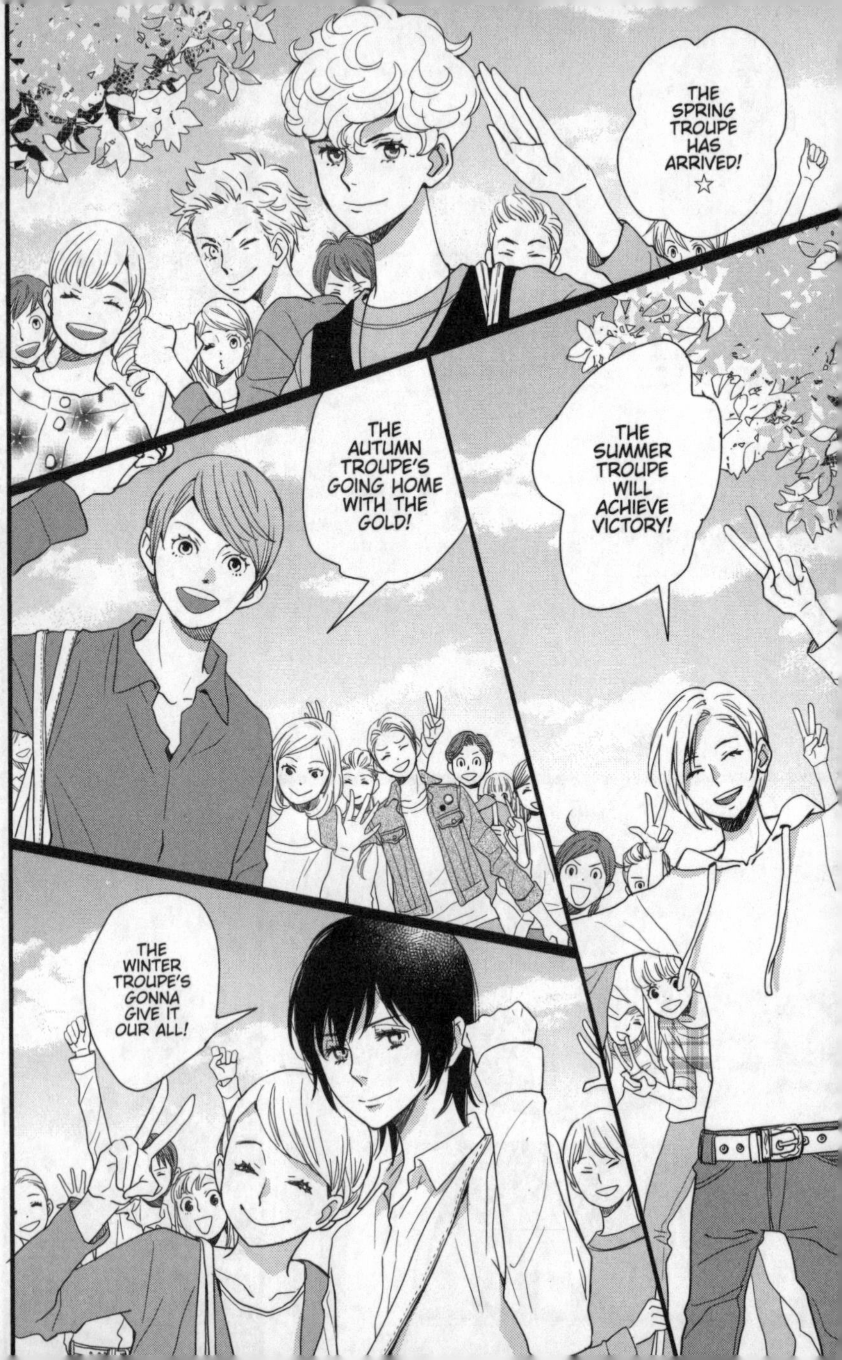
THE SPRING TROUPE HAS ARRIVED! ☆
THE SUMMER TROUPE WILL ACHIEVE VICTORY!
THE AUTUMN TROUPE'S GOING HOME WITH THE GOLD!
THE WINTER TROUPE'S GONNA GIVE IT OUR ALL!

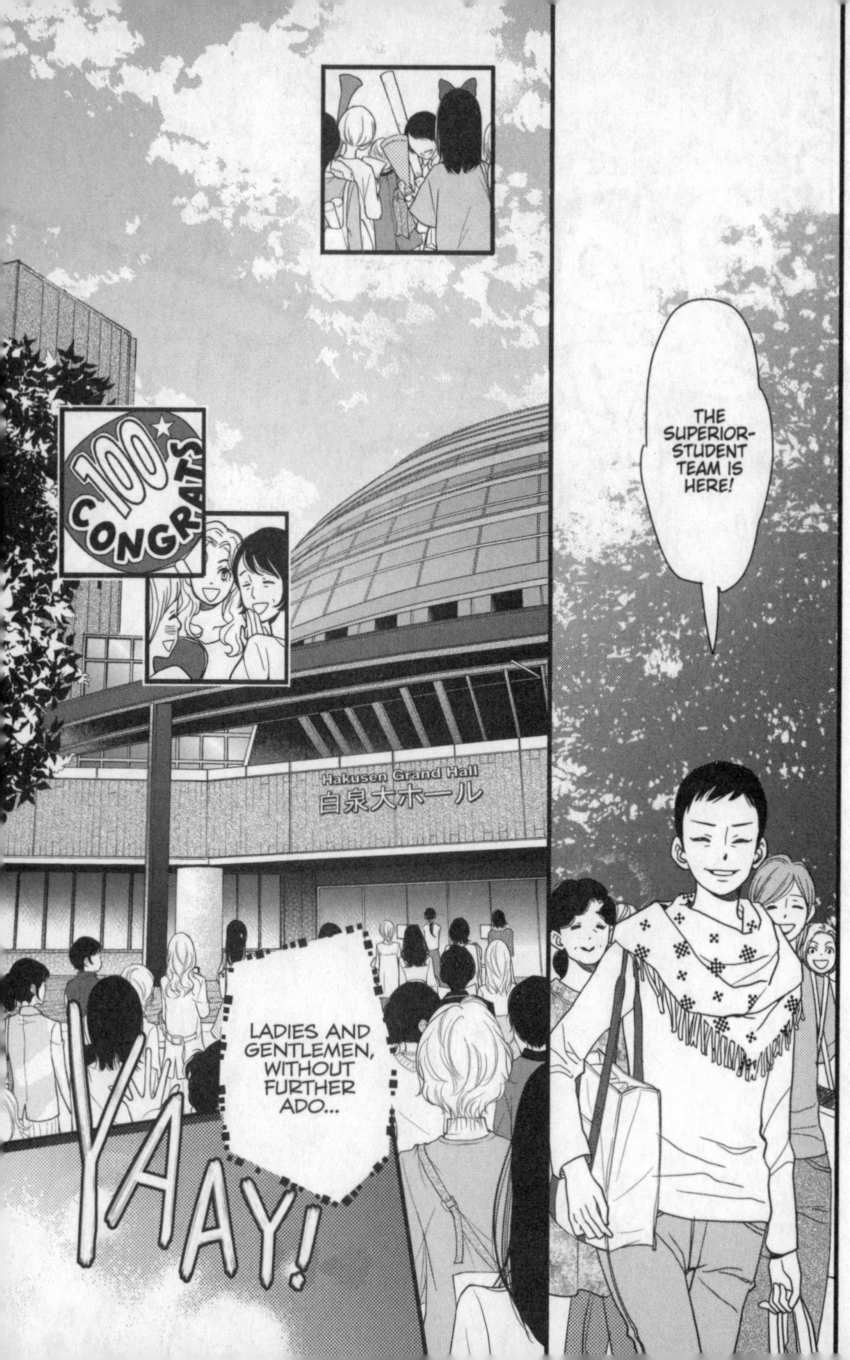
THE SUPERIOR-STUDENT TEAM IS HERE!
100 CONGRATS
Hakusen Grand Hall
白泉大ホール
LADIES AND GENTLEMEN, WITHOUT FURTHER ADO...
YAAY!

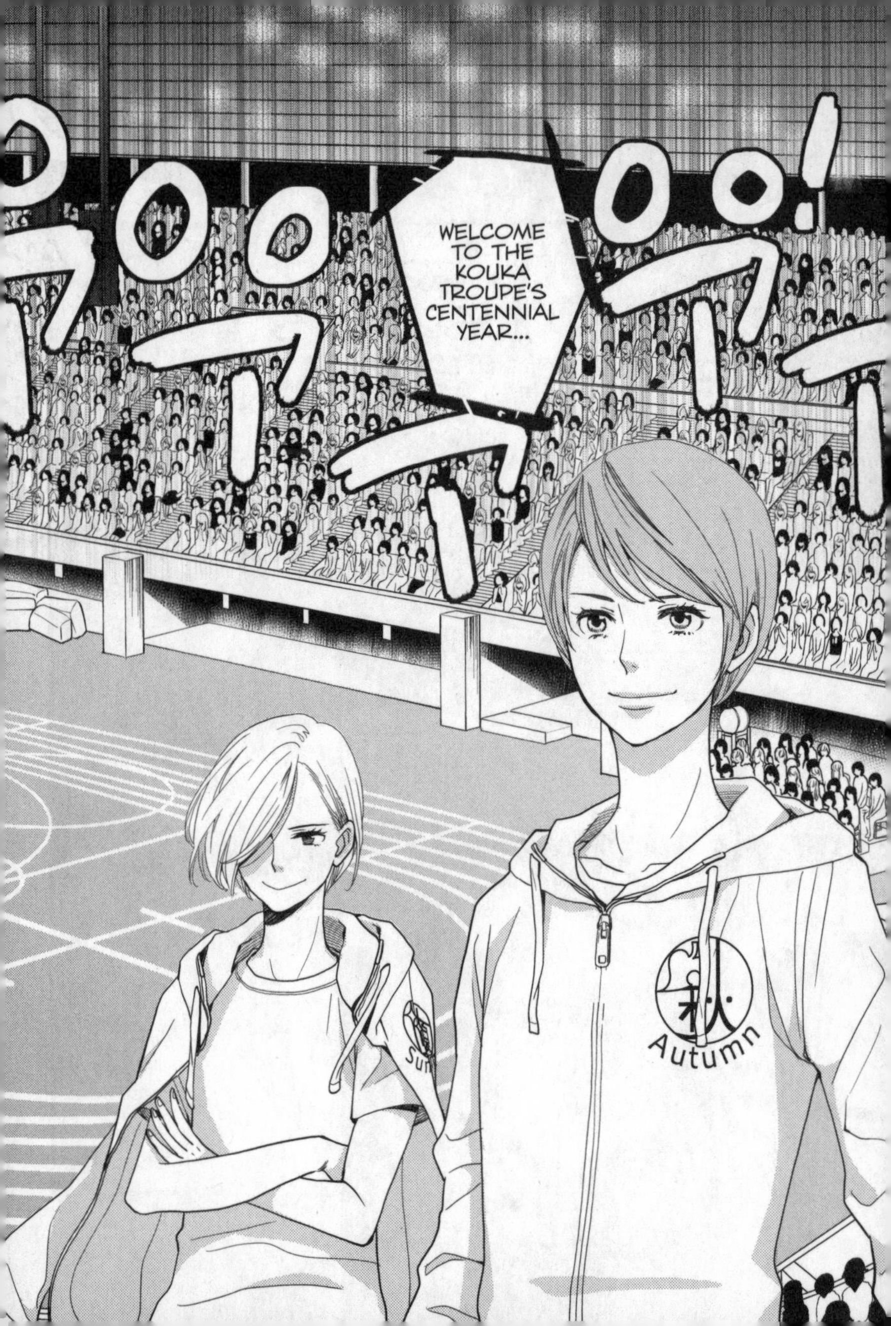
WELCOME TO THE KOUKA TROUPE'S CENTENNIAL YEAR...
Autumn

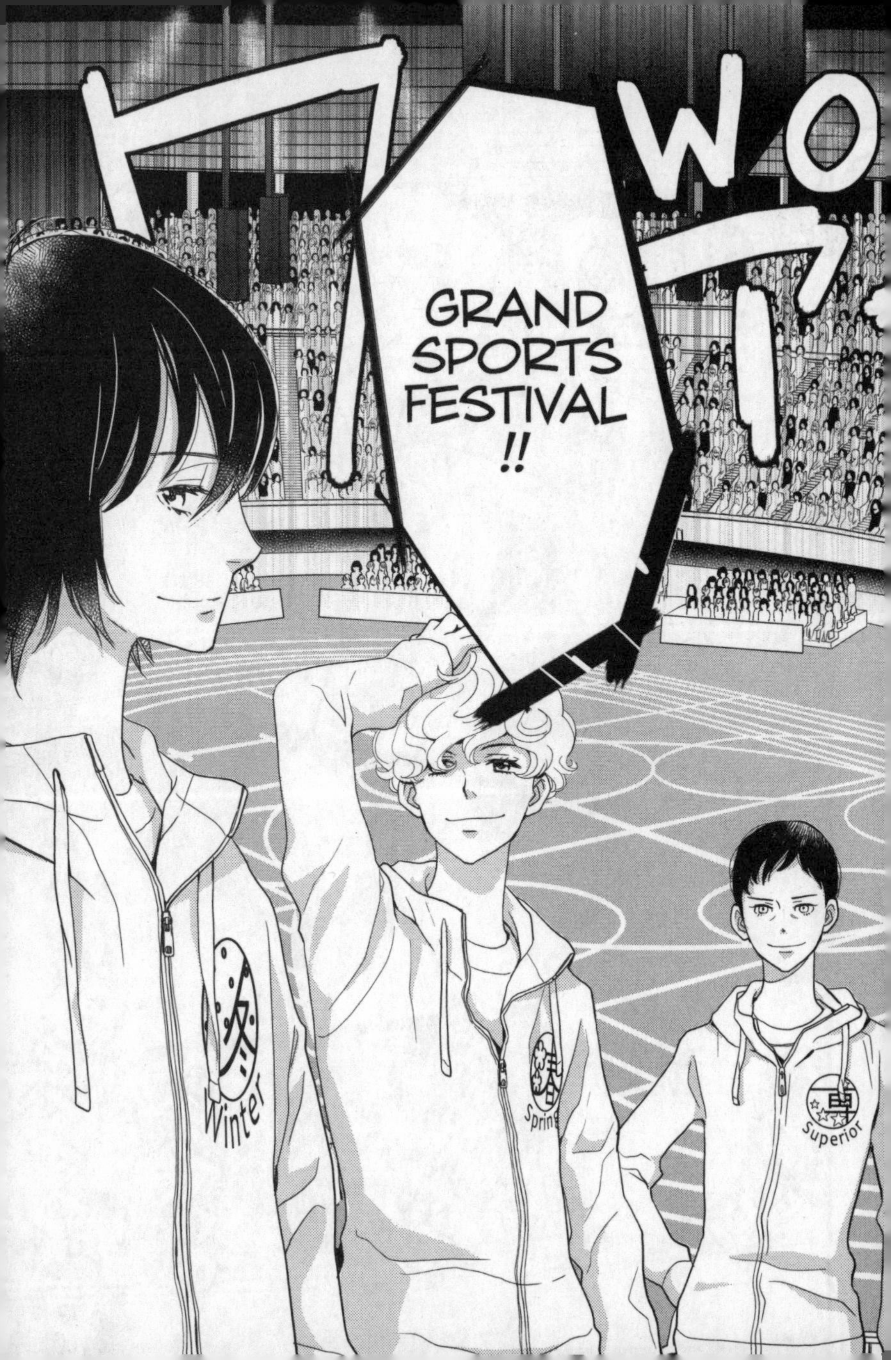
GRAND SPORTS FESTIVAL !!
WO
Winter
Spring
Superior

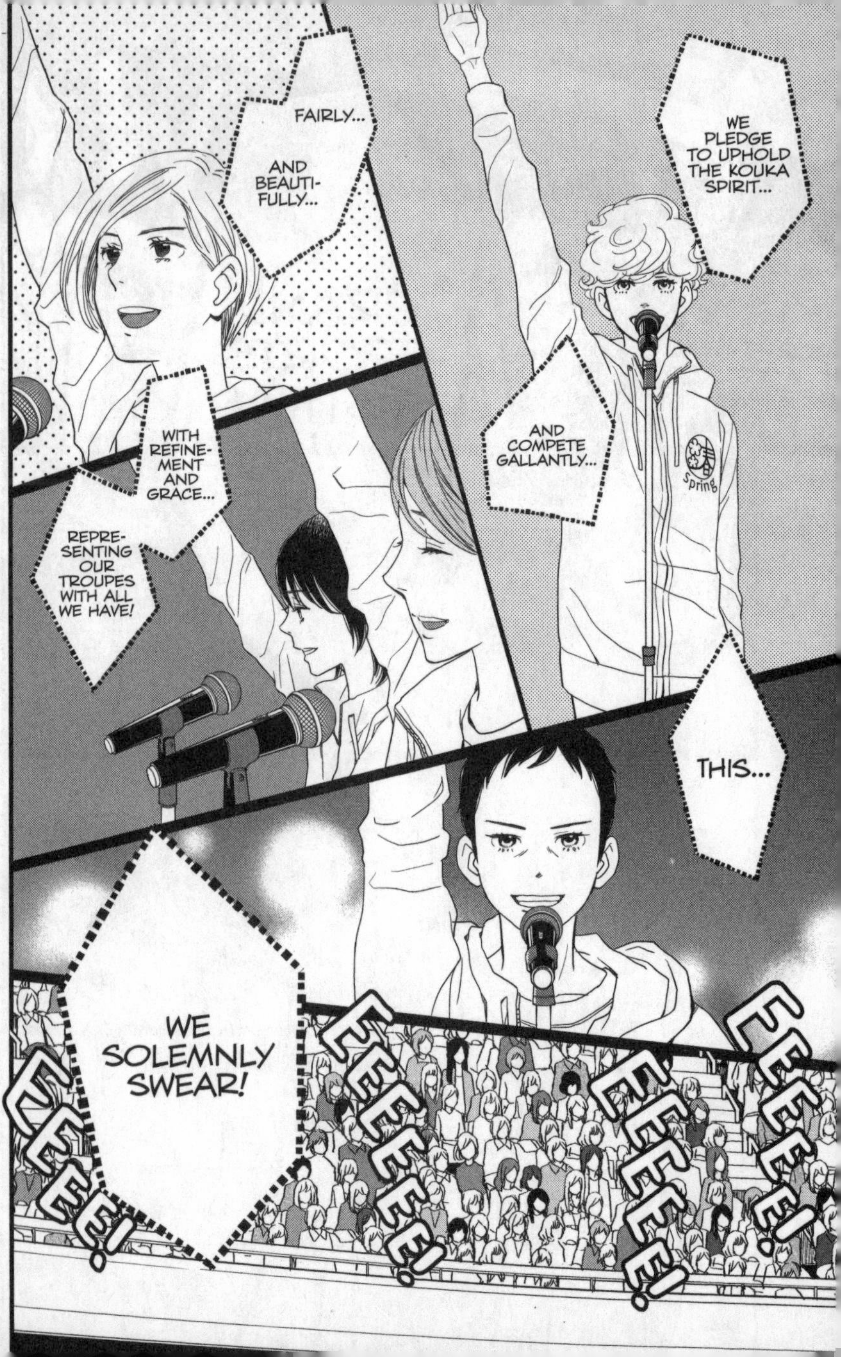
WE PLEDGE TO UPHOLD THE KOUKA SPIRIT...
AND COMPETE GALLANTLY...
FAIRLY...
AND BEAUTI-FULLY...
WITH REFINE-MENT AND GRACE...
REPRE-SENTING OUR TROUPES WITH ALL WE HAVE!
THIS...
WE SOLEMNLY SWEAR!
EEEEEE!
EEEEEEE!
EEEEEE!
EEEE!

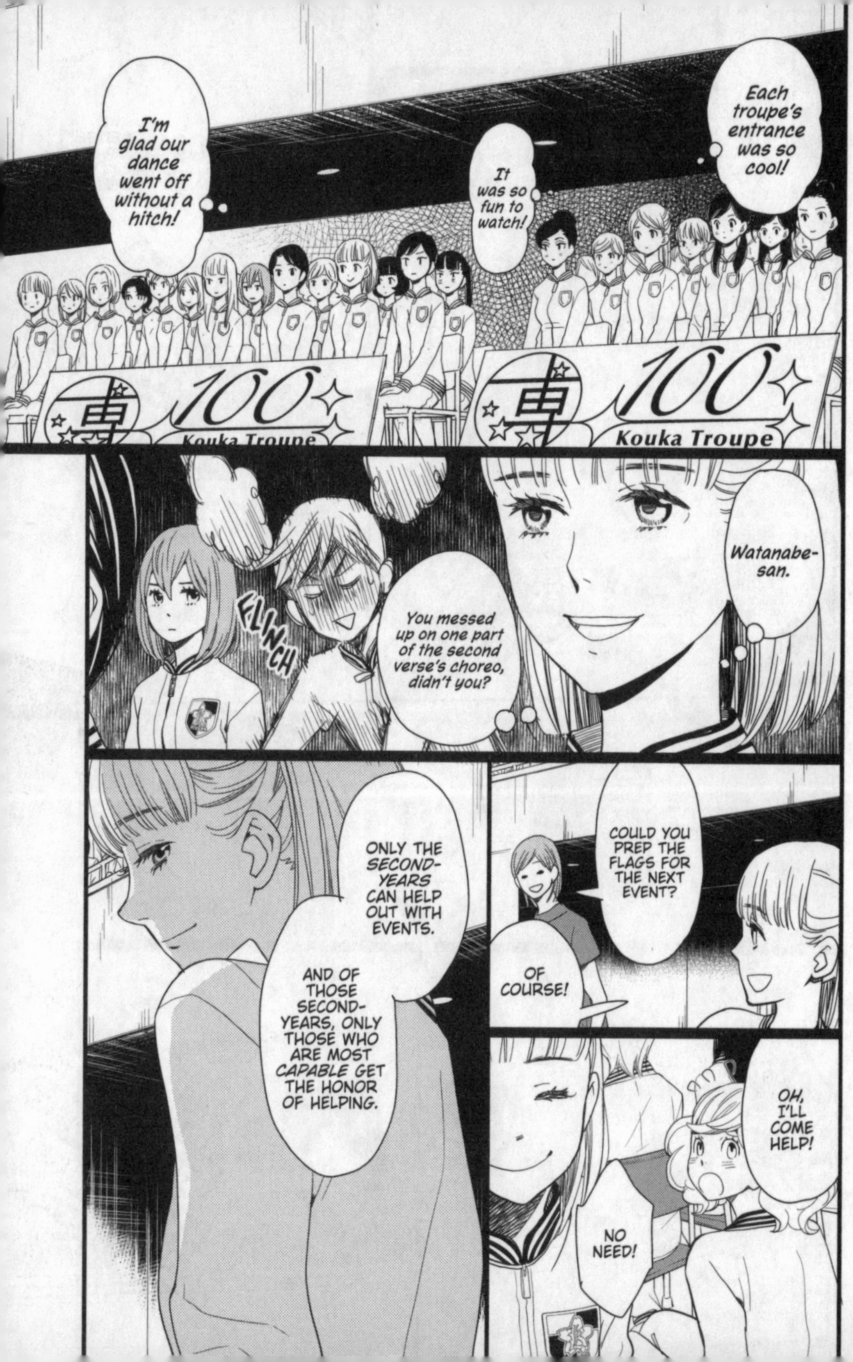

Each troupe's entrance was so cool!
It was so fun to watch!
I'm glad our dance went off without a hitch!
100
Kouka Troupe
100
Kouka Troupe
Watanabe-san.
You messed up on one part of the second verse's choreo, didn't you?
FLINCH
COULD YOU PREP THE FLAGS FOR THE NEXT EVENT?
OF COURSE!
OH, I'LL COME HELP!
NO NEED!
ONLY THE *SECOND-YEARS* CAN HELP OUT WITH EVENTS.
AND OF THOSE SECOND-YEARS, ONLY THOSE WHO ARE MOST *CAPABLE* GET THE HONOR OF HELPING.

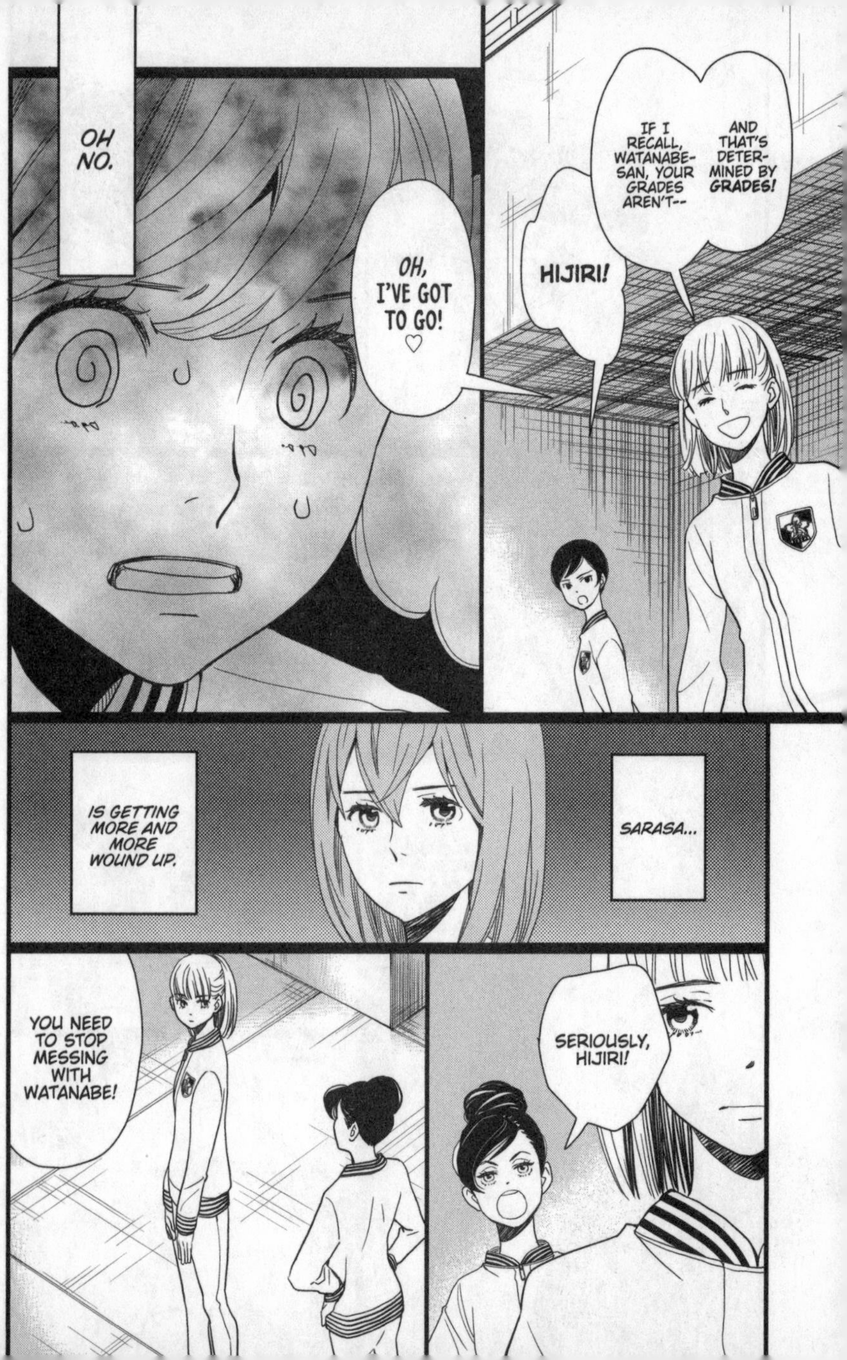
AND THAT'S DETERMINED BY GRADES!
IF I RECALL, WATANABE-SAN, YOUR GRADES AREN'T--
HIJIRI!
OH, I'VE GOT TO GO! ♡
OH NO.
SARASA...
IS GETTING MORE AND MORE WOUND UP.
SERIOUSLY, HIJIRI!
YOU NEED TO STOP MESSING WITH WATANABE!

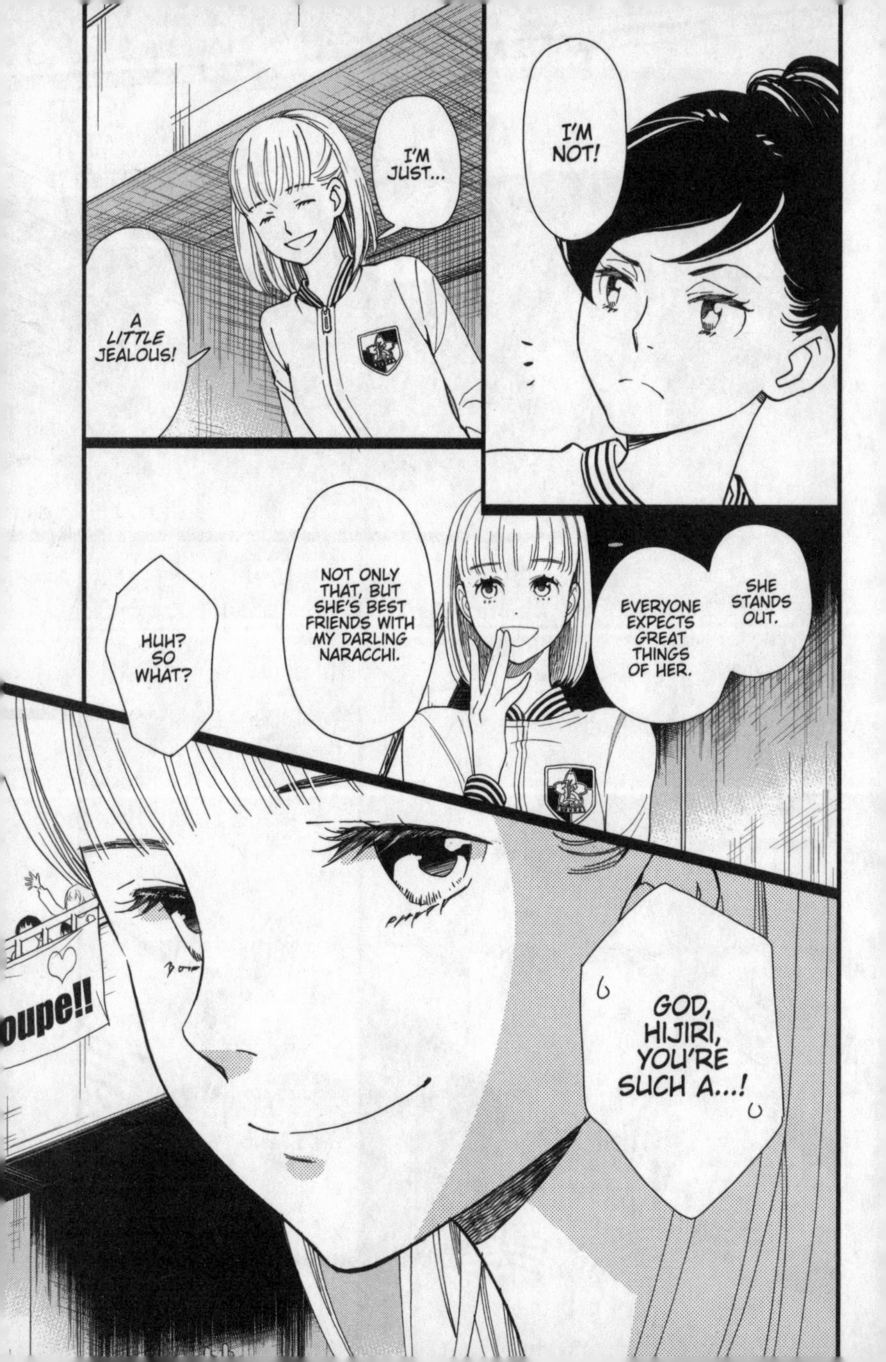
I'M NOT!
I'M JUST...
A LITTLE JEALOUS!
SHE STANDS OUT.
EVERYONE EXPECTS GREAT THINGS OF HER.
NOT ONLY THAT, BUT SHE'S BEST FRIENDS WITH MY DARLING NARACCHI.
HUH? SO WHAT?
oupe!!
GOD, HIJIRI, YOU'RE SUCH A...!

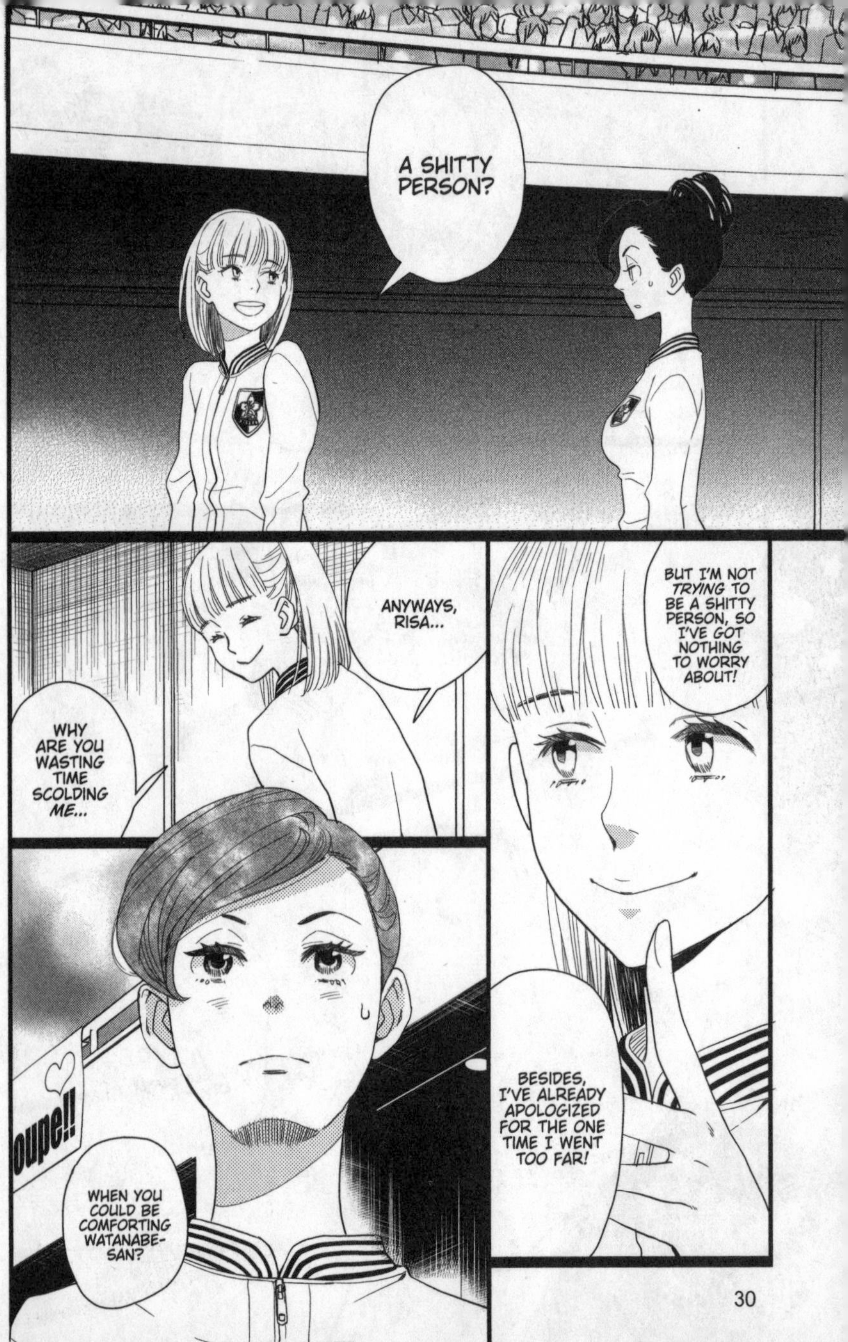
A SHITTY PERSON?
BUT I'M NOT *TRYING* TO BE A SHITTY PERSON, SO I'VE GOT NOTHING TO WORRY ABOUT!
BESIDES, I'VE ALREADY APOLOGIZED FOR THE ONE TIME I WENT TOO FAR!
ANYWAYS, RISA...
WHY ARE YOU WASTING TIME SCOLDING ME...
oupe!!
WHEN YOU COULD BE COMFORTING WATANABE-SAN?

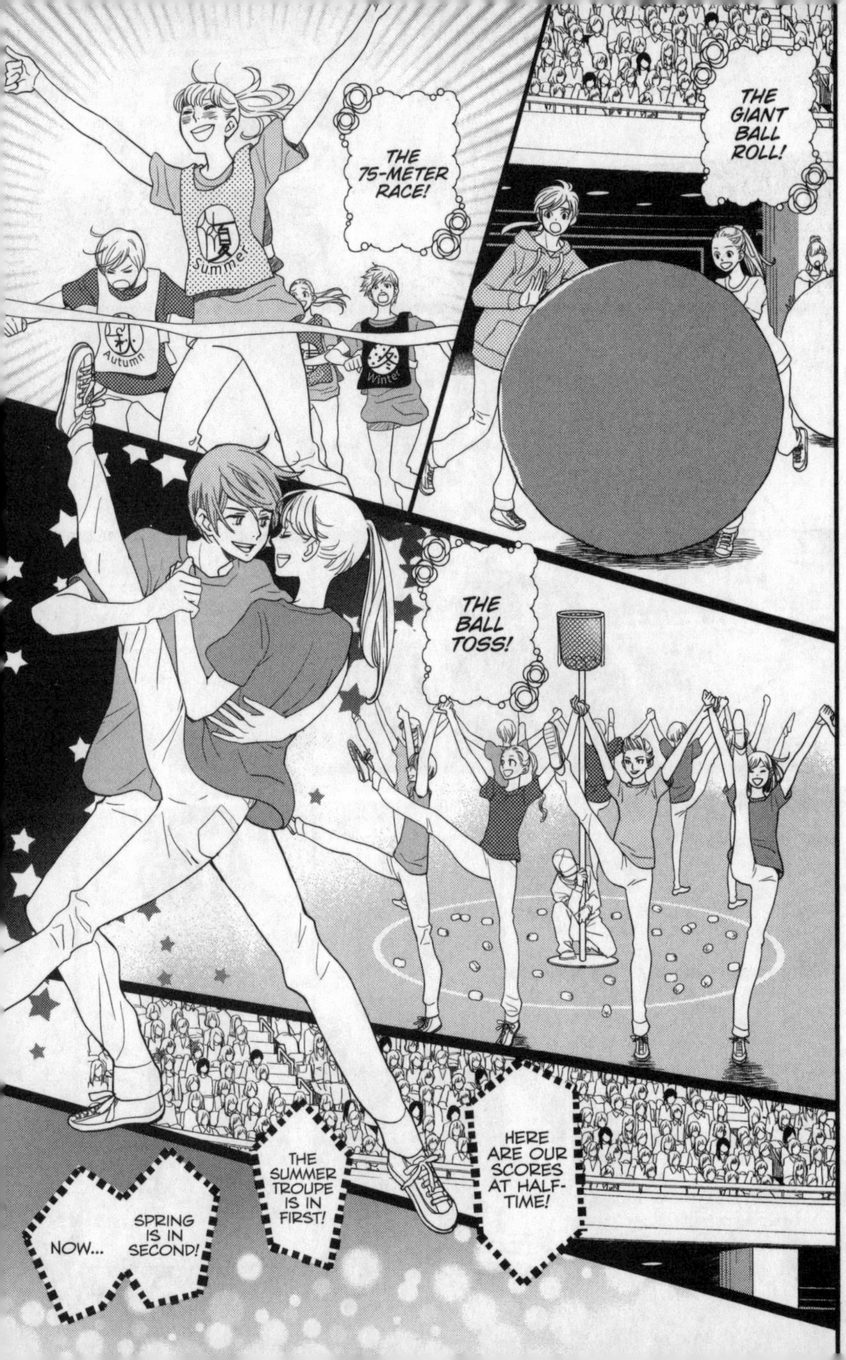
THE GIANT BALL ROLL!
THE 75-METER RACE!
Summer
Autumn
Winter
THE BALL TOSS!
HERE ARE OUR SCORES AT HALF-TIME!
THE SUMMER TROUPE IS IN FIRST!
SPRING IS IN SECOND!
NOW...

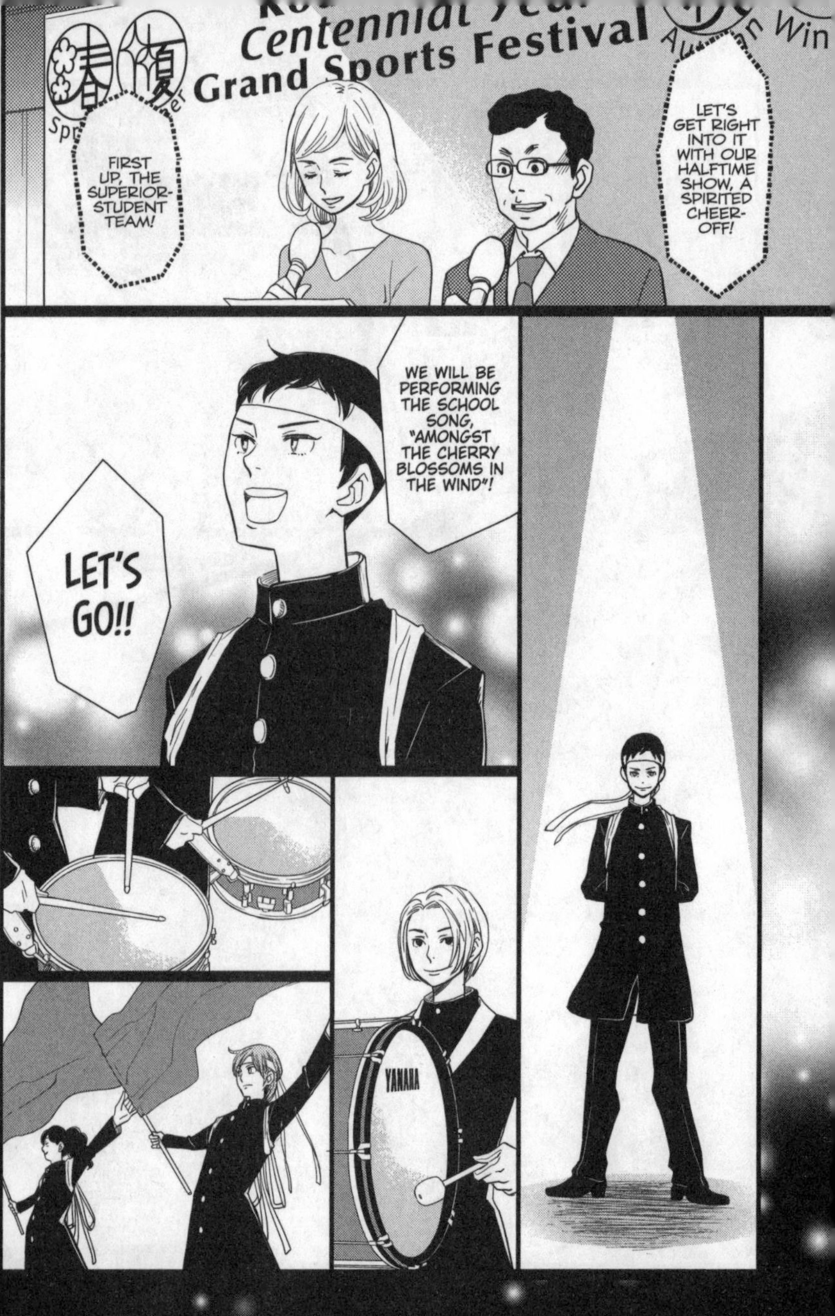
Centennial
Grand Sports Festival
LET'S GET RIGHT INTO IT WITH OUR HALFTIME SHOW, A SPIRITED CHEER-OFF!
FIRST UP, THE SUPERIOR-STUDENT TEAM!
WE WILL BE PERFORMING THE SCHOOL SONG, "AMONGST THE CHERRY BLOSSOMS IN THE WIND"!
LET'S GO!!
YAMAHA

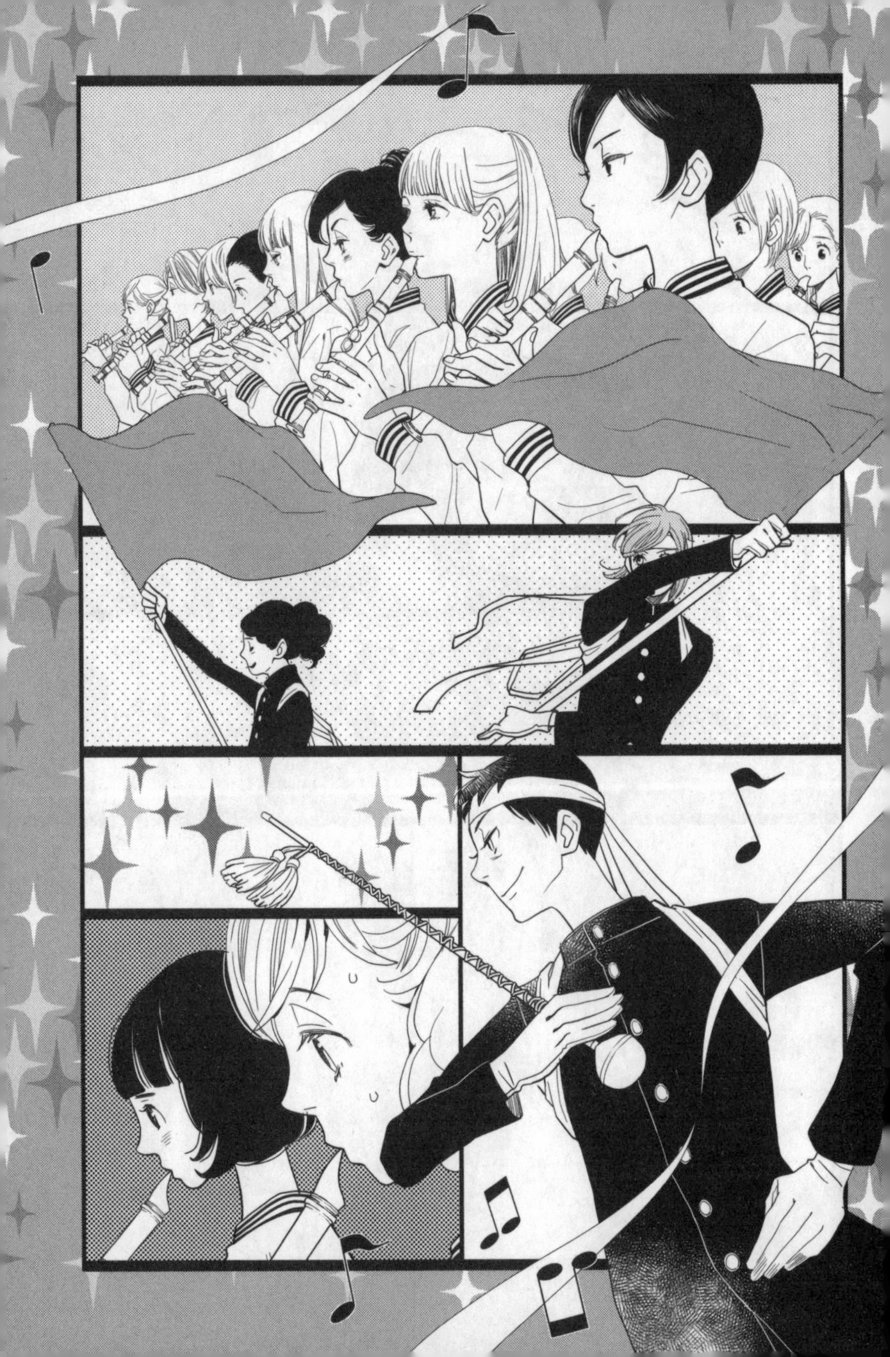

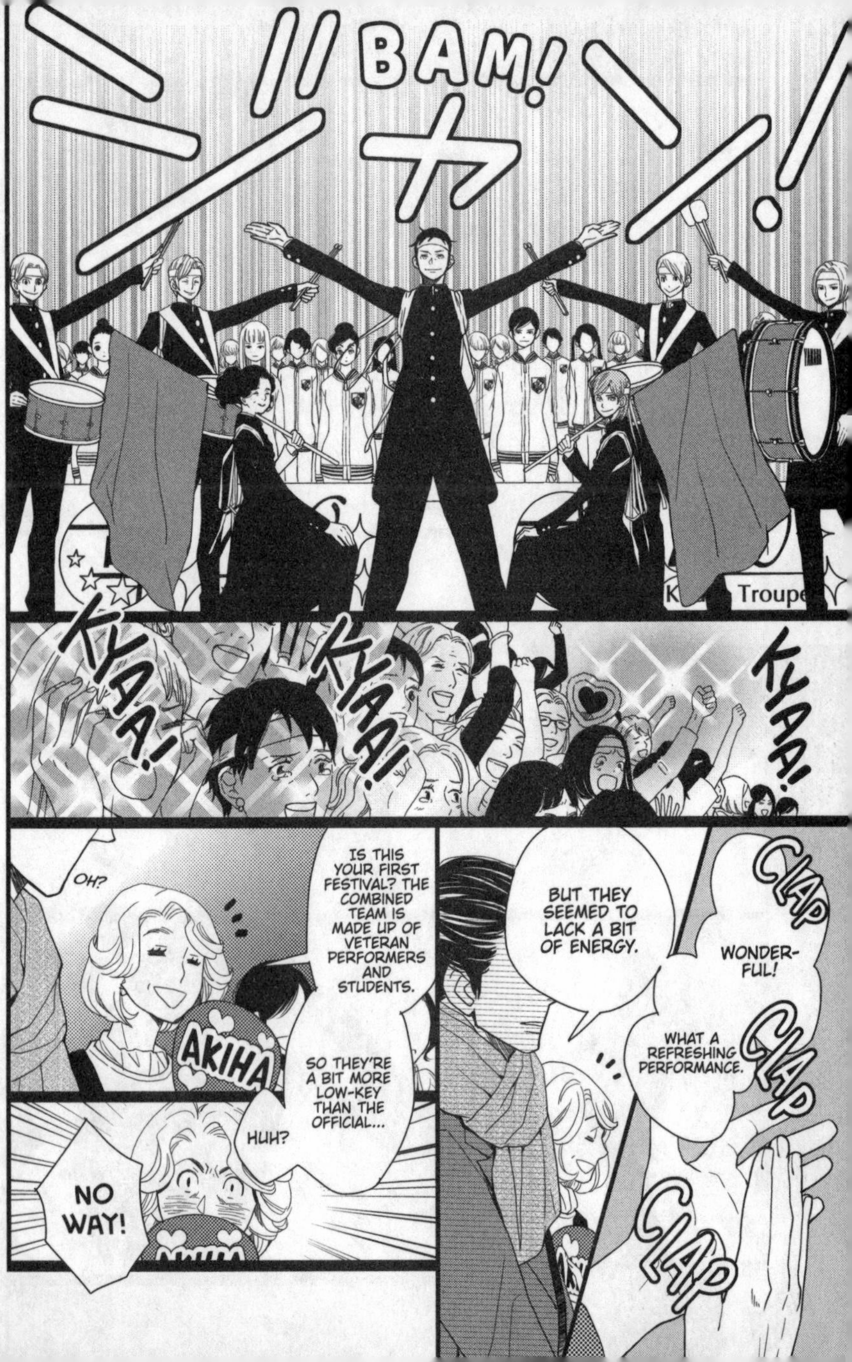
BAM!
Troupe
KYAAA!
KYAAA!
KYAAA!
CLAP
WONDERFUL!
WHAT A REFRESHING PERFORMANCE.
BUT THEY SEEMED TO LACK A BIT OF ENERGY.
CLAP
CLAP
CLAP
OH?
IS THIS YOUR FIRST FESTIVAL? THE COMBINED TEAM IS MADE UP OF VETERAN PERFORMERS AND STUDENTS.
SO THEY'RE A BIT MORE LOW-KEY THAN THE OFFICIAL...
AKIHA
HUH?
NO WAY!

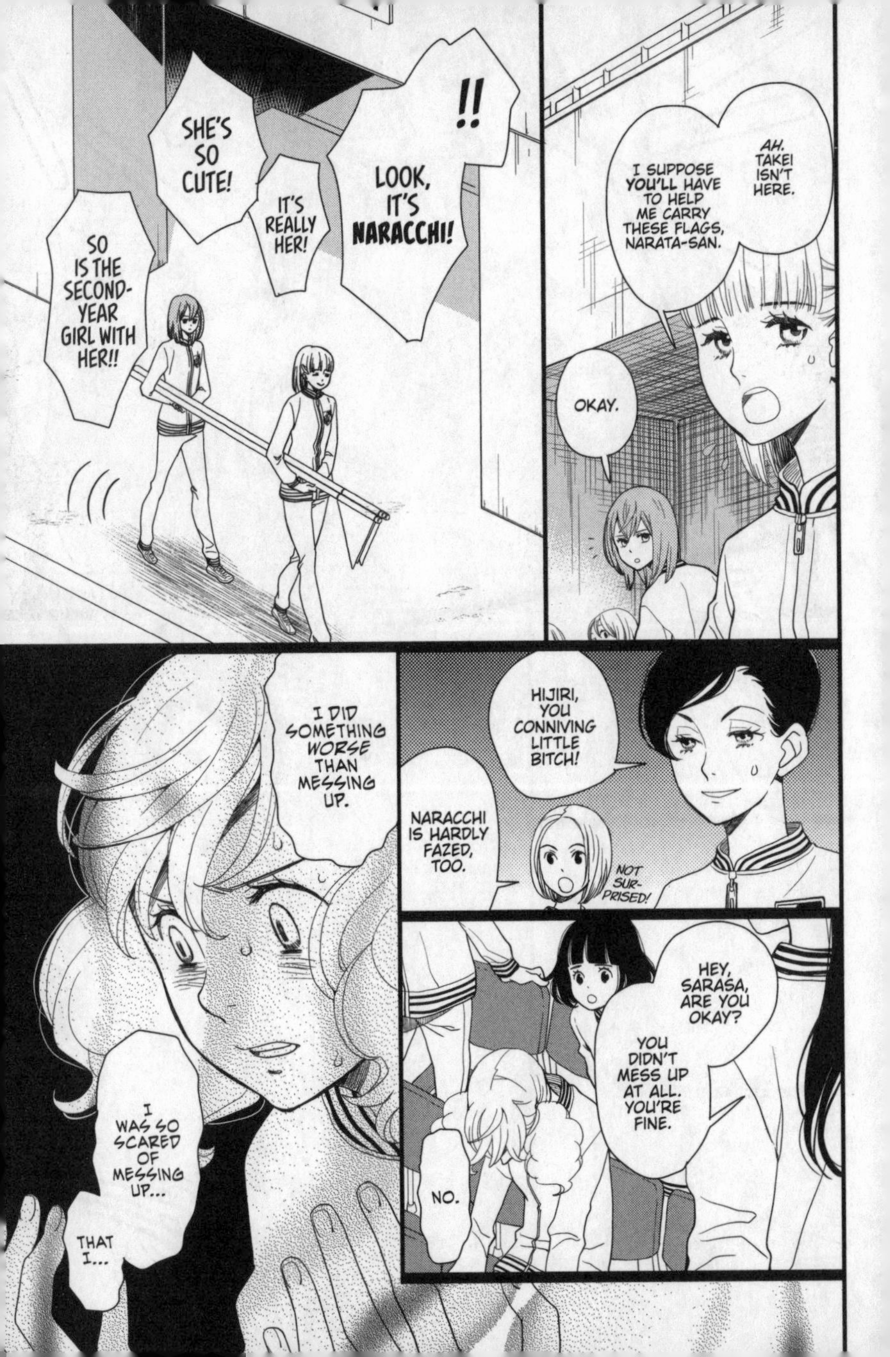
AH. TAKEI ISN'T HERE.
I SUPPOSE YOU'LL HAVE TO HELP ME CARRY THESE FLAGS, NARATA-SAN.
OKAY.
!!
LOOK, IT'S NARACCHI!
SHE'S SO CUTE!
IT'S REALLY HER!
SO IS THE SECOND-YEAR GIRL WITH HER!!
HIJIRI, YOU CONNIVING LITTLE BITCH!
NARACCHI IS HARDLY FAZED, TOO.
NOT SURPRISED!
HEY, SARASA, ARE YOU OKAY?
YOU DIDN'T MESS UP AT ALL. YOU'RE FINE.
NO.
I DID SOMETHING WORSE THAN MESSING UP.
I WAS SO SCARED OF MESSING UP...
THAT I...

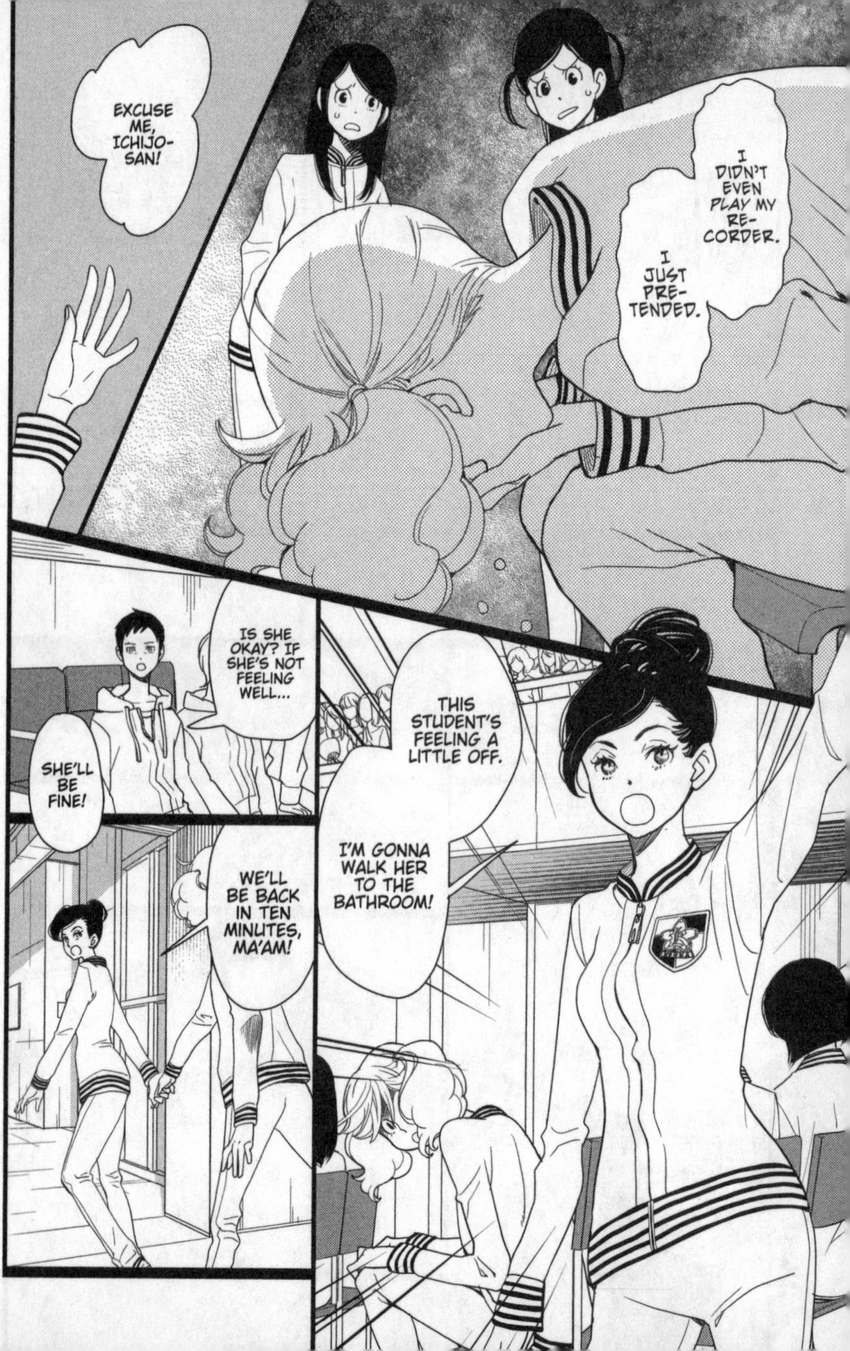
I DIDN'T EVEN PLAY MY RE-CORDER.
I JUST PRE-TENDED.
EXCUSE ME, ICHIJO-SAN!
THIS STUDENT'S FEELING A LITTLE OFF.
I'M GONNA WALK HER TO THE BATHROOM!
IS SHE OKAY? IF SHE'S NOT FEELING WELL...
SHE'LL BE FINE!
WE'LL BE BACK IN TEN MINUTES, MA'AM!

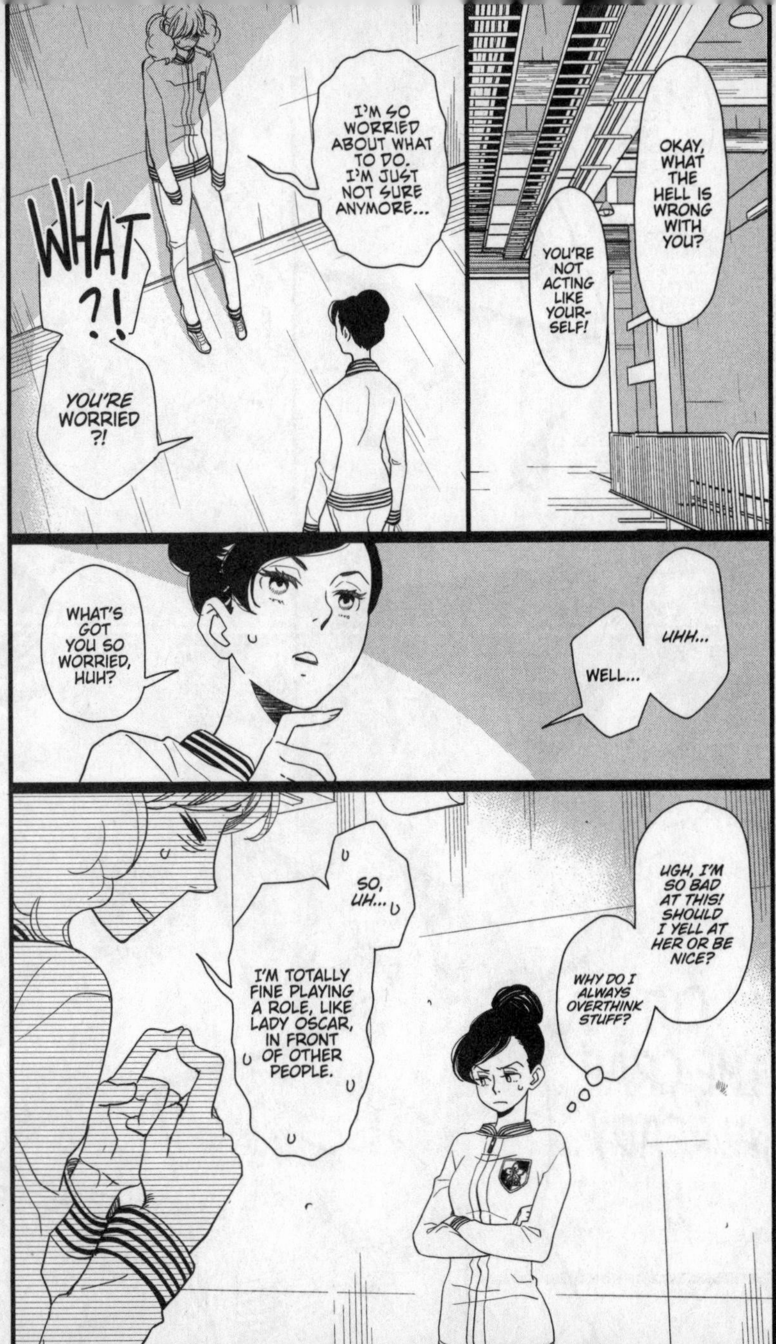
OKAY, WHAT THE HELL IS WRONG WITH YOU?
YOU'RE NOT ACTING LIKE YOUR-SELF!
I'M SO WORRIED ABOUT WHAT TO DO. I'M JUST NOT SURE ANYMORE...
WHAT ?!
YOU'RE WORRIED ?!
WHAT'S GOT YOU SO WORRIED, HUH?
UHH...
WELL...
UGH, I'M SO BAD AT THIS! SHOULD I YELL AT HER OR BE NICE?
WHY DO I ALWAYS OVERTHINK STUFF?
SO, UH...
I'M TOTALLY FINE PLAYING A ROLE, LIKE LADY OSCAR, IN FRONT OF OTHER PEOPLE.

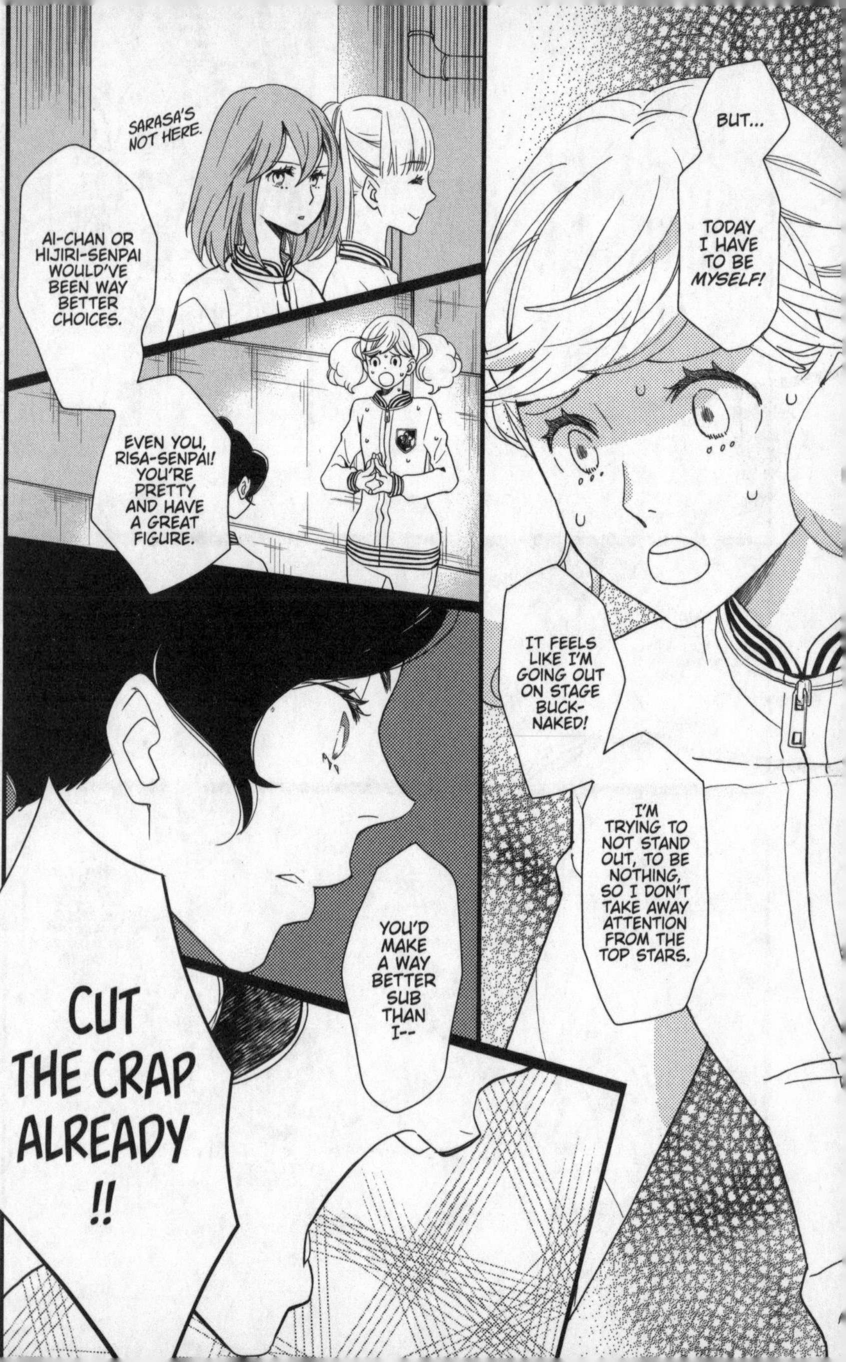
BUT...
TODAY I HAVE TO BE MYSELF!
IT FEELS LIKE I'M GOING OUT ON STAGE BUCK-NAKED!
I'M TRYING TO NOT STAND OUT, TO BE NOTHING, SO I DON'T TAKE AWAY ATTENTION FROM THE TOP STARS.
SARASA'S NOT HERE.
AI-CHAN OR HIJIRI-SENPAI WOULD'VE BEEN WAY BETTER CHOICES.
EVEN YOU, RISA-SENPAI! YOU'RE PRETTY AND HAVE A GREAT FIGURE.
YOU'D MAKE A WAY BETTER SUB THAN I--
CUT THE CRAP ALREADY !!

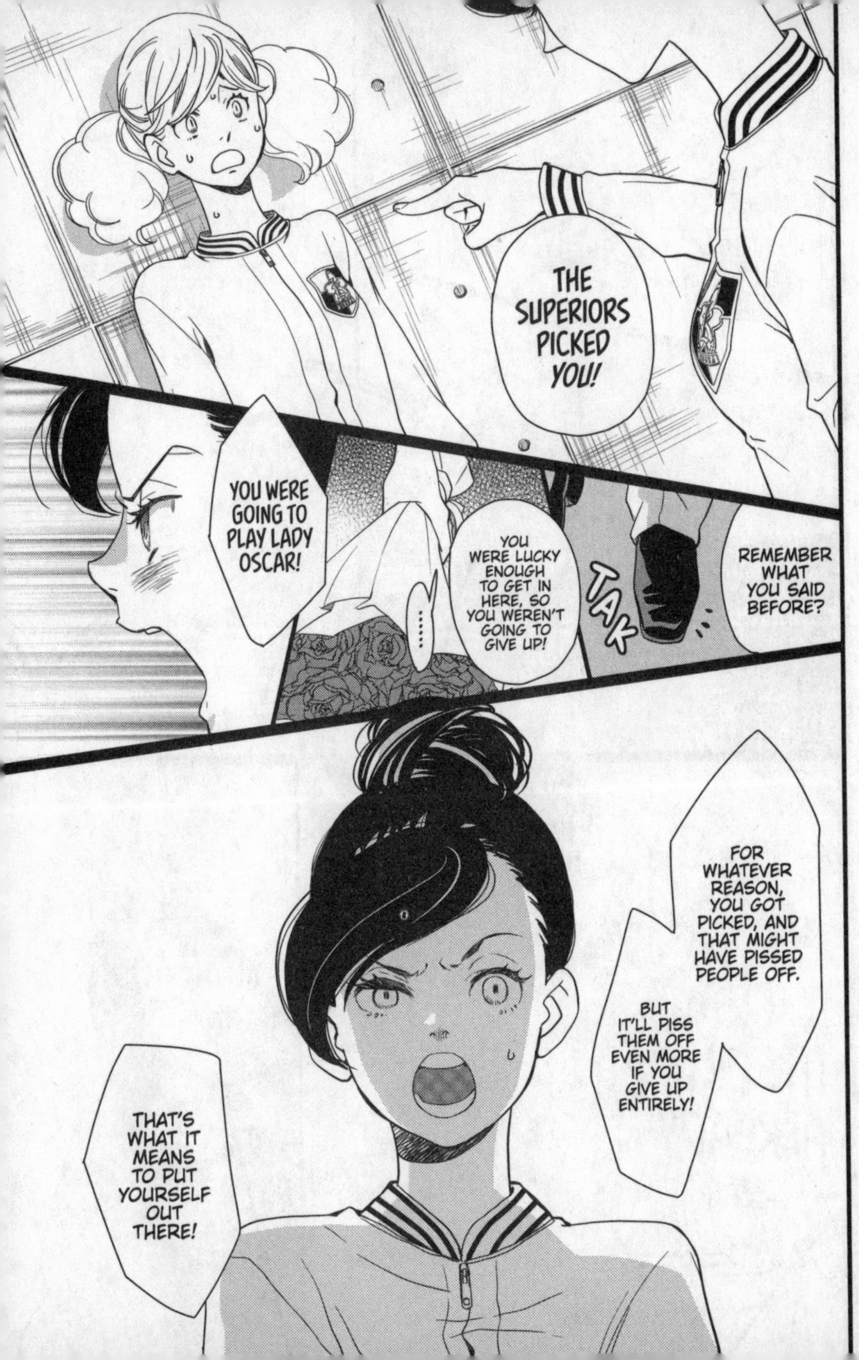
THE SUPERIORS PICKED YOU!
REMEMBER WHAT YOU SAID BEFORE?
TAK
YOU WERE LUCKY ENOUGH TO GET IN HERE, SO YOU WEREN'T GOING TO GIVE UP!
......
YOU WERE GOING TO PLAY LADY OSCAR!
FOR WHATEVER REASON, YOU GOT PICKED, AND THAT MIGHT HAVE PISSED PEOPLE OFF.
BUT IT'LL PISS THEM OFF EVEN MORE IF YOU GIVE UP ENTIRELY!
THAT'S WHAT IT MEANS TO PUT YOURSELF OUT THERE!

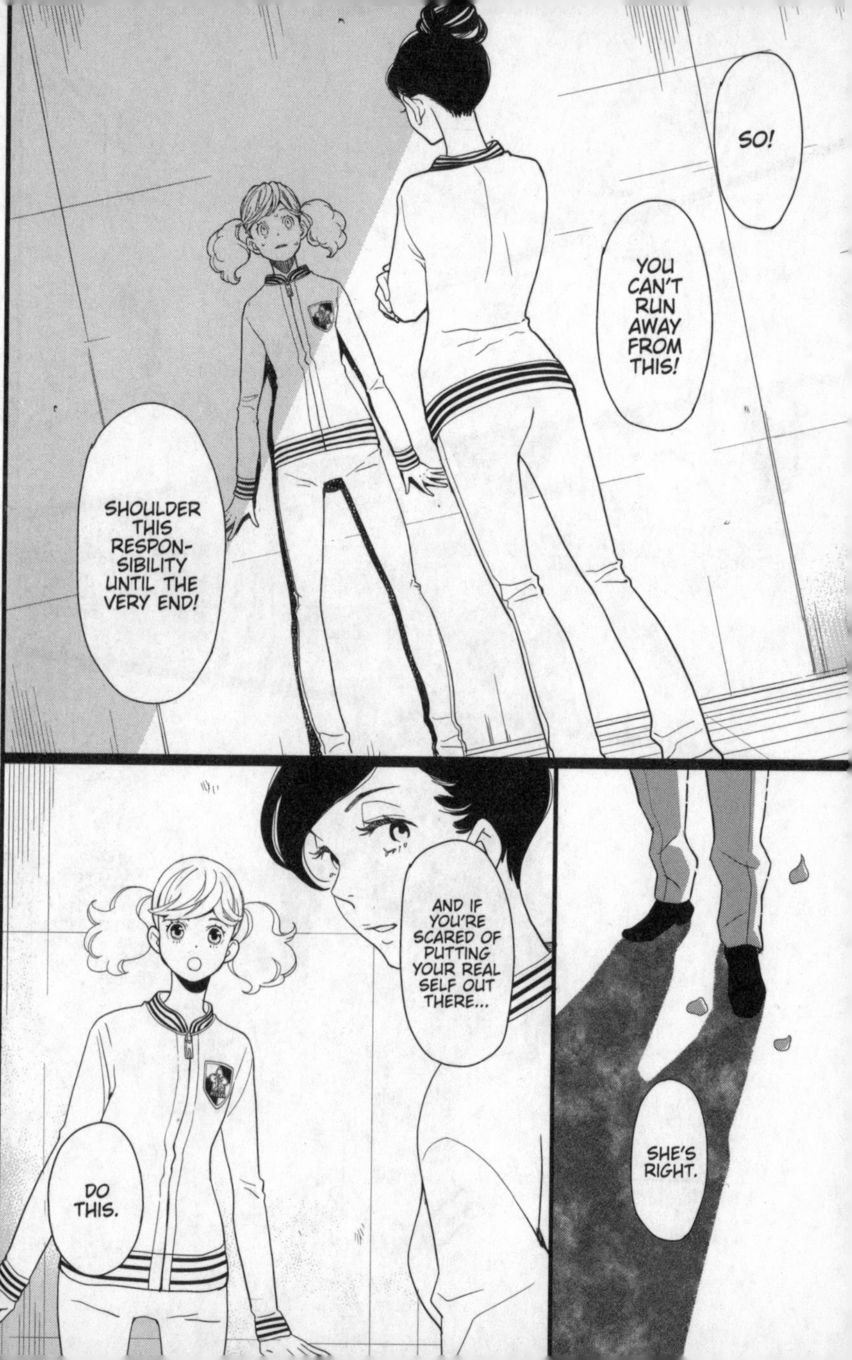
SO!
YOU CAN'T RUN AWAY FROM THIS!
SHOULDER THIS RESPON-SIBILITY UNTIL THE VERY END!
SHE'S RIGHT.
AND IF YOU'RE SCARED OF PUTTING YOUR REAL SELF OUT THERE...
DO THIS.

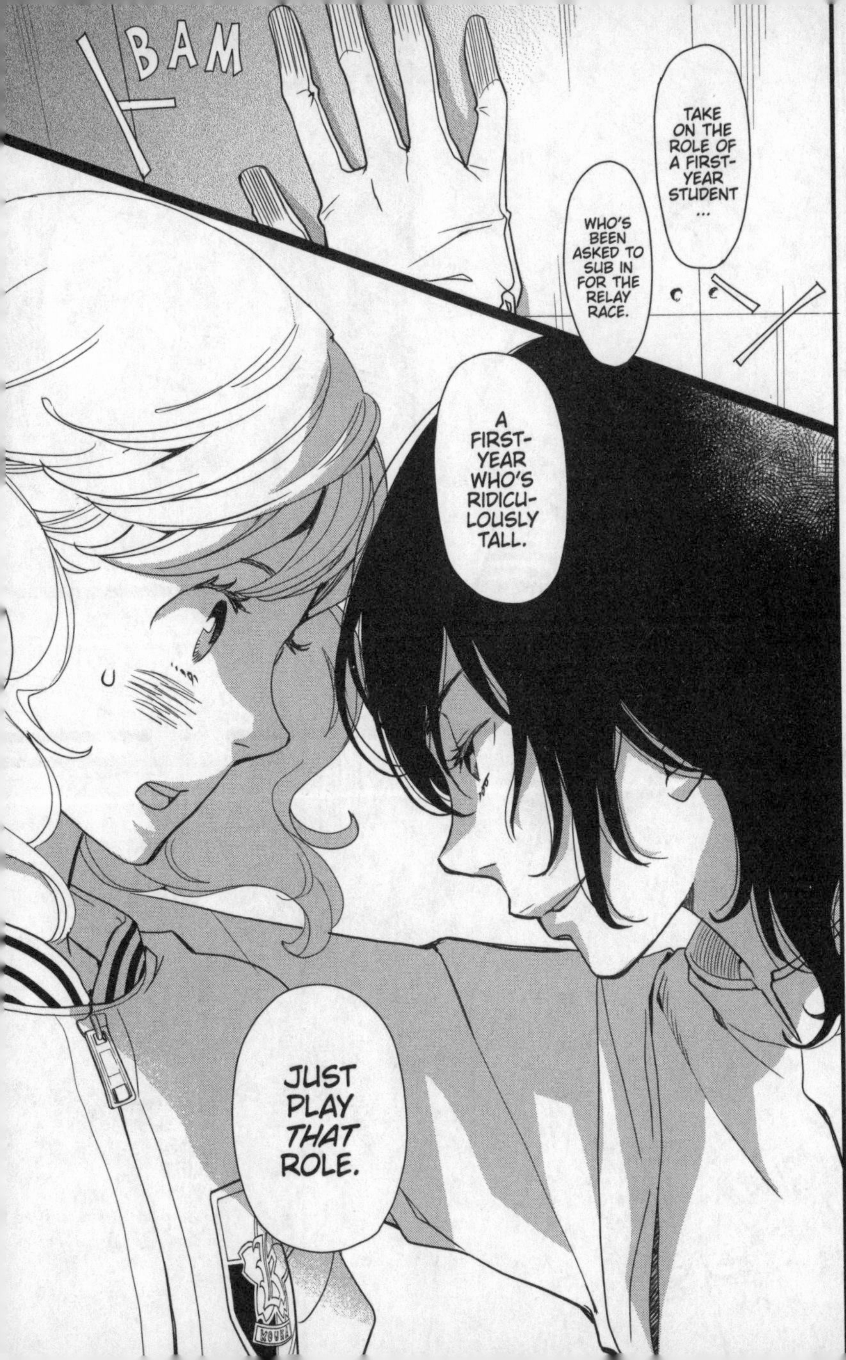
TAKE ON THE ROLE OF A FIRST-YEAR STUDENT...
WHO'S BEEN ASKED TO SUB IN FOR THE RELAY RACE.
BAM
A FIRST-YEAR WHO'S RIDICULOUSLY TALL.
JUST PLAY *THAT* ROLE.

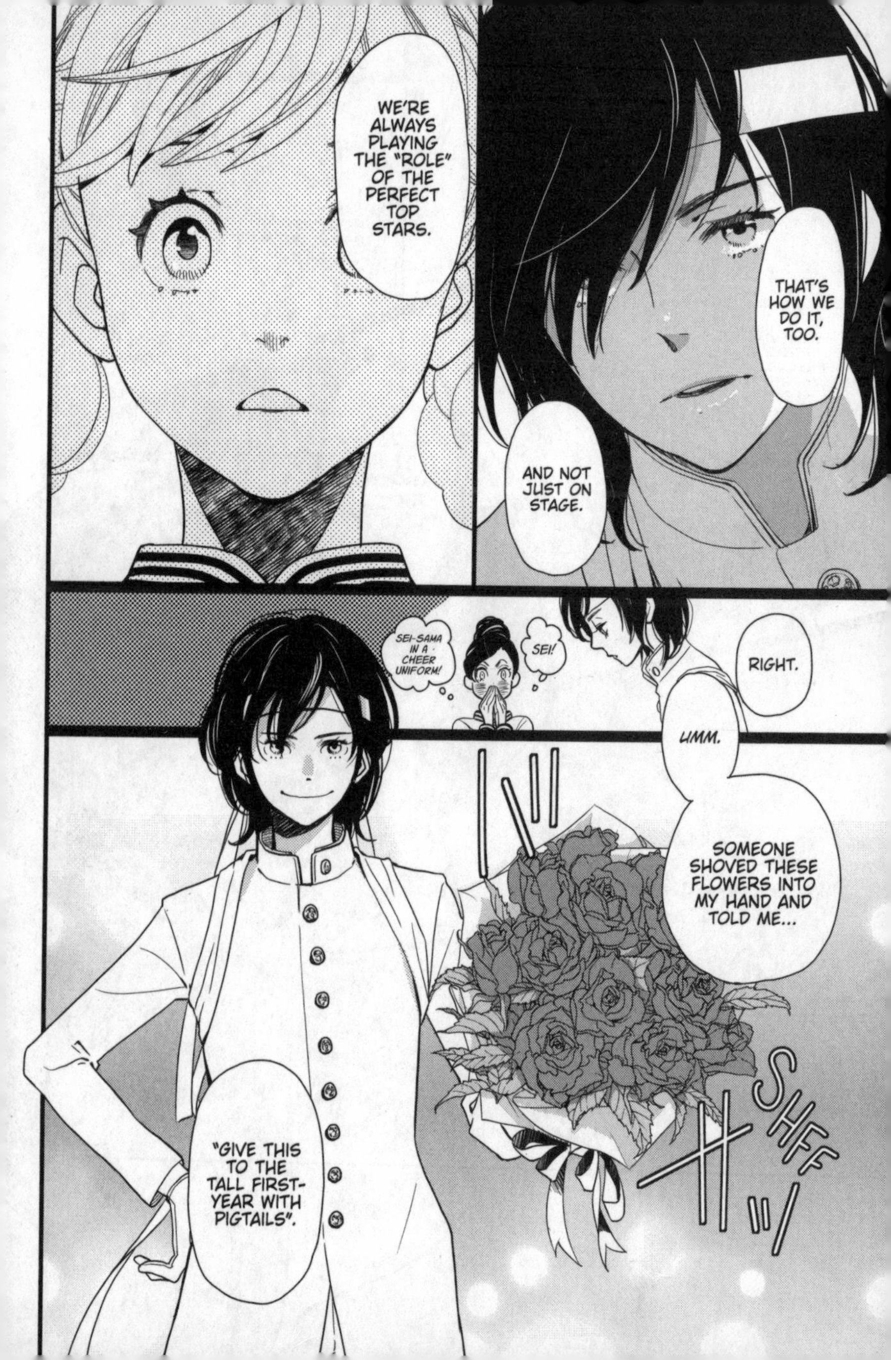
THAT'S HOW WE DO IT, TOO.
AND NOT JUST ON STAGE.
WE'RE ALWAYS PLAYING THE "ROLE" OF THE PERFECT TOP STARS.
RIGHT.
SEI!
SEI-SAMA IN A CHEER UNIFORM!
UMM.
SOMEONE SHOVED THESE FLOWERS INTO MY HAND AND TOLD ME...
SHFF
"GIVE THIS TO THE TALL FIRST-YEAR WITH PIGTAILS".

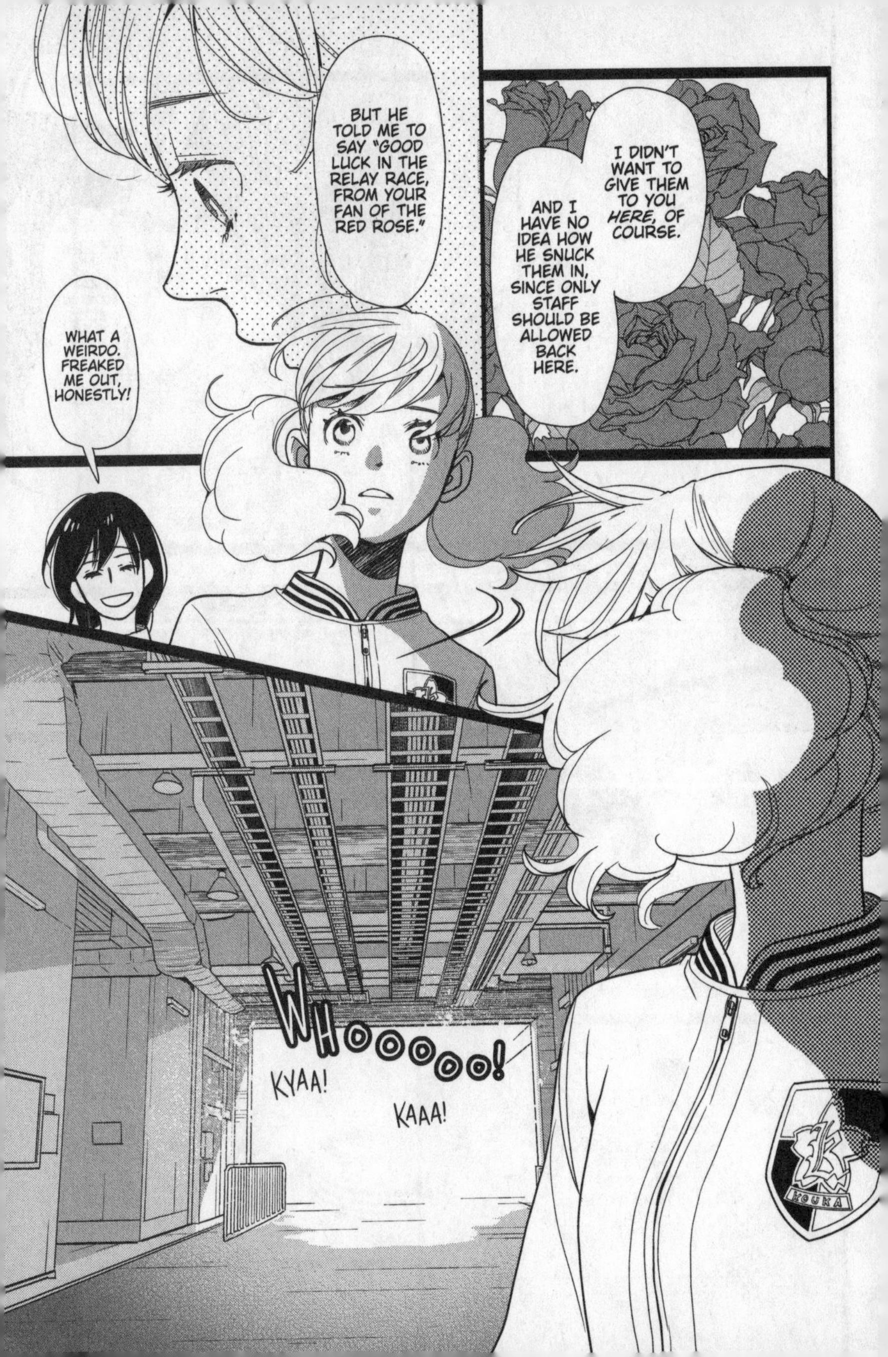
I DIDN'T WANT TO GIVE THEM TO YOU *HERE*, OF COURSE.
AND I HAVE NO IDEA HOW HE SNUCK THEM IN, SINCE ONLY STAFF SHOULD BE ALLOWED BACK HERE.
BUT HE TOLD ME TO SAY "GOOD LUCK IN THE RELAY RACE, FROM YOUR FAN OF THE RED ROSE."
WHAT A WEIRDO. FREAKED ME OUT, HONESTLY!
WHOOOOOO!
KYAA!
KAAA!
KOUKA

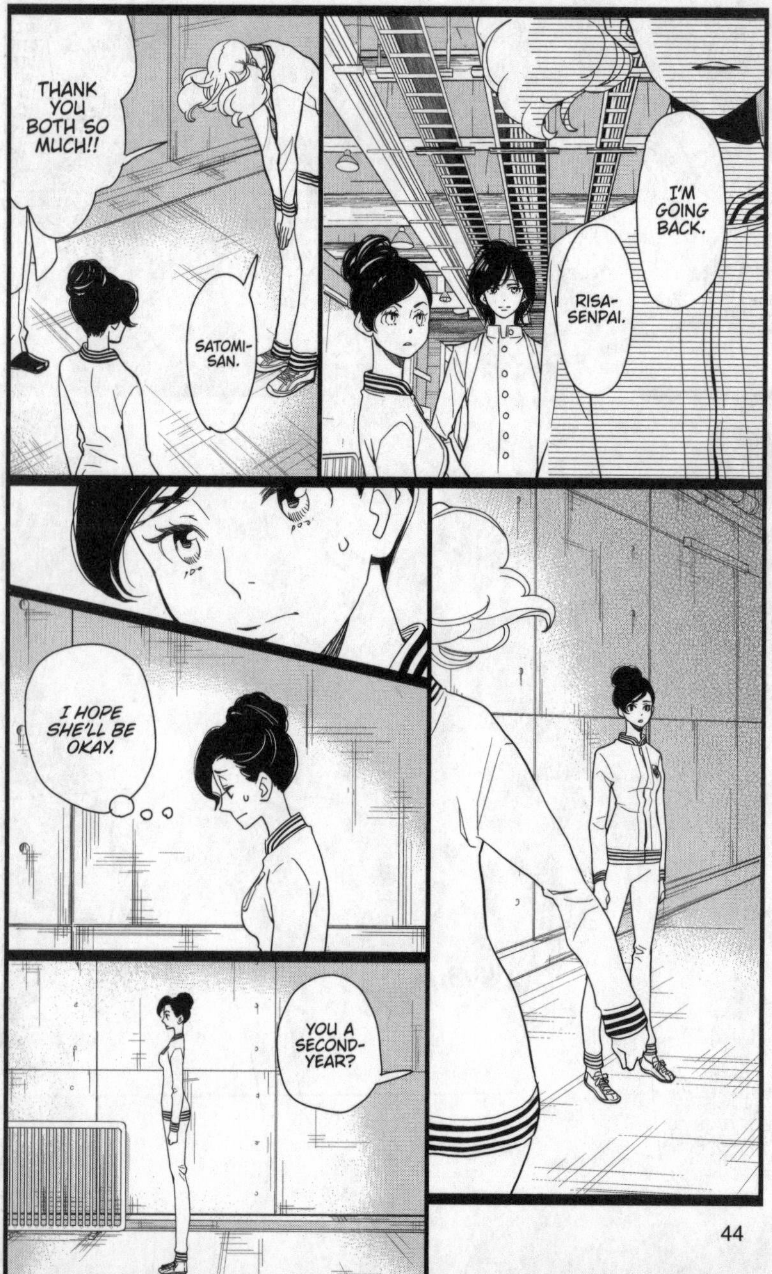
I'M GOING BACK.
RISA-SENPAI.
THANK YOU BOTH SO MUCH!!
SATOMI-SAN.
I HOPE SHE'LL BE OKAY.
YOU A SECOND-YEAR?

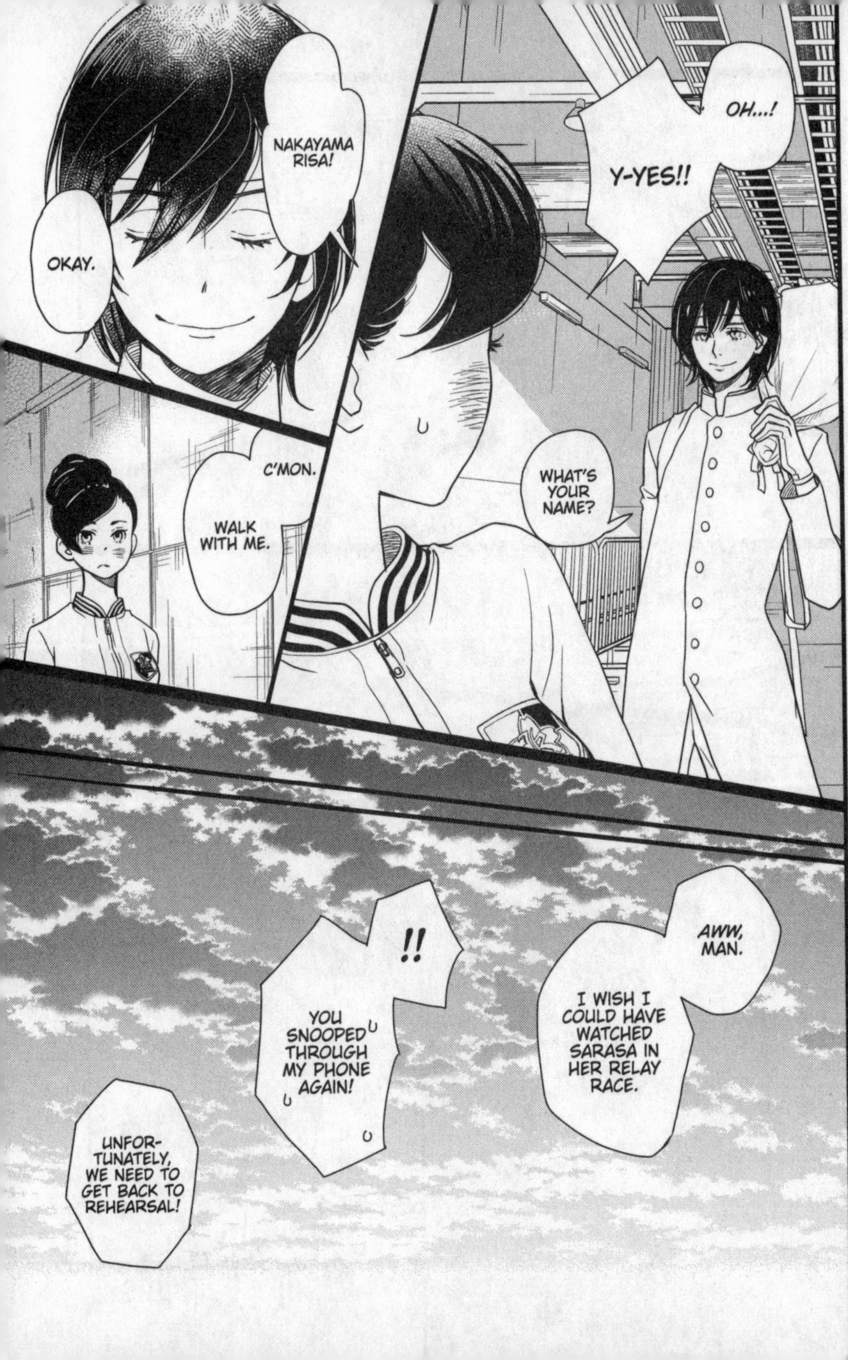
OH...!
Y-YES!!
WHAT'S YOUR NAME?
NAKAYAMA RISA!
OKAY.
C'MON.
WALK WITH ME.
AWW, MAN.
I WISH I COULD HAVE WATCHED SARASA IN HER RELAY RACE.
!!
YOU SNOOPED THROUGH MY PHONE AGAIN!
UNFOR-TUNATELY, WE NEED TO GET BACK TO REHEARSAL!

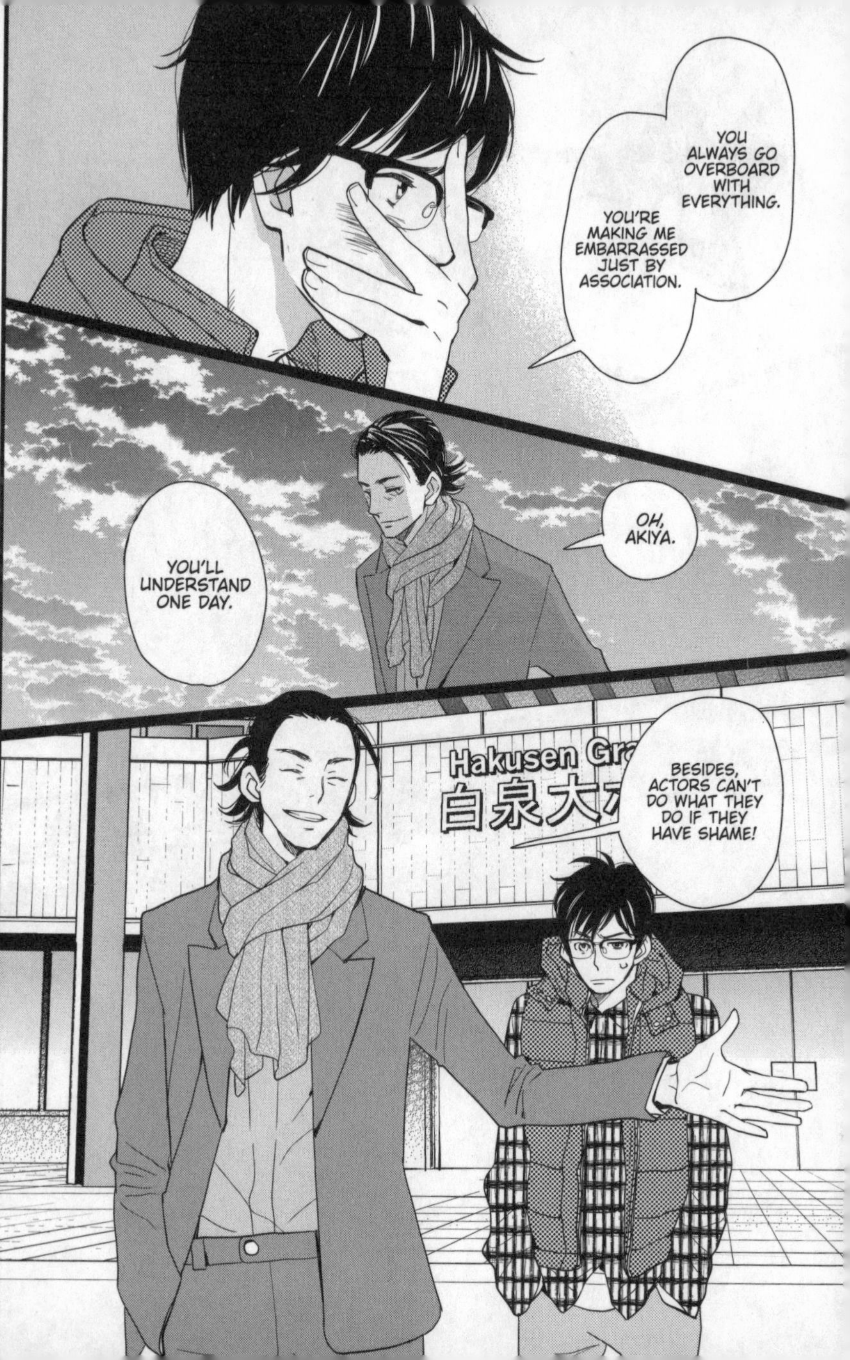
YOU ALWAYS GO OVERBOARD WITH EVERYTHING.
YOU'RE MAKING ME EMBARRASSED JUST BY ASSOCIATION.
OH, AKIYA.
YOU'LL UNDERSTAND ONE DAY.
Hakusen Gra
白泉大
BESIDES, ACTORS CAN'T DO WHAT THEY DO IF THEY HAVE SHAME!

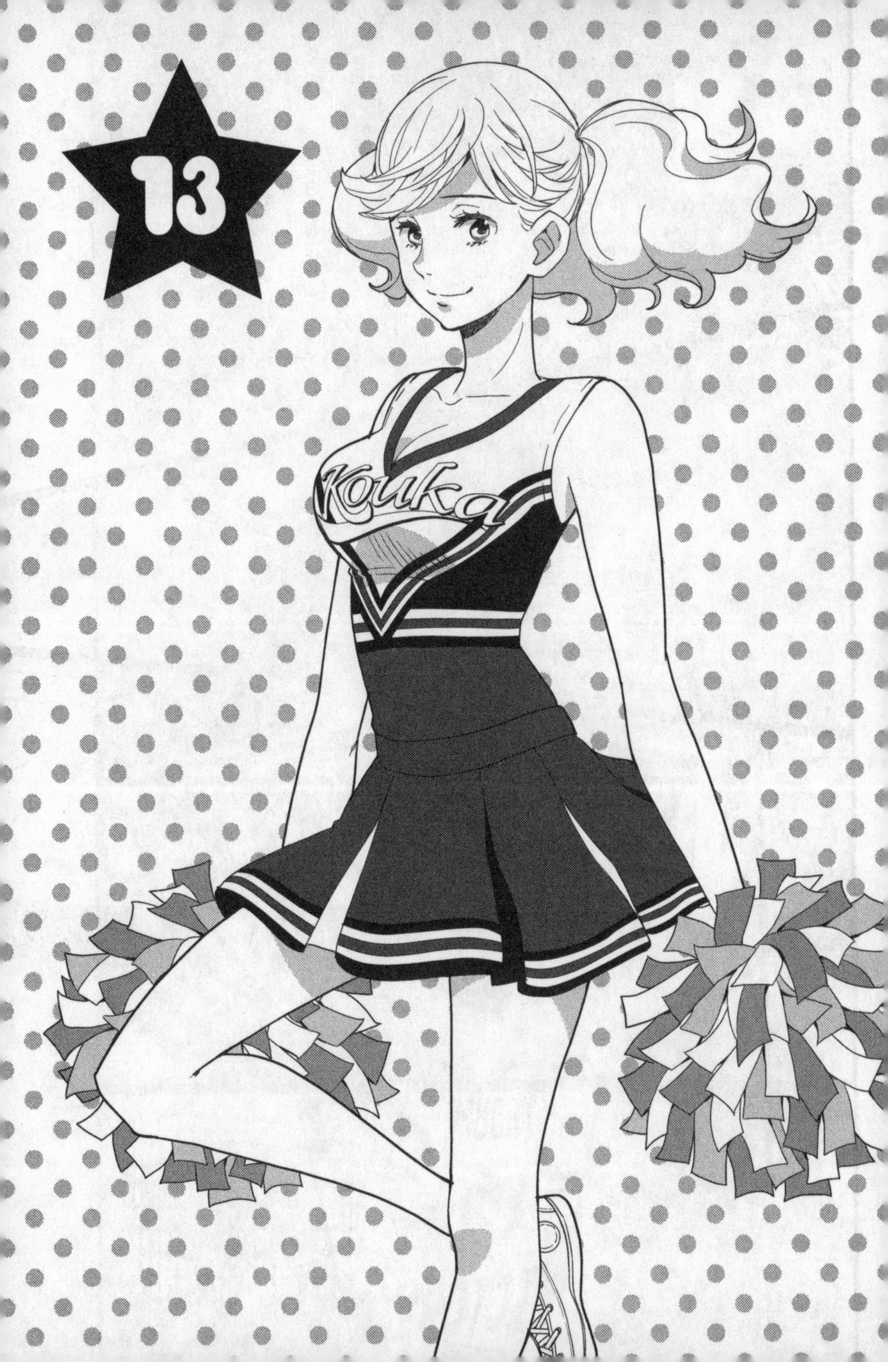
13
Kouka

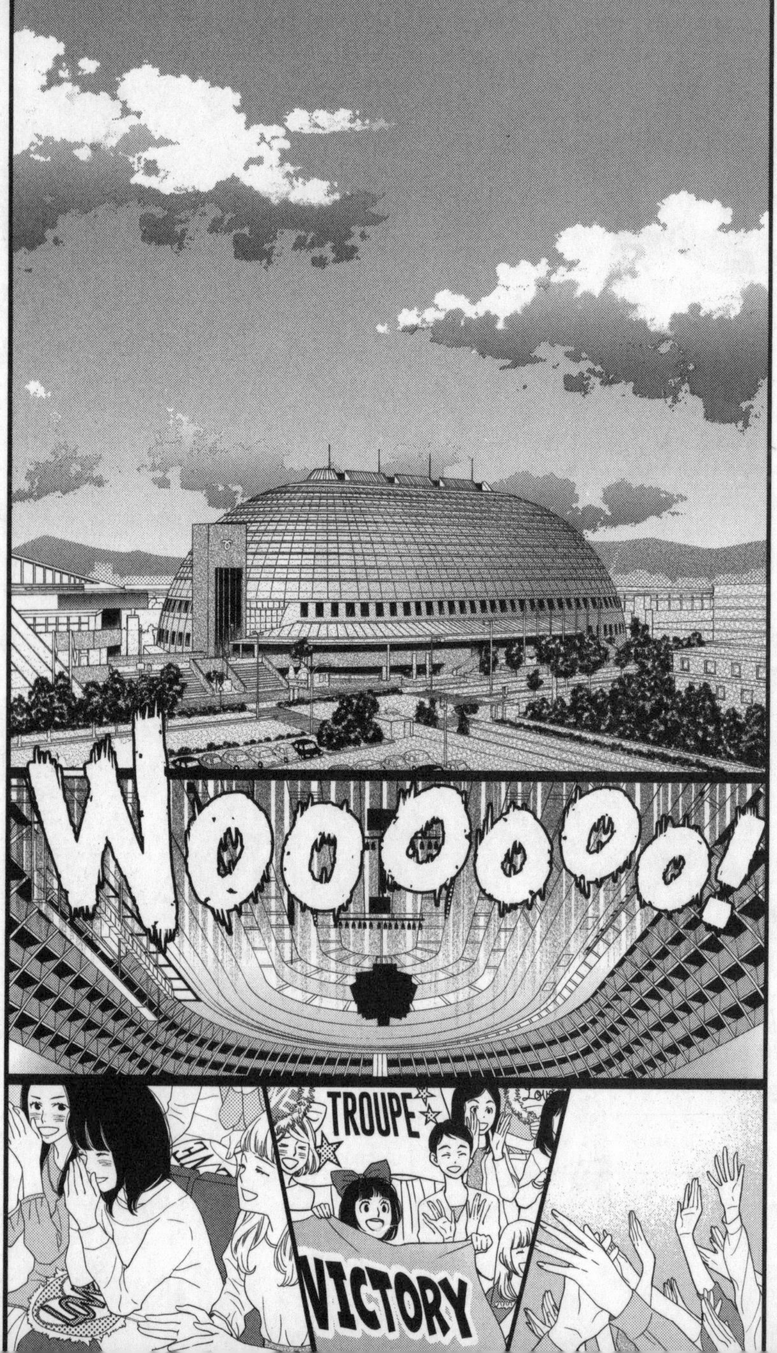
Woooooo!
TROUPE
VICTORY

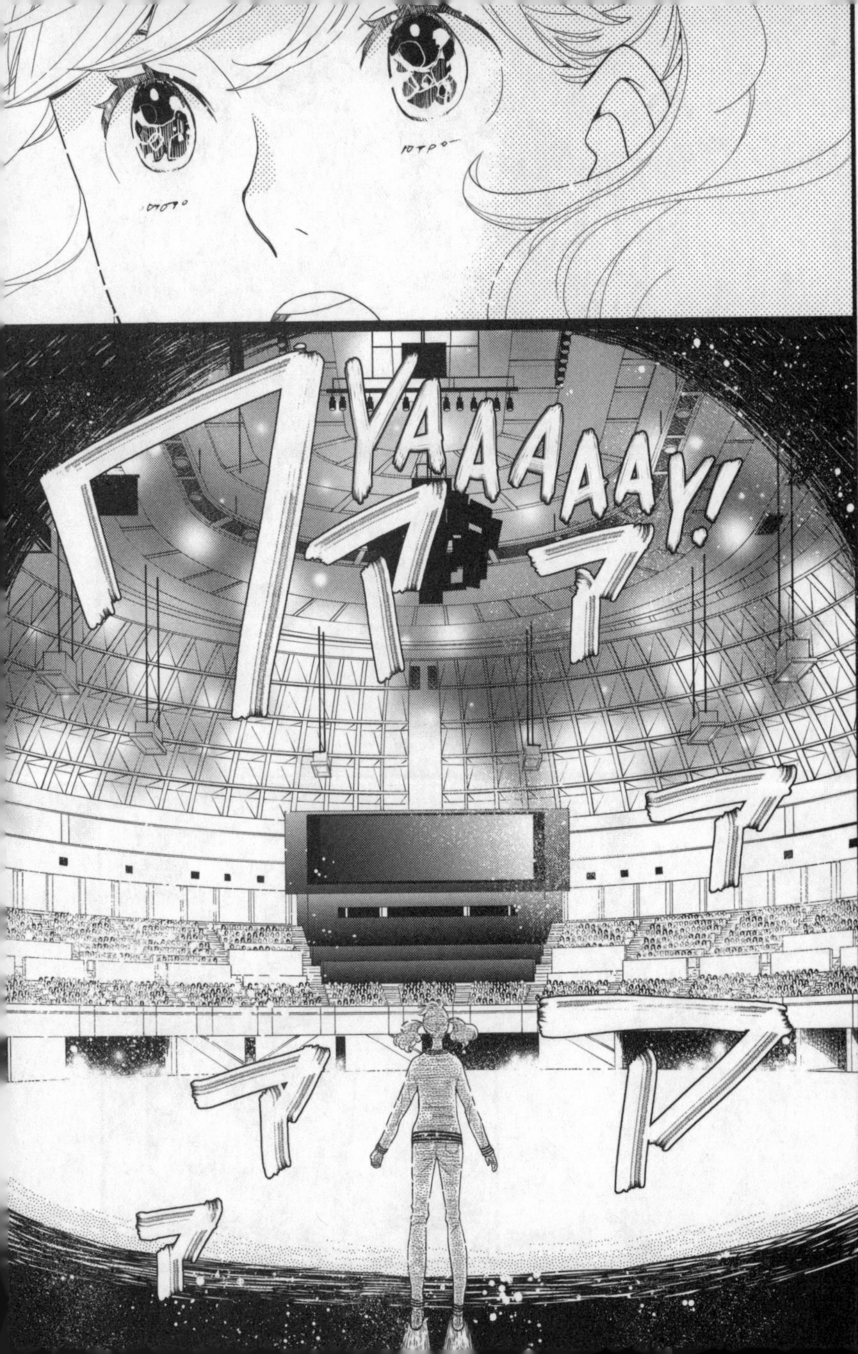
YAAAAAY!

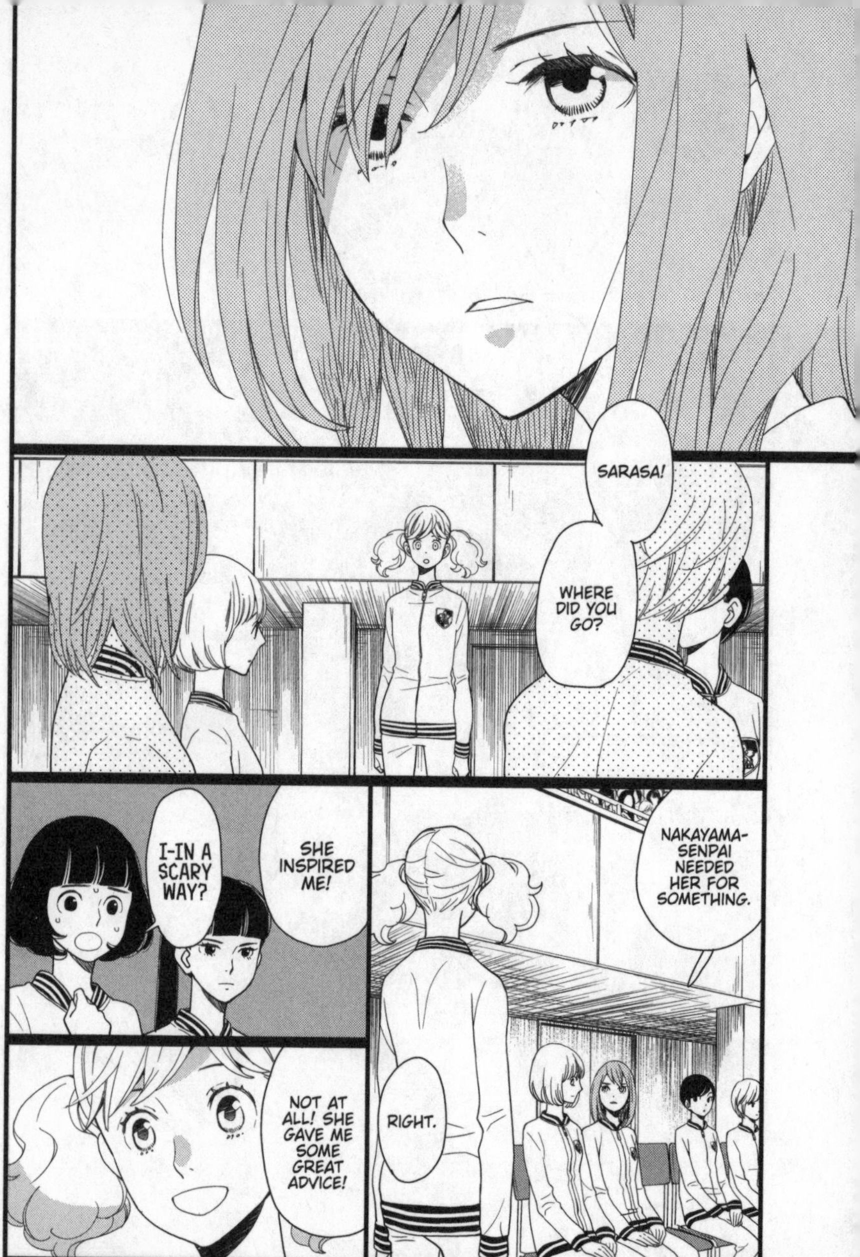
SARASA!
WHERE DID YOU GO?
NAKAYAMA-SENPAI NEEDED HER FOR SOMETHING.
RIGHT.
SHE INSPIRED ME!
I-IN A SCARY WAY?
NOT AT ALL! SHE GAVE ME SOME GREAT ADVICE!

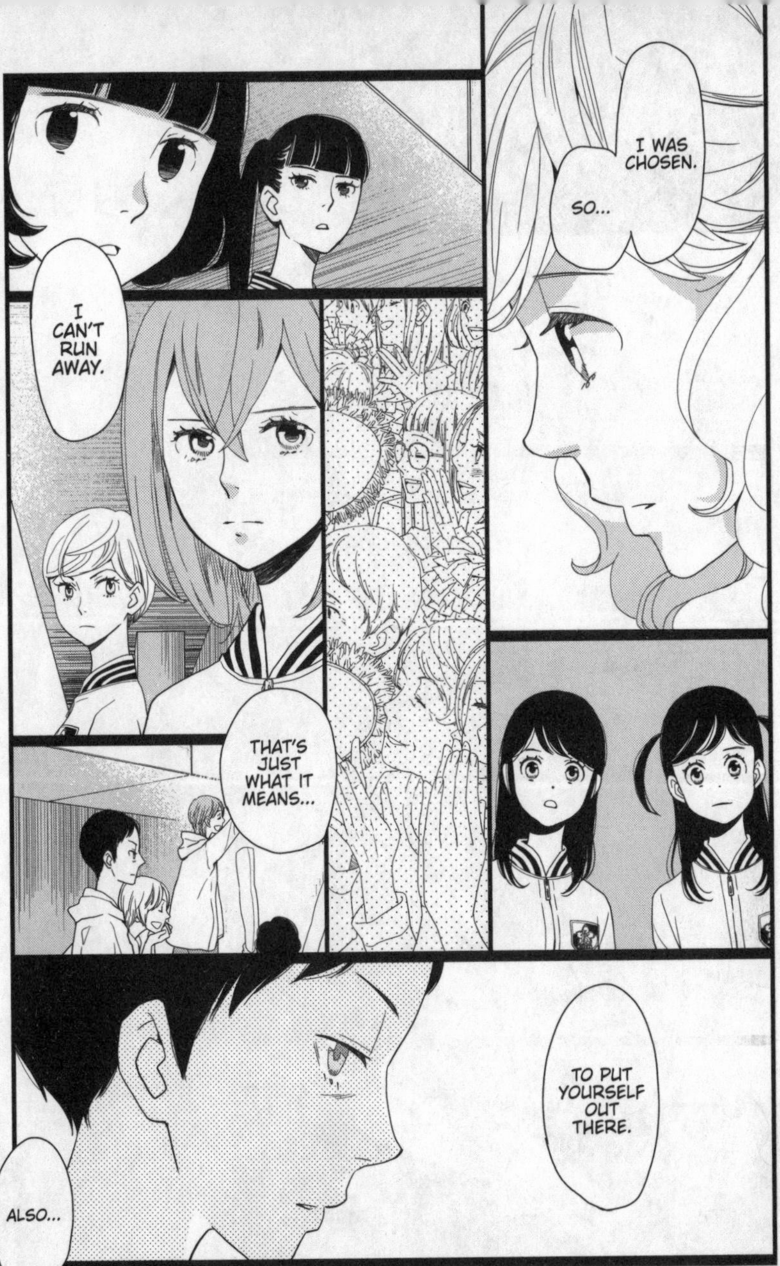
I WAS CHOSEN.
SO...
I CAN'T RUN AWAY.
THAT'S JUST WHAT IT MEANS...
TO PUT YOURSELF OUT THERE.
ALSO...

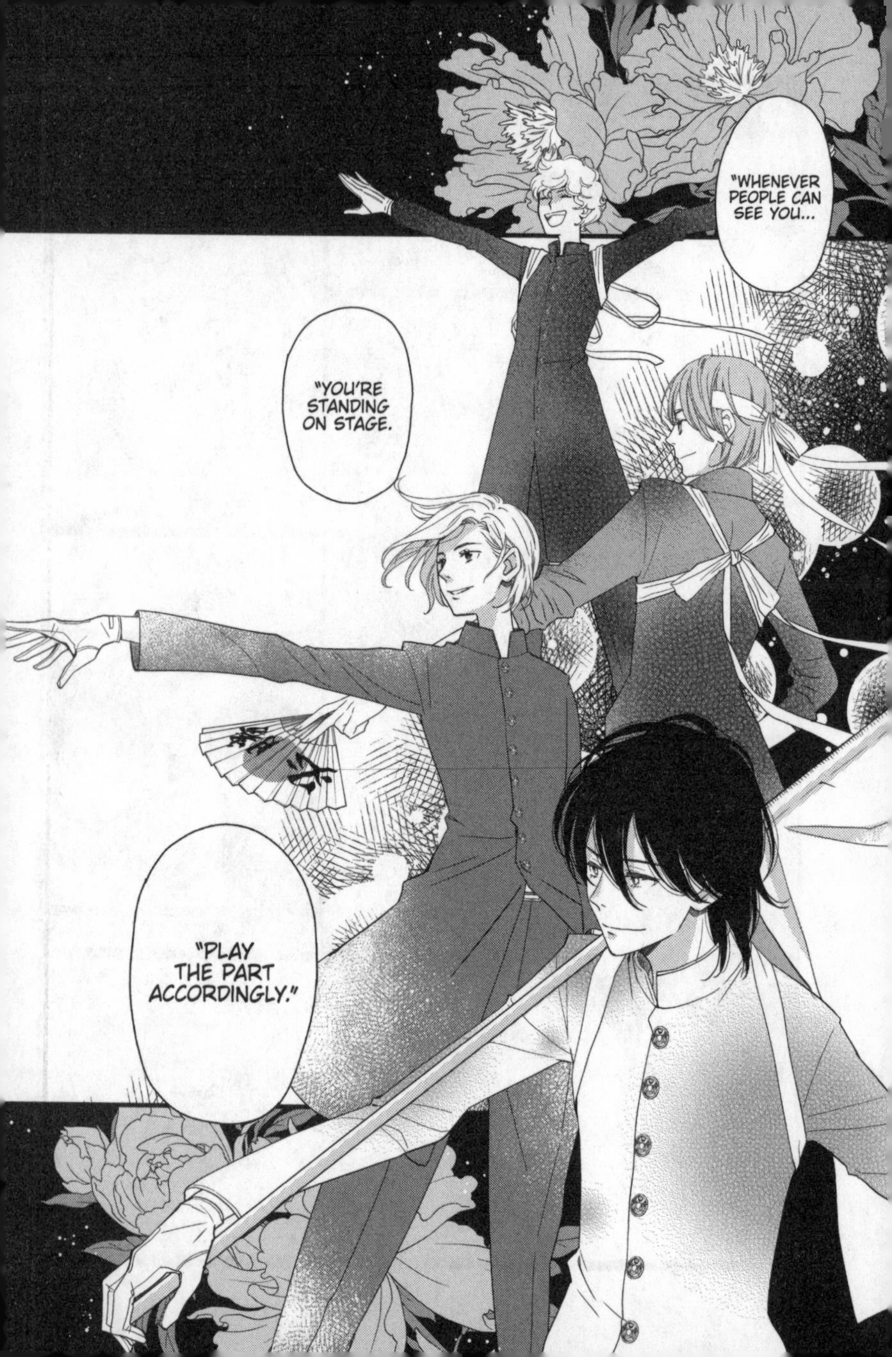
"WHENEVER PEOPLE CAN SEE YOU...
"YOU'RE STANDING ON STAGE.
"PLAY THE PART ACCORDINGLY."

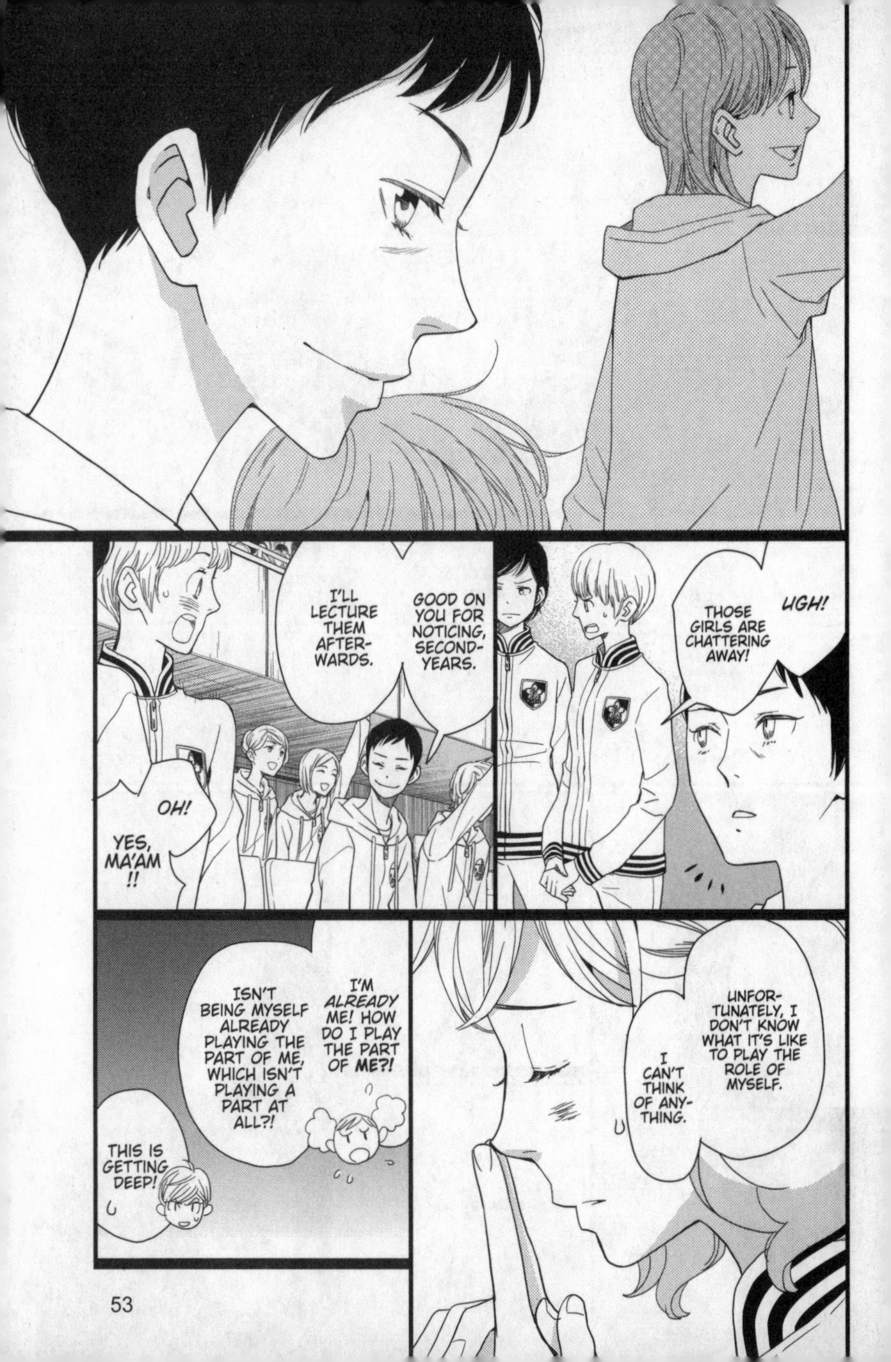
UGH!
THOSE GIRLS ARE CHATTERING AWAY!
GOOD ON YOU FOR NOTICING, SECOND-YEARS.
I'LL LECTURE THEM AFTERWARDS.
OH!
YES, MA'AM!!
UNFORTUNATELY, I DON'T KNOW WHAT IT'S LIKE TO PLAY THE ROLE OF MYSELF.
I CAN'T THINK OF ANYTHING.
I'M *ALREADY* ME! HOW DO I PLAY THE PART OF **ME**?!
ISN'T BEING MYSELF ALREADY PLAYING THE PART OF ME, WHICH ISN'T PLAYING A PART AT ALL?!
THIS IS GETTING DEEP!

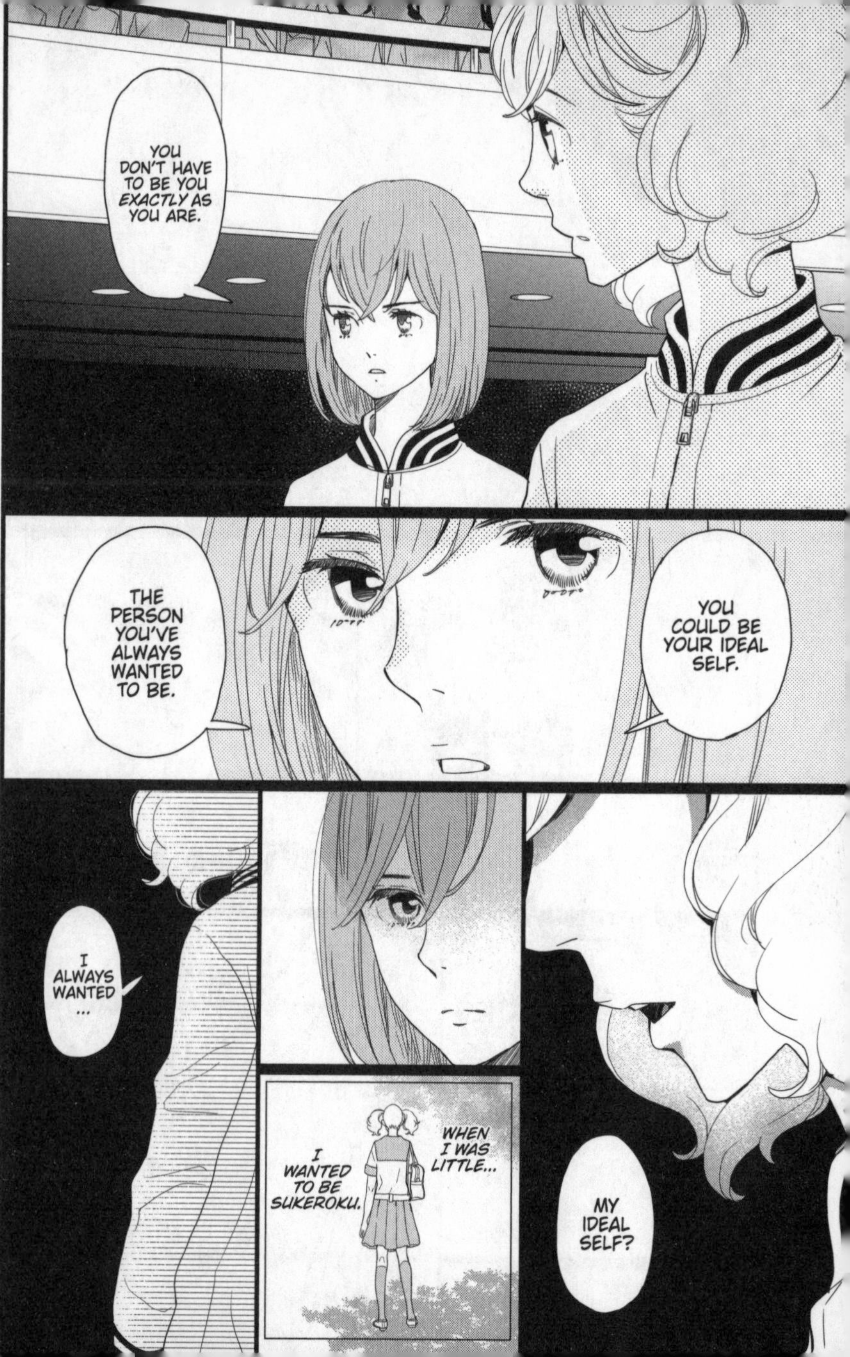
YOU DON'T HAVE TO BE YOU *EXACTLY* AS YOU ARE.
YOU COULD BE YOUR IDEAL SELF.
THE PERSON YOU'VE ALWAYS WANTED TO BE.
MY IDEAL SELF?
WHEN I WAS LITTLE...
I WANTED TO BE SUKEROKU.
I ALWAYS WANTED ...

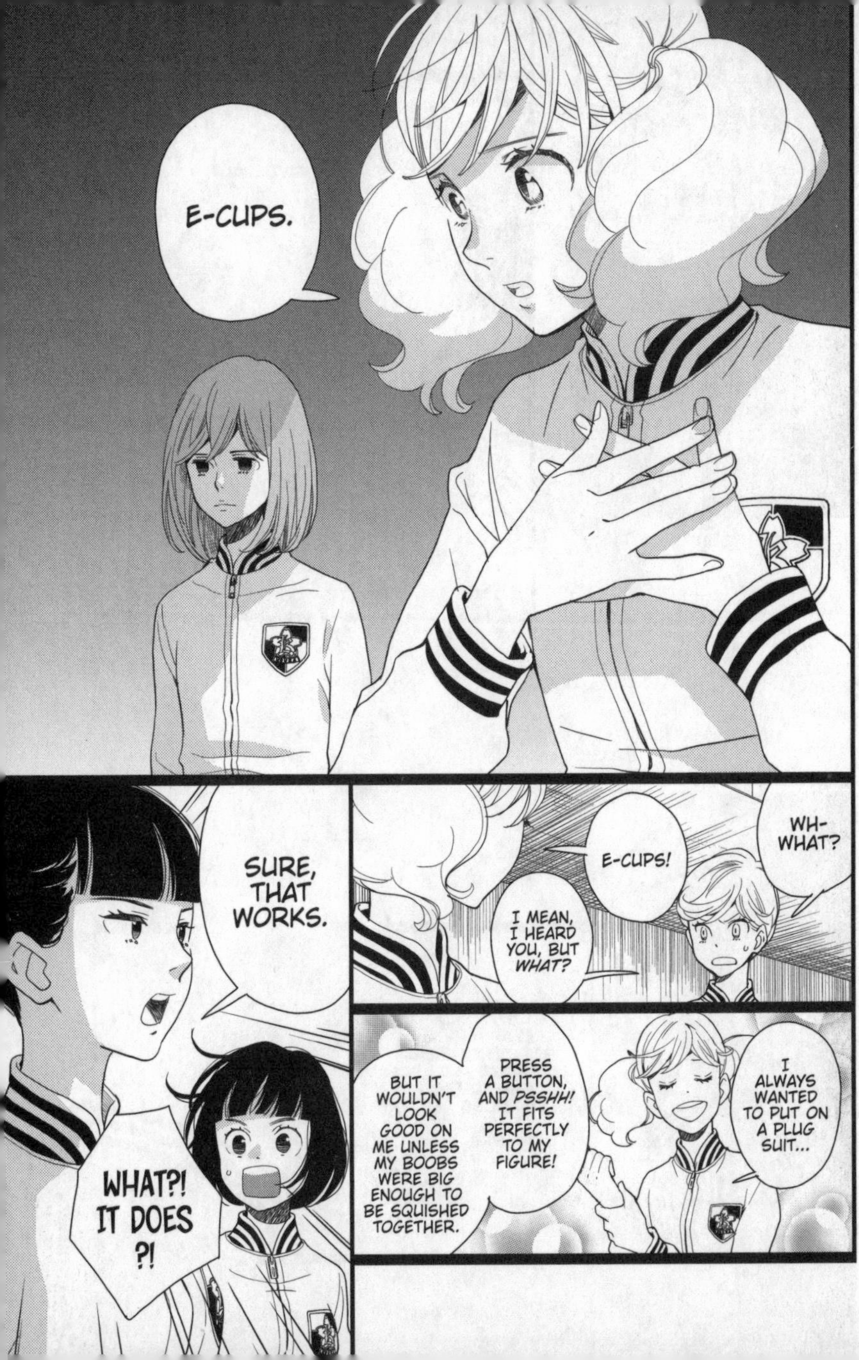
E-CUPS.
WH-WHAT?
E-CUPS!
I MEAN, I HEARD YOU, BUT *WHAT?*
I ALWAYS WANTED TO PUT ON A PLUG SUIT...
PRESS A BUTTON, AND *PSSHH!* IT FITS PERFECTLY TO MY FIGURE!
BUT IT WOULDN'T LOOK GOOD ON ME UNLESS MY BOOBS WERE BIG ENOUGH TO BE SQUISHED TOGETHER.
SURE, THAT WORKS.
WHAT?! IT DOES ?!

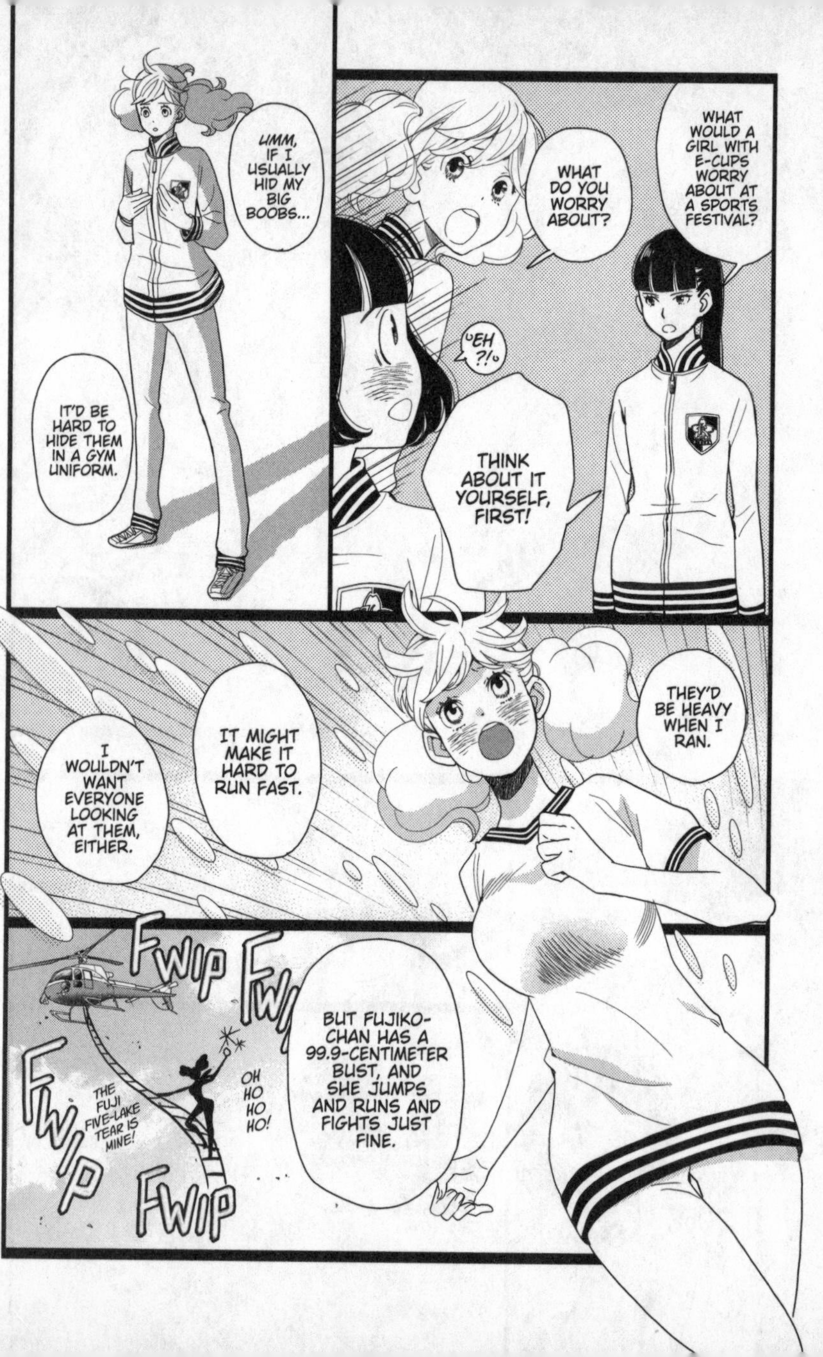
WHAT WOULD A GIRL WITH E-CUPS WORRY ABOUT AT A SPORTS FESTIVAL?
WHAT DO YOU WORRY ABOUT?
EH ?!
THINK ABOUT IT YOURSELF, FIRST!
UMM, IF I USUALLY HID MY BIG BOOBS...
IT'D BE HARD TO HIDE THEM IN A GYM UNIFORM.
THEY'D BE HEAVY WHEN I RAN.
IT MIGHT MAKE IT HARD TO RUN FAST.
I WOULDN'T WANT EVERYONE LOOKING AT THEM, EITHER.
FWIP FWIP
BUT FUJIKO-CHAN HAS A 99.9-CENTIMETER BUST, AND SHE JUMPS AND RUNS AND FIGHTS JUST FINE.
OH HO HO HO!
THE FUJI FIVE-LAKE TEAR IS MINE!
FWIP FWIP

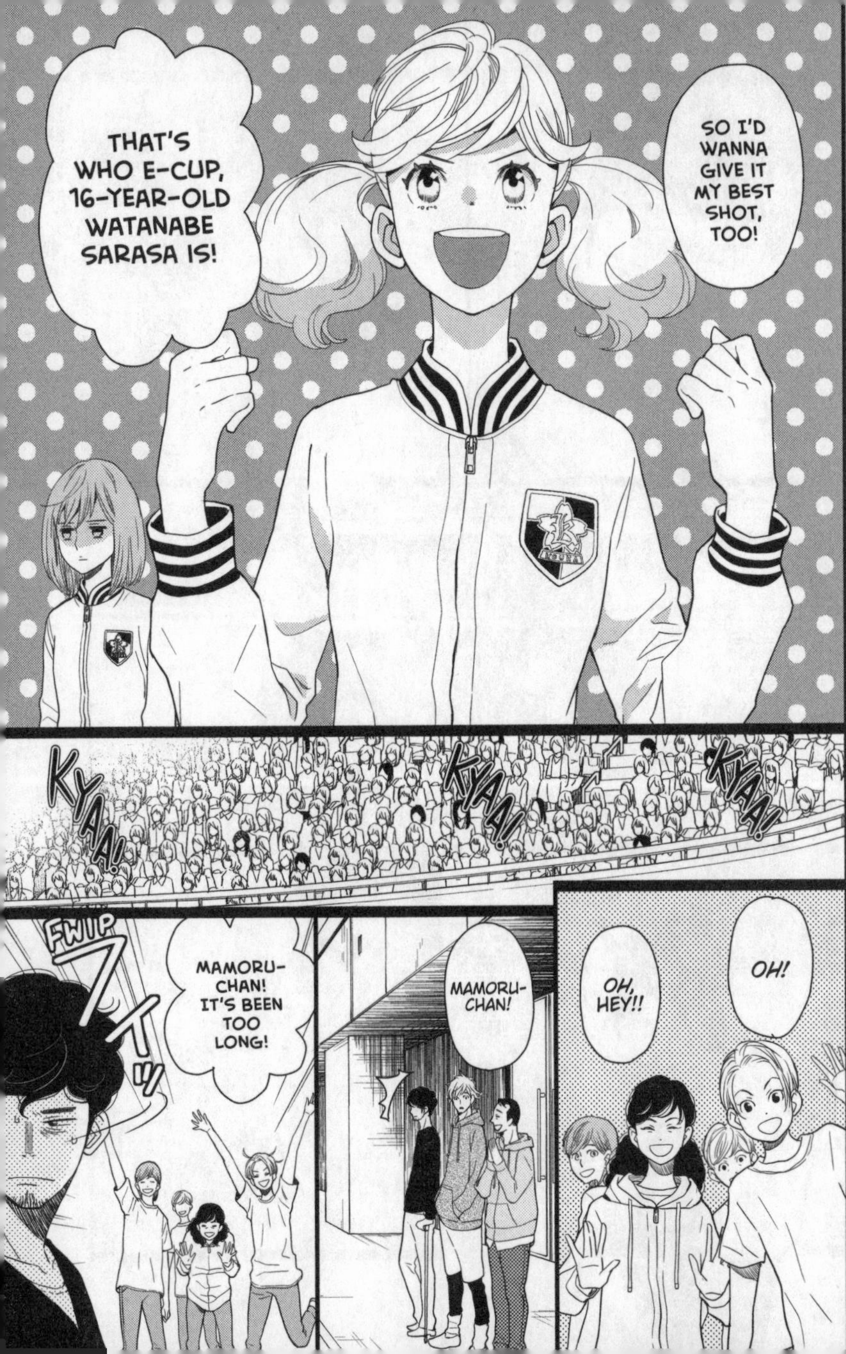
SO I'D WANNA GIVE IT MY BEST SHOT, TOO!
THAT'S WHO E-CUP, 16-YEAR-OLD WATANABE SARASA IS!
KYAA!
KYAA!
KYAA!
OH!
OH, HEY!!
MAMORU-CHAN!
FWIP
MAMORU-CHAN! IT'S BEEN TOO LONG!

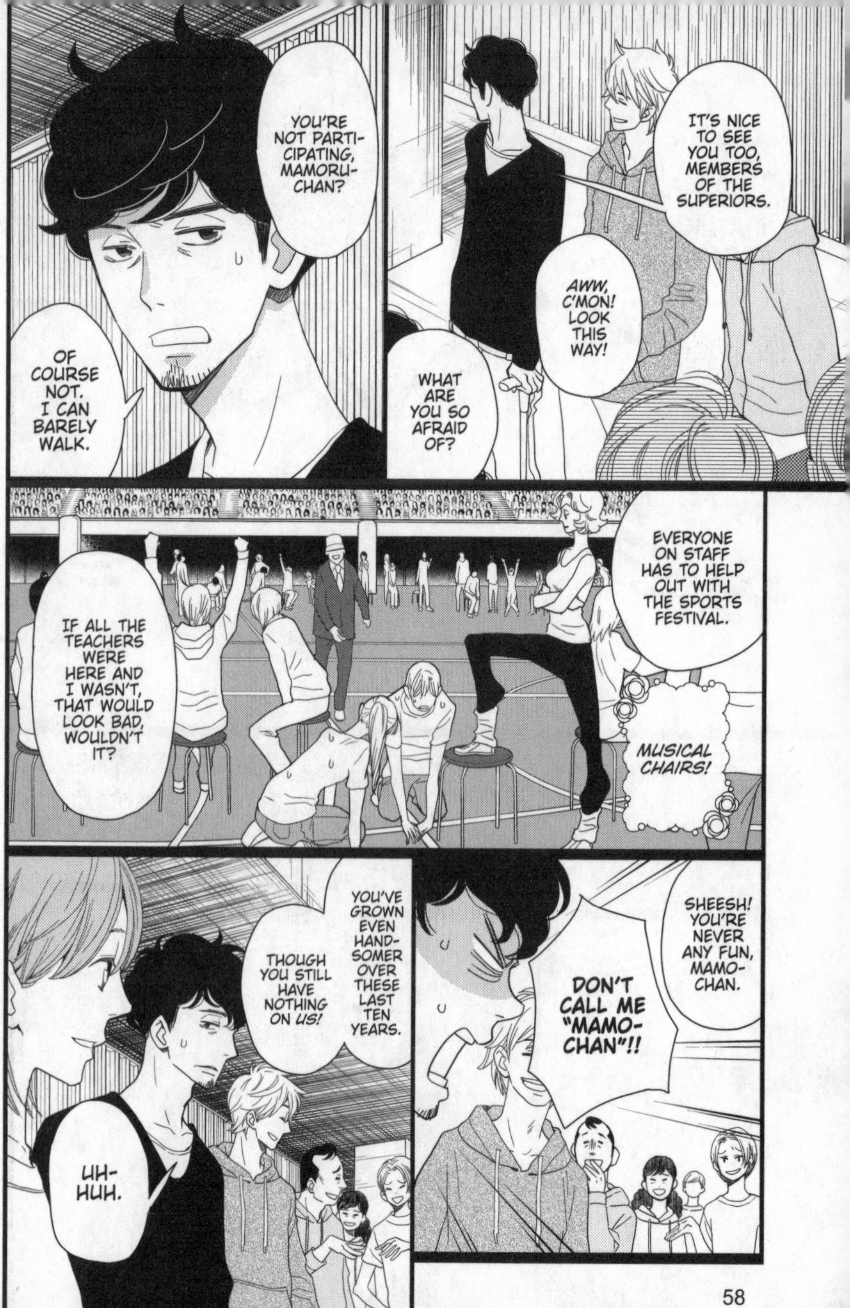
IT'S NICE TO SEE YOU TOO, MEMBERS OF THE SUPERIORS.
AWW, C'MON! LOOK THIS WAY!
WHAT ARE YOU SO AFRAID OF?
YOU'RE NOT PARTI-CIPATING, MAMORU-CHAN?
OF COURSE NOT. I CAN BARELY WALK.
EVERYONE ON STAFF HAS TO HELP OUT WITH THE SPORTS FESTIVAL.
MUSICAL CHAIRS!
IF ALL THE TEACHERS WERE HERE AND I WASN'T, THAT WOULD LOOK BAD, WOULDN'T IT?
SHEESH! YOU'RE NEVER ANY FUN, MAMO-CHAN.
DON'T CALL ME "MAMO-CHAN"!!
YOU'VE GROWN EVEN HAND-SOMER OVER THESE LAST TEN YEARS.
THOUGH YOU STILL HAVE NOTHING ON *US!*
UH-HUH.

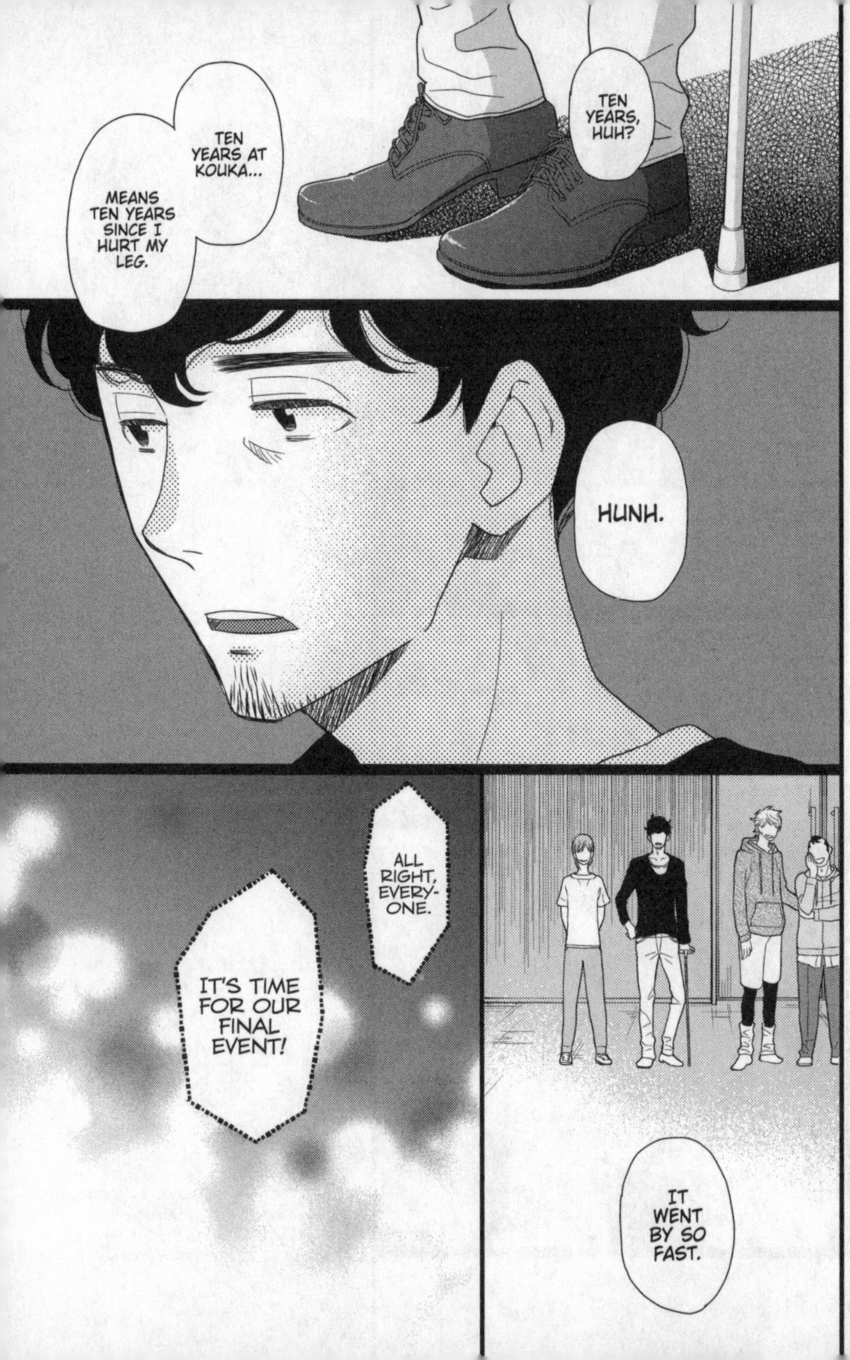
TEN YEARS, HUH?
TEN YEARS AT KOUKA...
MEANS TEN YEARS SINCE I HURT MY LEG.
HUNH.
IT WENT BY SO FAST.
ALL RIGHT, EVERY-ONE.
IT'S TIME FOR OUR FINAL EVENT!

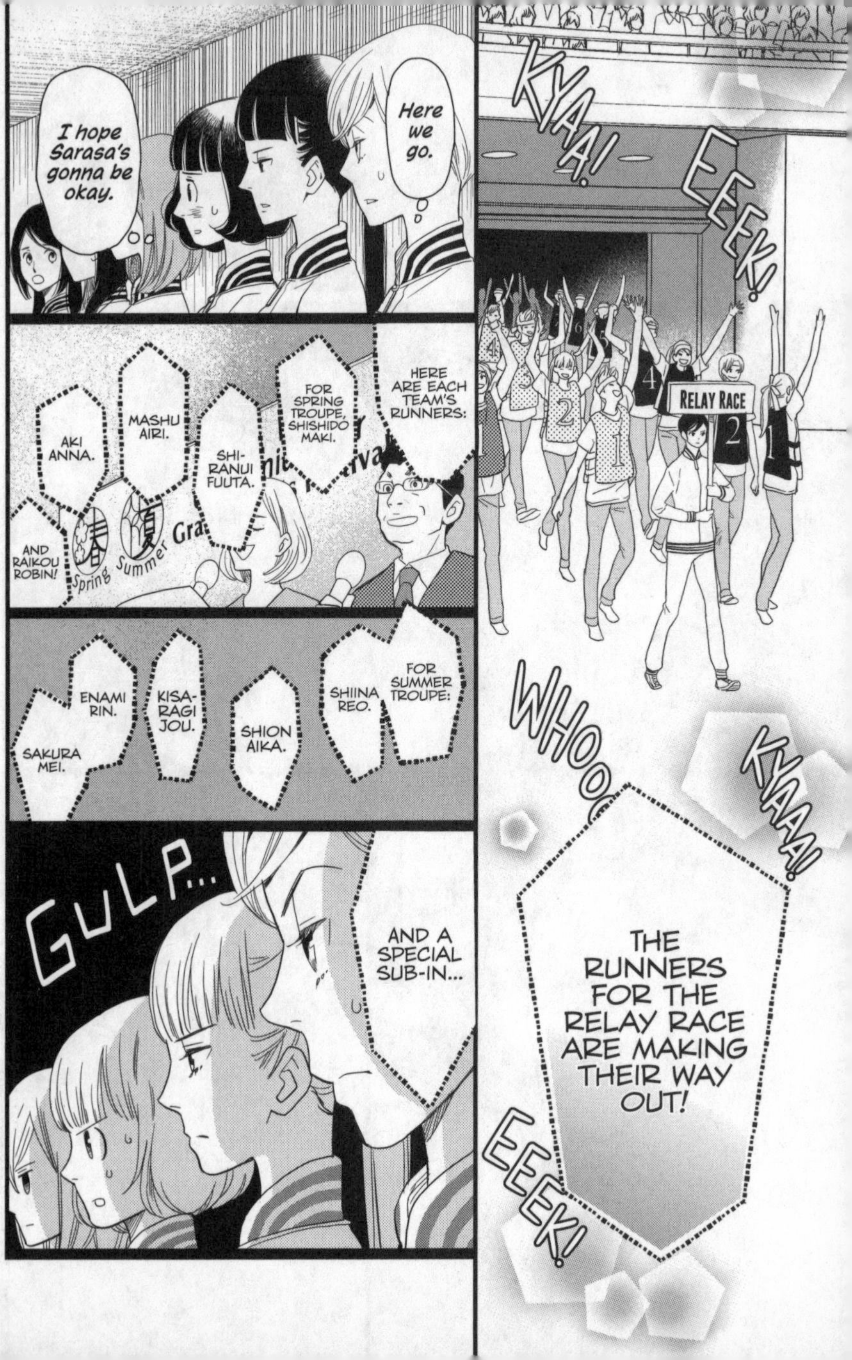
KYAA!
EEEK!
RELAY RACE
WHOO...
KYAAA!
THE RUNNERS FOR THE RELAY RACE ARE MAKING THEIR WAY OUT!
EEEK!
Here we go.
I hope Sarasa's gonna be okay.
HERE ARE EACH TEAM'S RUNNERS:
FOR SPRING TROUPE, SHISHIDO MAKI.
SHI-RANUI FUUTA.
MASHU AIRI.
AKI ANNA.
AND RAIKOU ROBIN!
春 Spring
夏 Summer
FOR SUMMER TROUPE:
SHIINA REO.
SHION AIKA.
KISA-RAGI JOU.
ENAMI RIN.
SAKURA MEI.
AND A SPECIAL SUB-IN...
GULP...

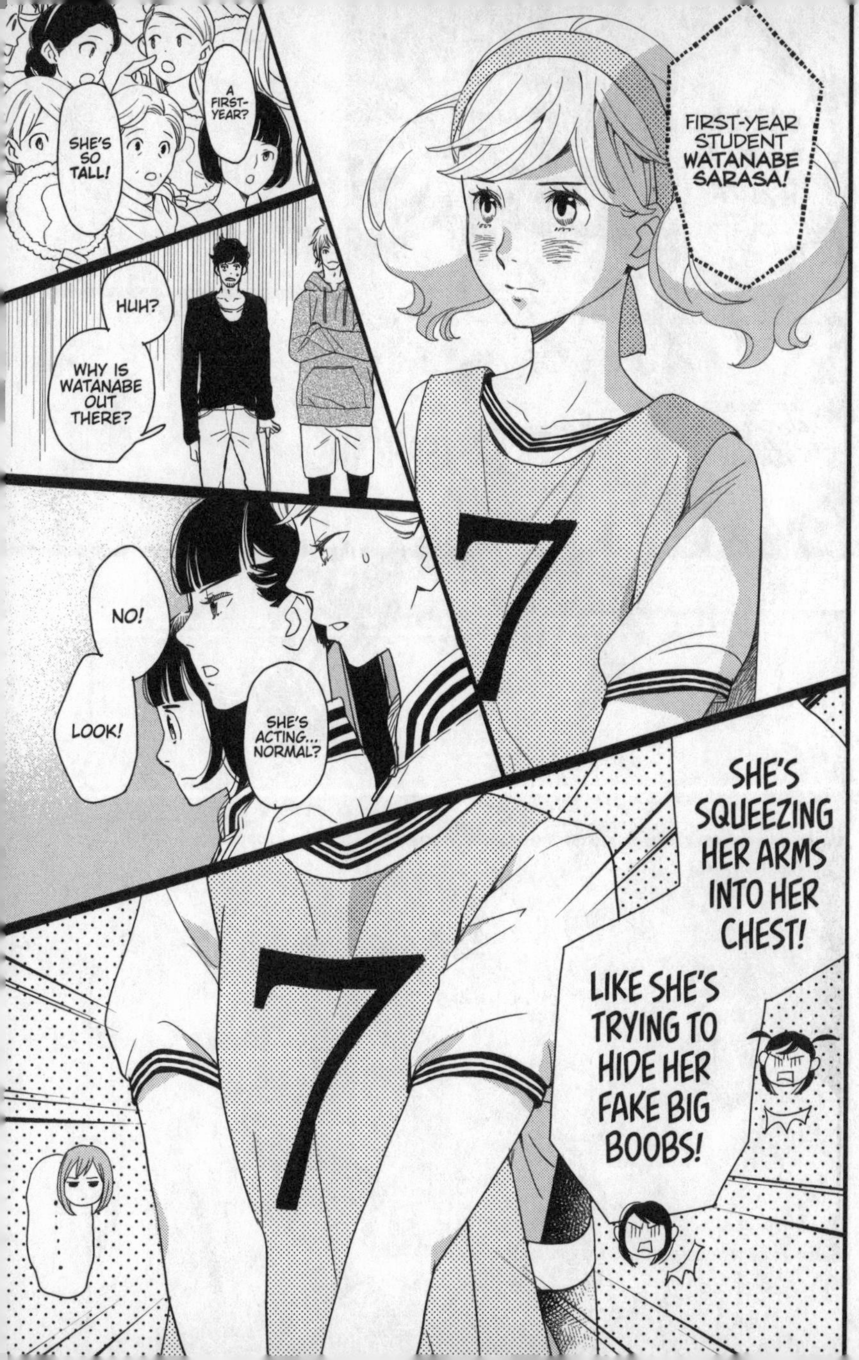
FIRST-YEAR STUDENT WATANABE SARASA!
A FIRST-YEAR?
SHE'S SO TALL!
HUH?
WHY IS WATANABE OUT THERE?
SHE'S ACTING... NORMAL?
NO!
LOOK!
SHE'S SQUEEZING HER ARMS INTO HER CHEST!
LIKE SHE'S TRYING TO HIDE HER FAKE BIG BOOBS!

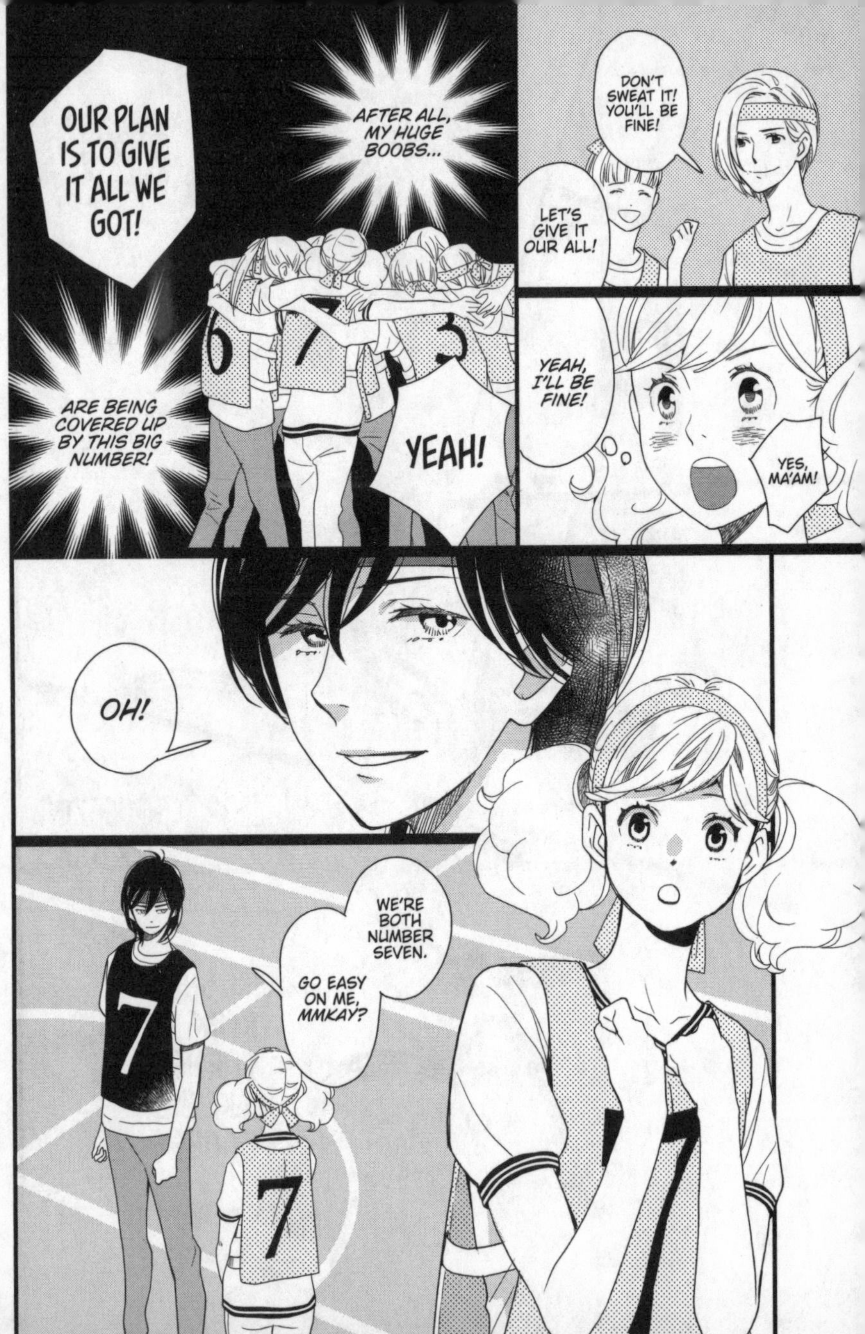
DON'T SWEAT IT! YOU'LL BE FINE!
LET'S GIVE IT OUR ALL!
YES, MA'AM!
YEAH, I'LL BE FINE!
OUR PLAN IS TO GIVE IT ALL WE GOT!
YEAH!
AFTER ALL, MY HUGE BOOBS...
ARE BEING COVERED UP BY THIS BIG NUMBER!
OH!
WE'RE BOTH NUMBER SEVEN.
GO EASY ON ME, MMKAY?

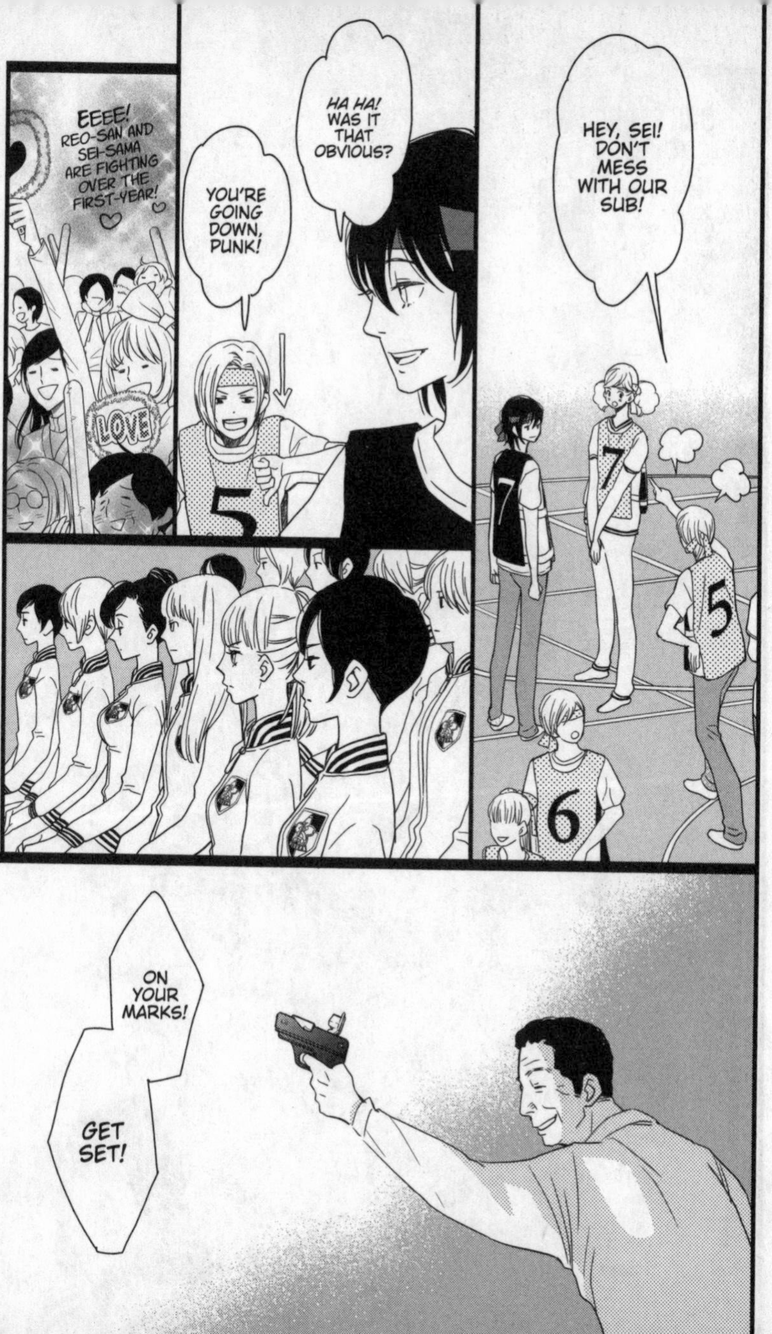
HEY, SEI! DON'T MESS WITH OUR SUB!
HA HA! WAS IT THAT OBVIOUS?
YOU'RE GOING DOWN, PUNK!
EEEE! REO-SAN AND SEI-SAMA ARE FIGHTING OVER THE FIRST-YEAR!
LOVE
ON YOUR MARKS!
GET SET!

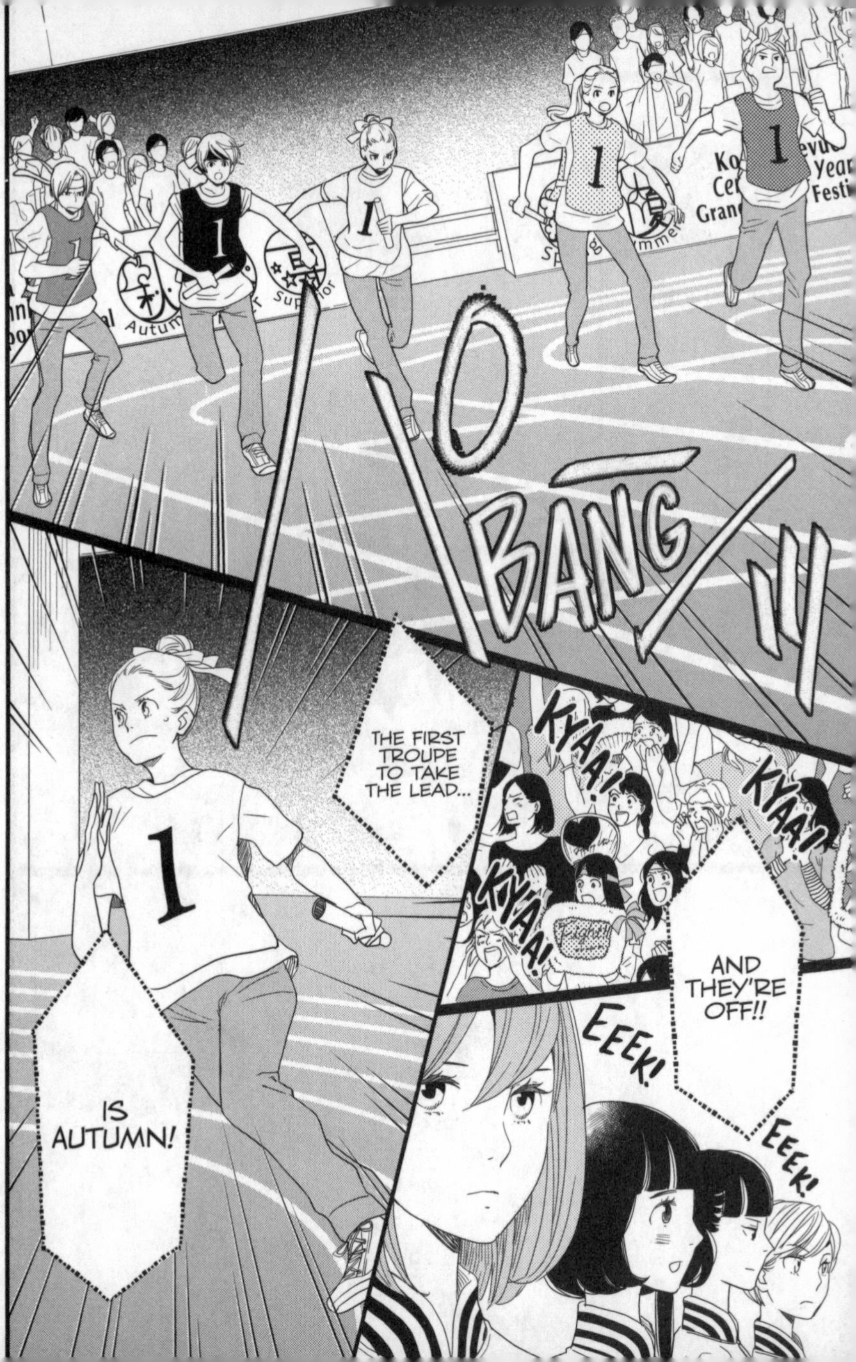
BANG!!
KYAA!
KYAA!
KYAA!
AND THEY'RE OFF!!
EEEK!
EEEK!
THE FIRST TROUPE TO TAKE THE LEAD...
IS AUTUMN!

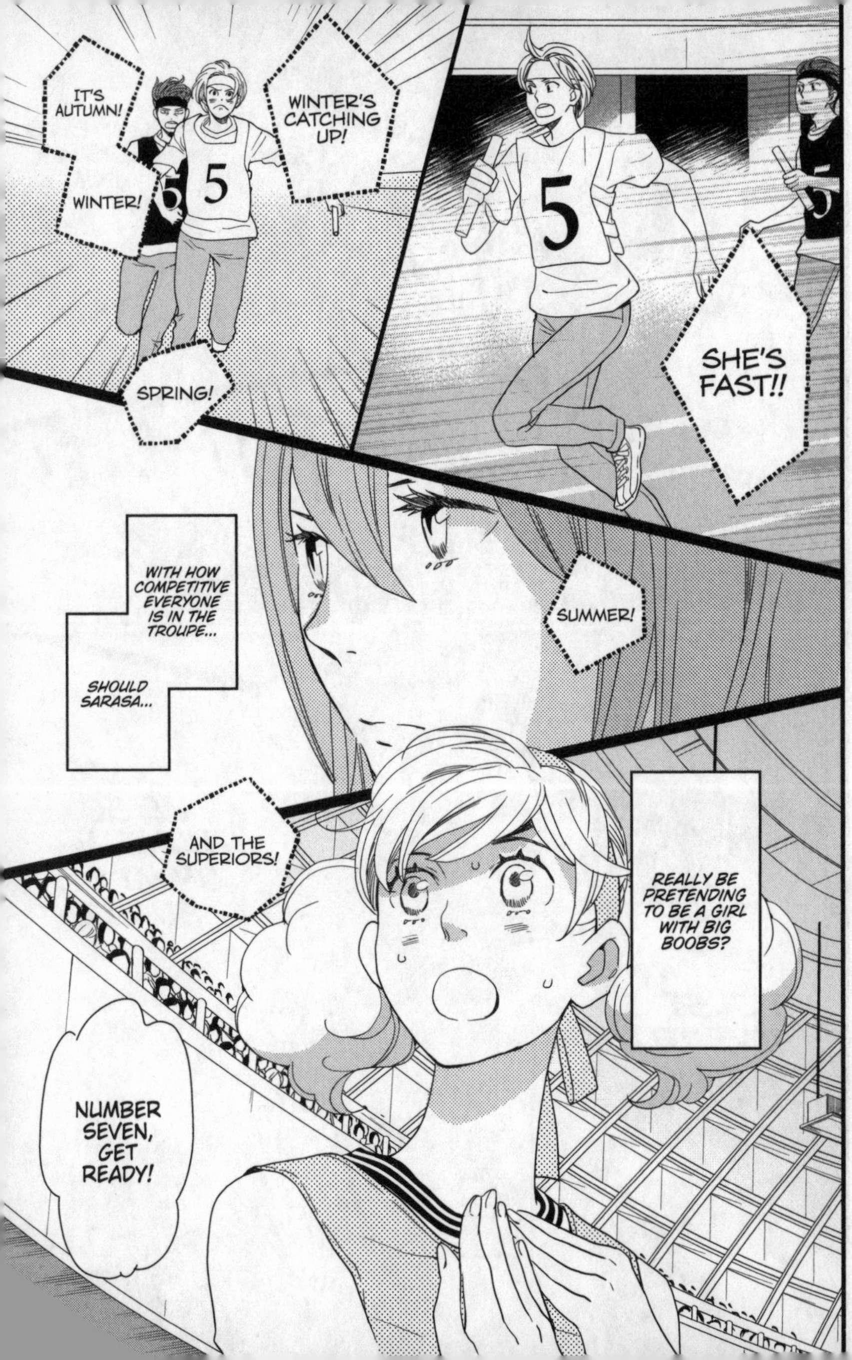
SHE'S FAST!!
WINTER'S CATCHING UP!
IT'S AUTUMN!
WINTER!
SPRING!
SUMMER!
WITH HOW COMPETITIVE EVERYONE IS IN THE TROUPE...
SHOULD SARASA...
REALLY BE PRETENDING TO BE A GIRL WITH BIG BOOBS?
AND THE SUPERIORS!
NUMBER SEVEN, GET READY!

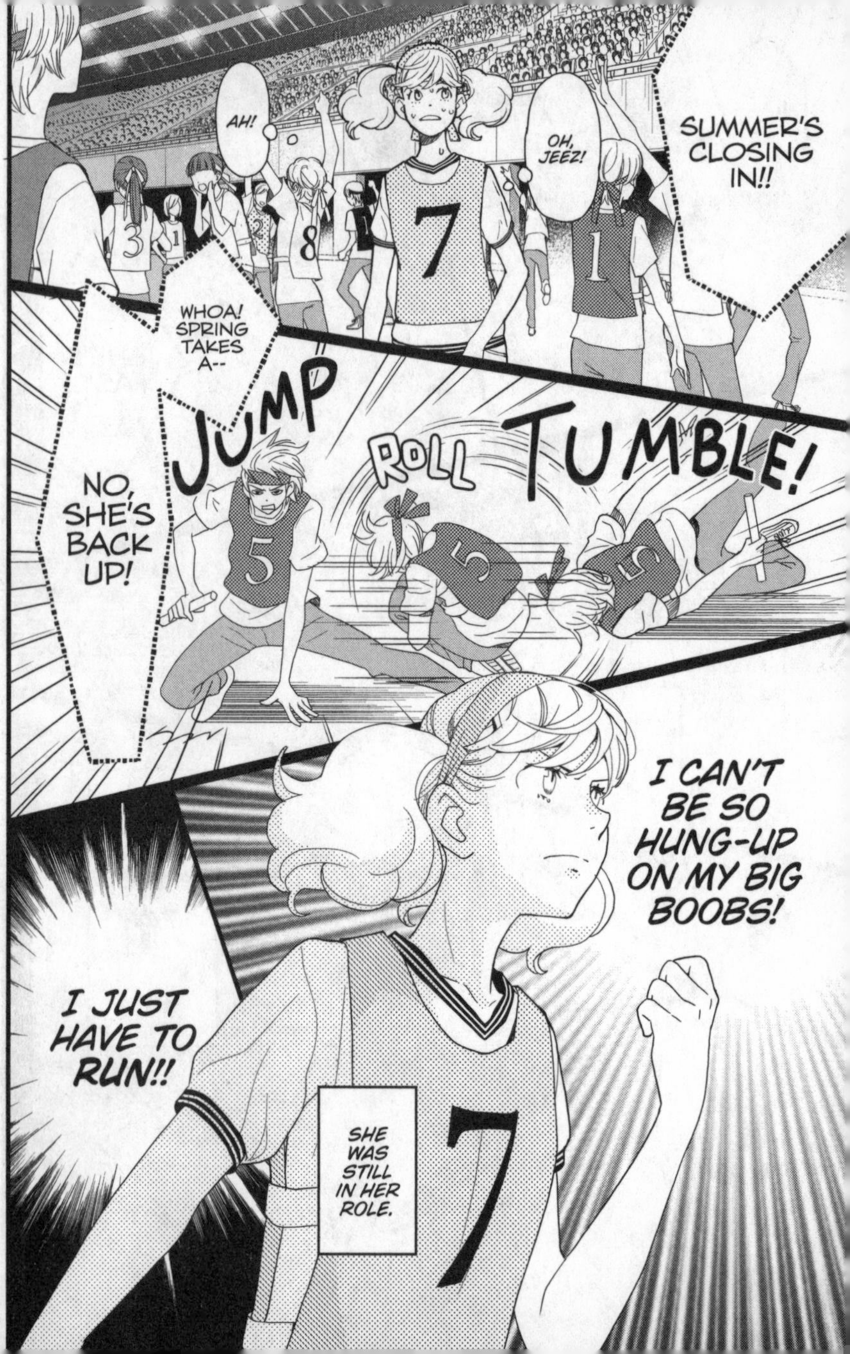
SUMMER'S CLOSING IN!!
OH, JEEZ!
AH!
WHOA! SPRING TAKES A--
JUMP
ROLL
TUMBLE!
NO, SHE'S BACK UP!
I CAN'T BE SO HUNG-UP ON MY BIG BOOBS!
I JUST HAVE TO RUN!!
SHE WAS STILL IN HER ROLE.

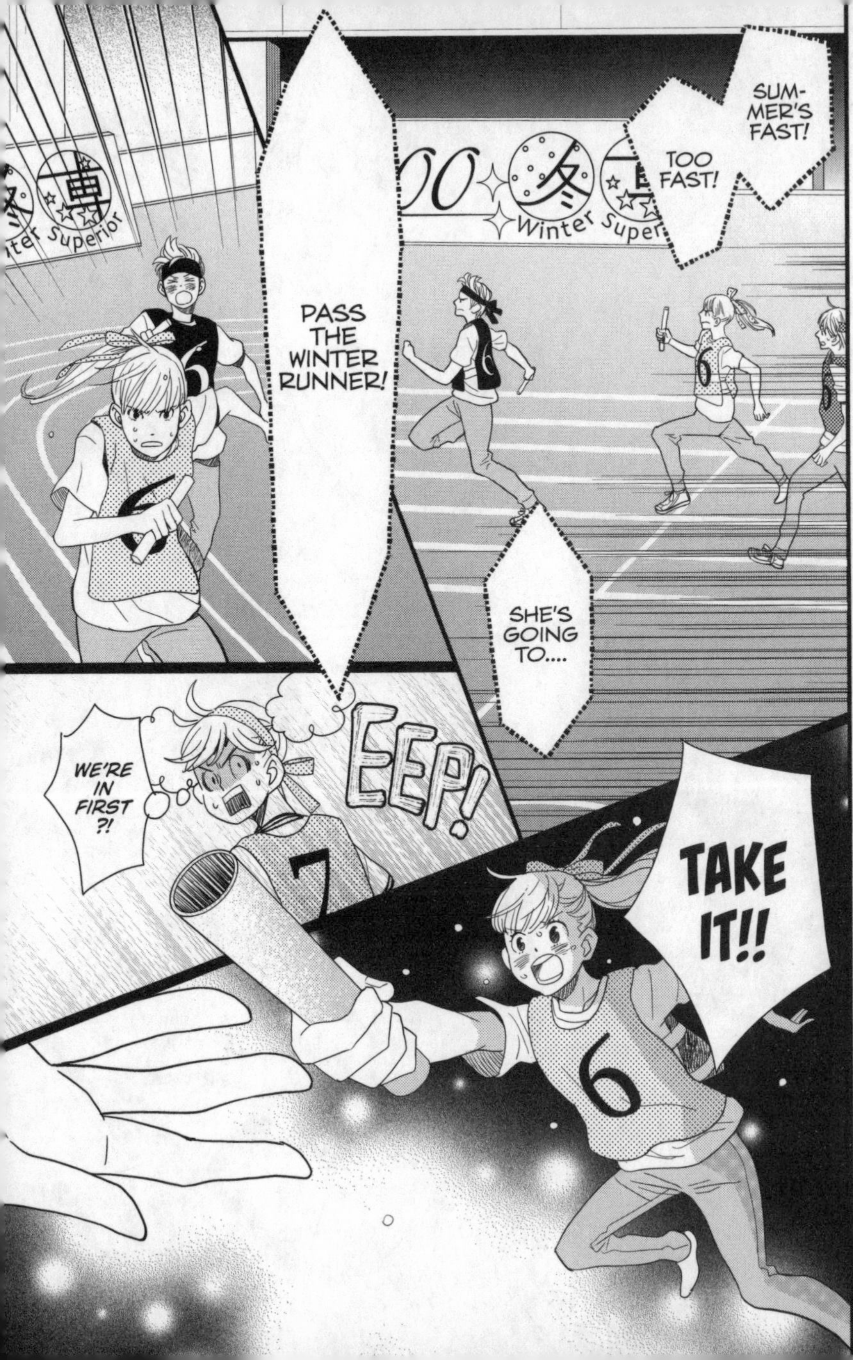
SUM-
MER'S
FAST!
TOO
FAST!
PASS
THE
WINTER
RUNNER!
Winter Superior
SHE'S
GOING
TO....
TAKE
IT!!
EEP!
WE'RE
IN
FIRST
?!

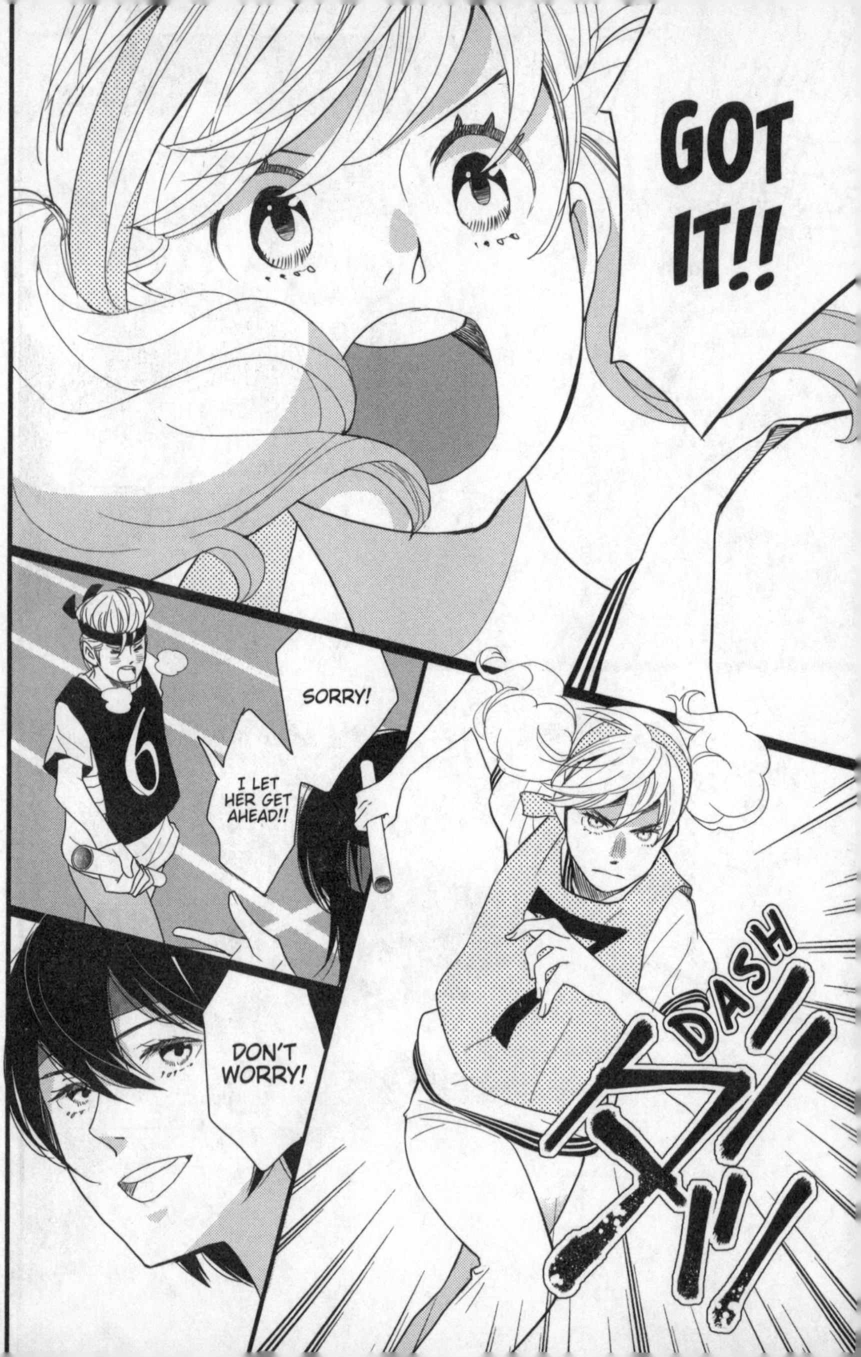
GOT IT!!
DASH
SORRY!
I LET HER GET AHEAD!!
DON'T WORRY!

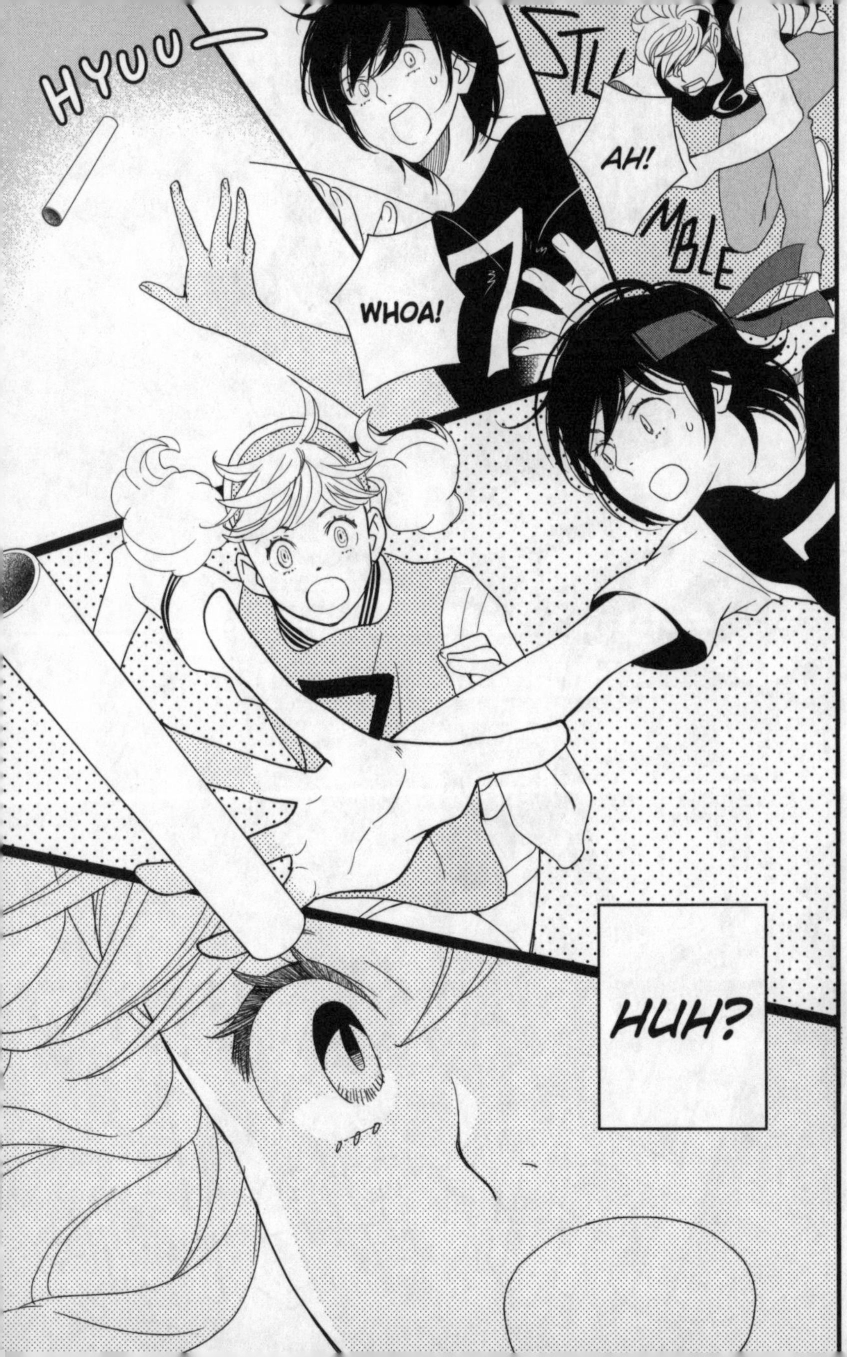
STU
AH!
MBLE
WHOA!
HYUU
HUH?

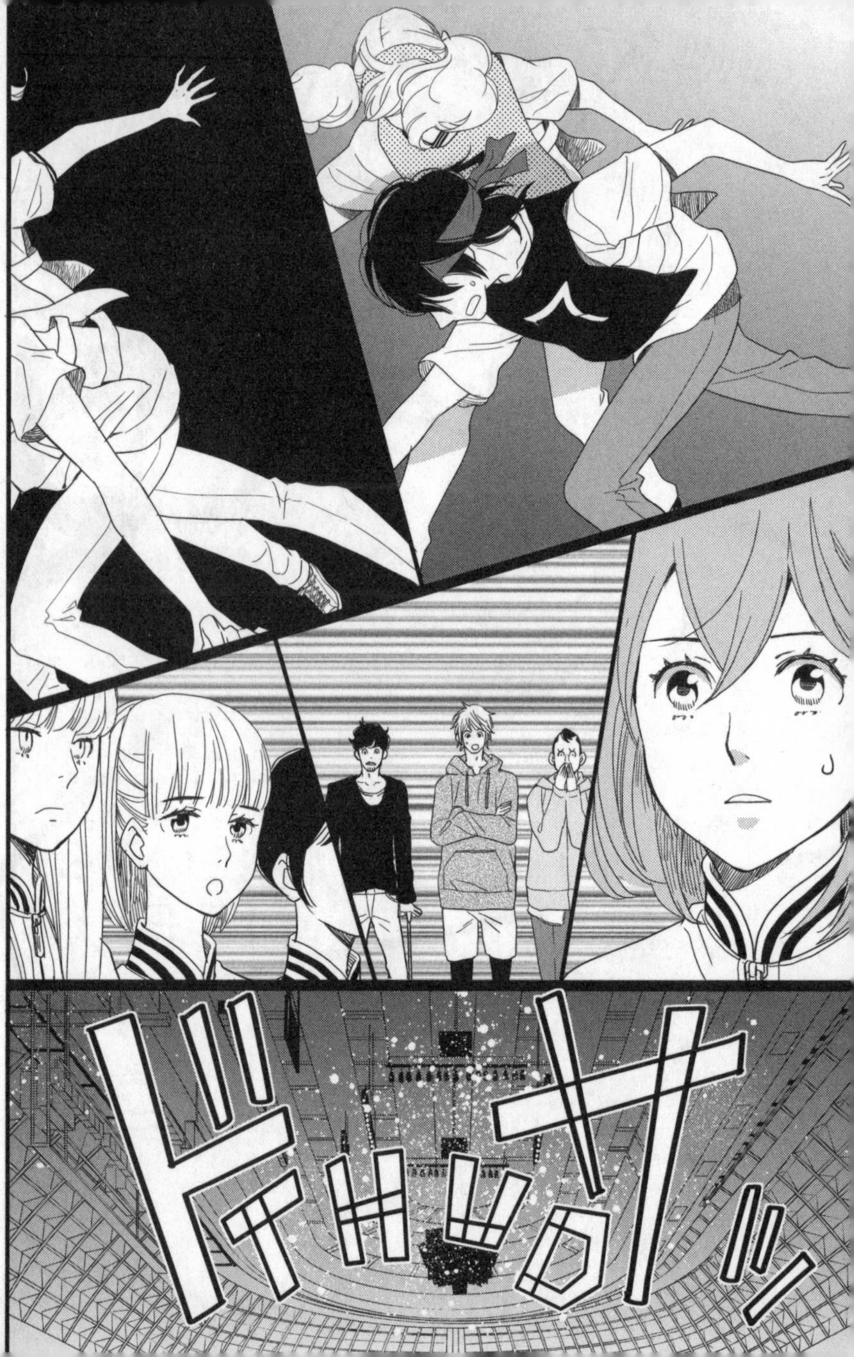

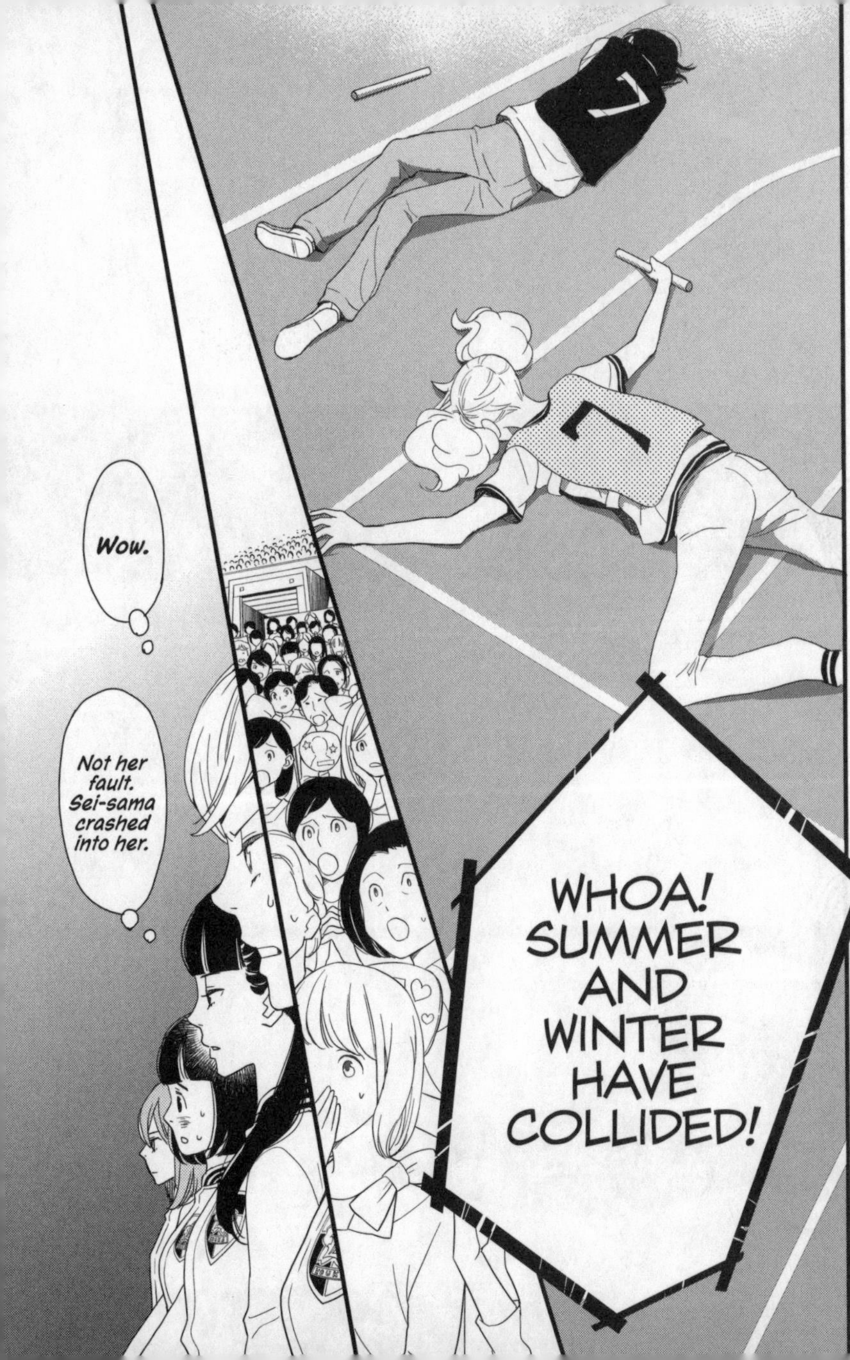
WHOA! SUMMER AND WINTER HAVE COLLIDED!
Wow.
Not her fault. Sei-sama crashed into her.

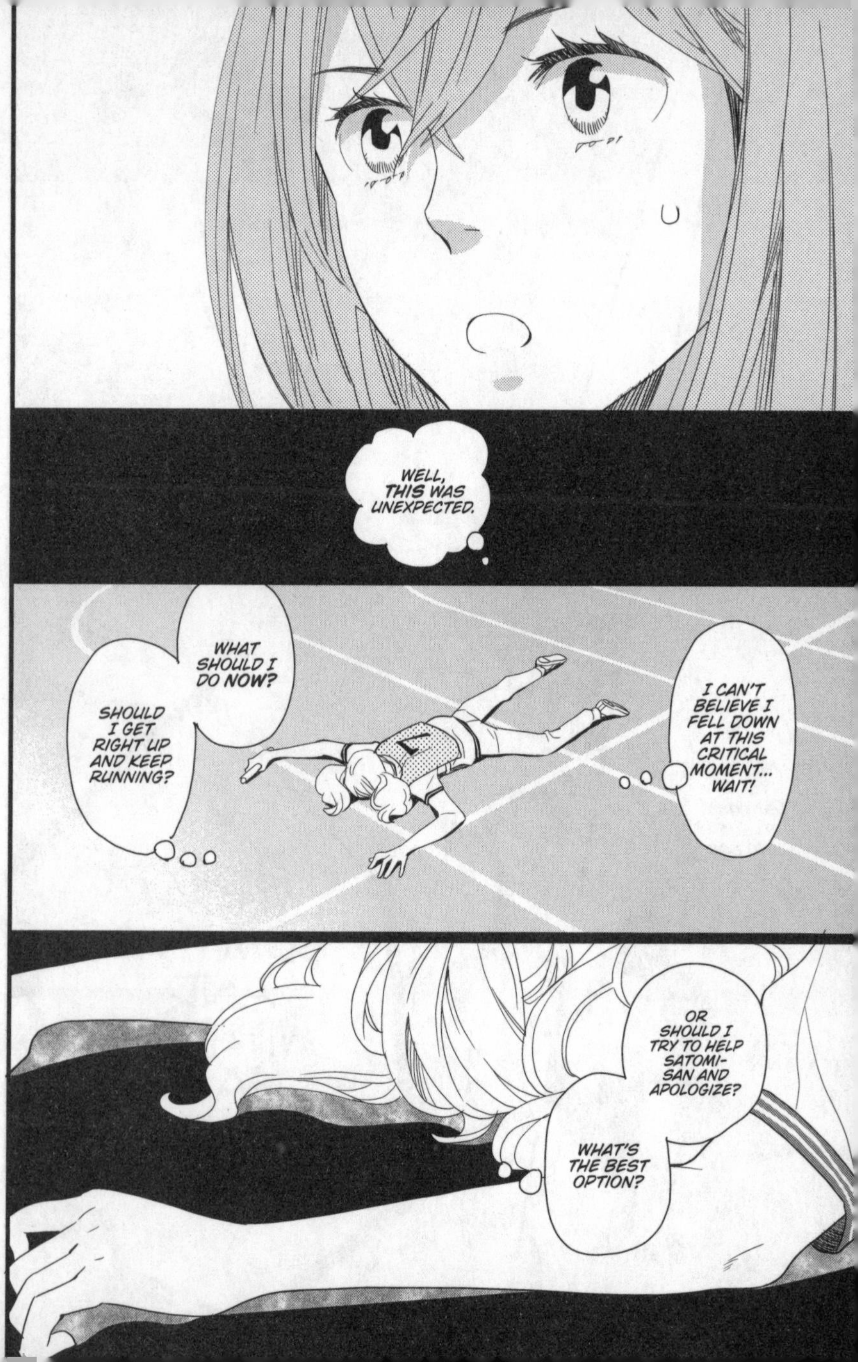
WELL, THIS WAS UNEXPECTED.
I CAN'T BELIEVE I FELL DOWN AT THIS CRITICAL MOMENT... WAIT!
WHAT SHOULD I DO NOW?
SHOULD I GET RIGHT UP AND KEEP RUNNING?
OR SHOULD I TRY TO HELP SATOMI-SAN AND APOLOGIZE?
WHAT'S THE BEST OPTION?

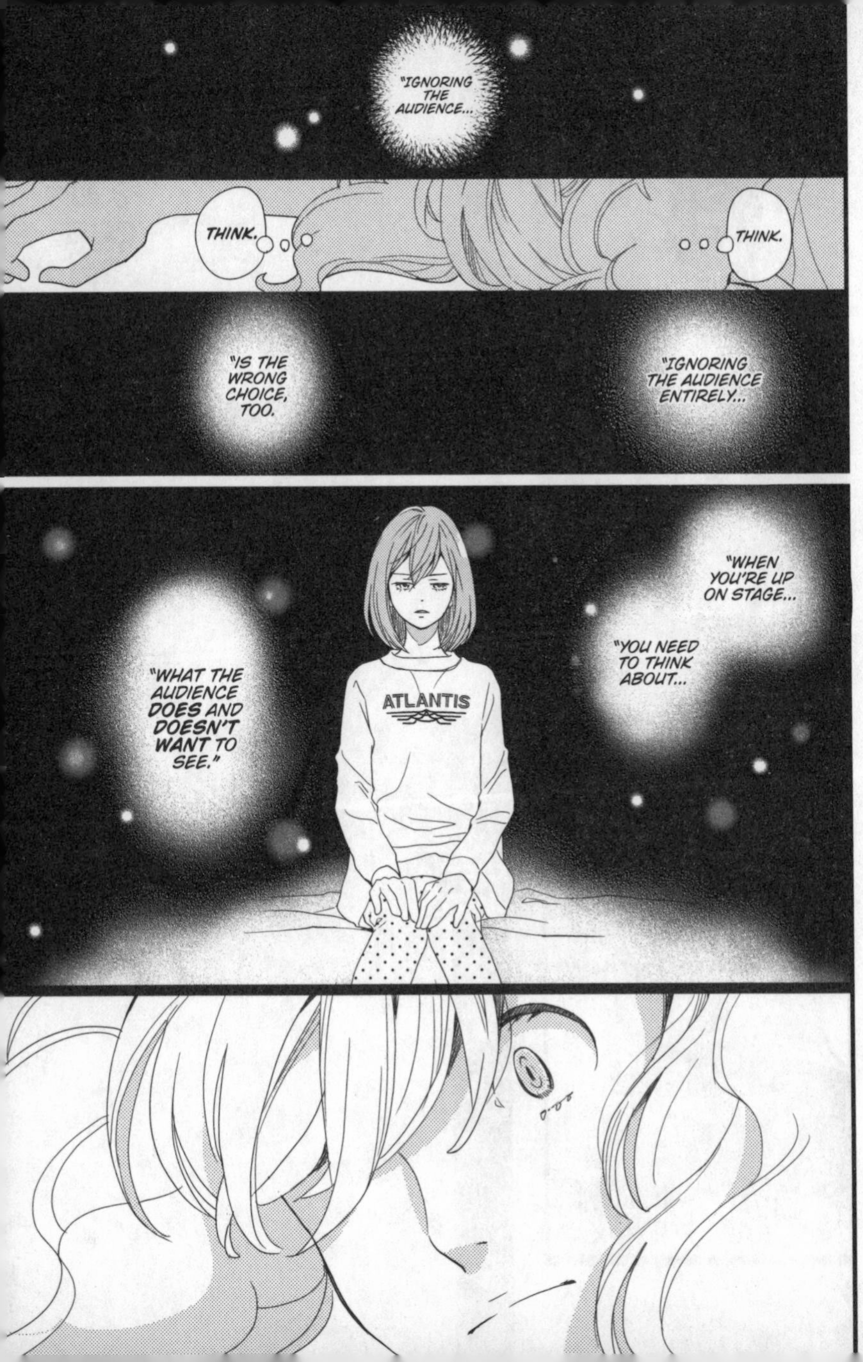
"IGNORING THE AUDIENCE...
THINK.
THINK.
"IGNORING THE AUDIENCE ENTIRELY...
"IS THE WRONG CHOICE, TOO.
"WHEN YOU'RE UP ON STAGE...
"YOU NEED TO THINK ABOUT...
ATLANTIS
"WHAT THE AUDIENCE DOES AND DOESN'T WANT TO SEE."

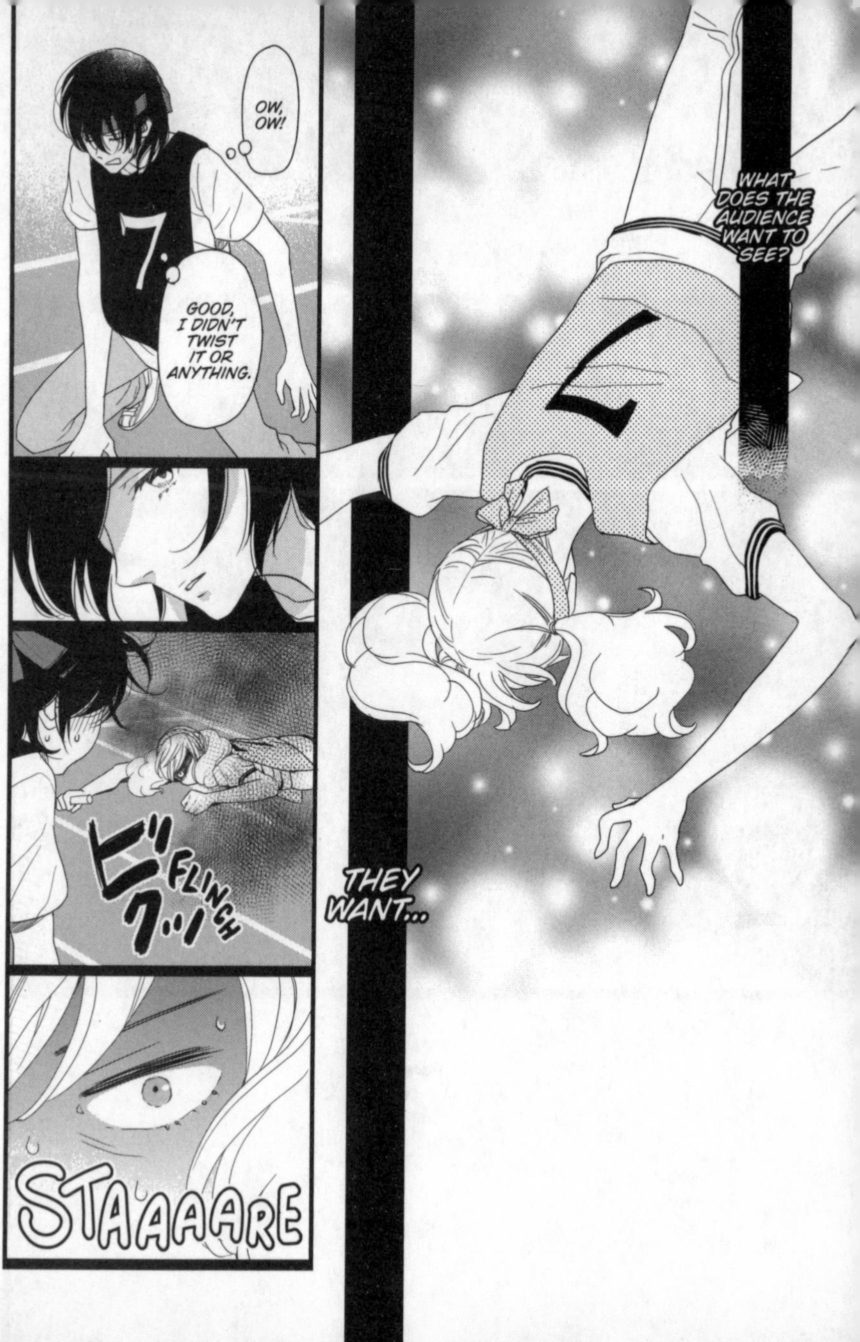
WHAT DOES THE AUDIENCE WANT TO SEE?
THEY WANT...
OW, OW!
GOOD, I DIDN'T TWIST IT OR ANYTHING.
ビクッ
FLINCH
STAAAARE

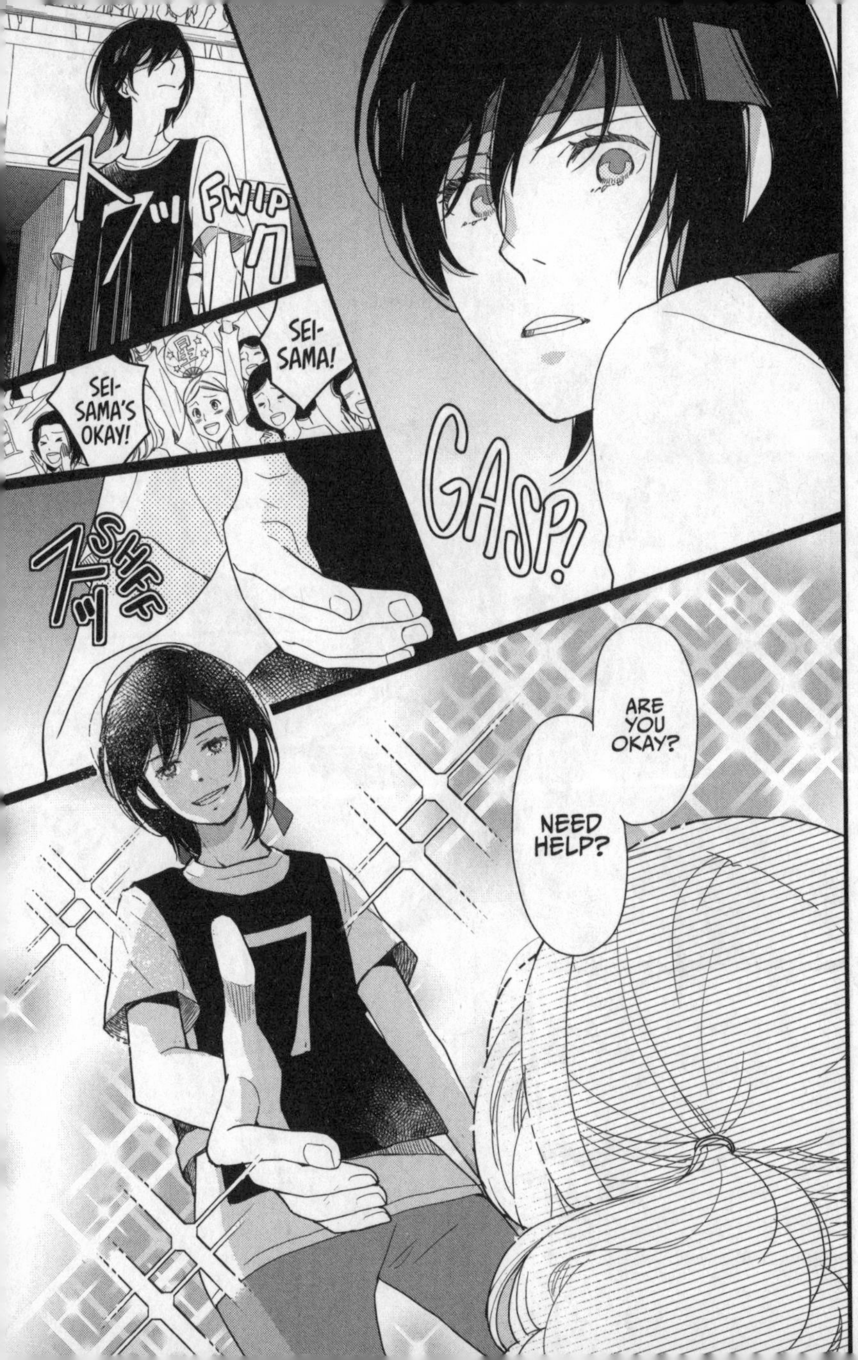
GASP!
FWIP
SEI-SAMA!
SEI-SAMA'S OKAY!
SHFF
ARE YOU OKAY?
NEED HELP?

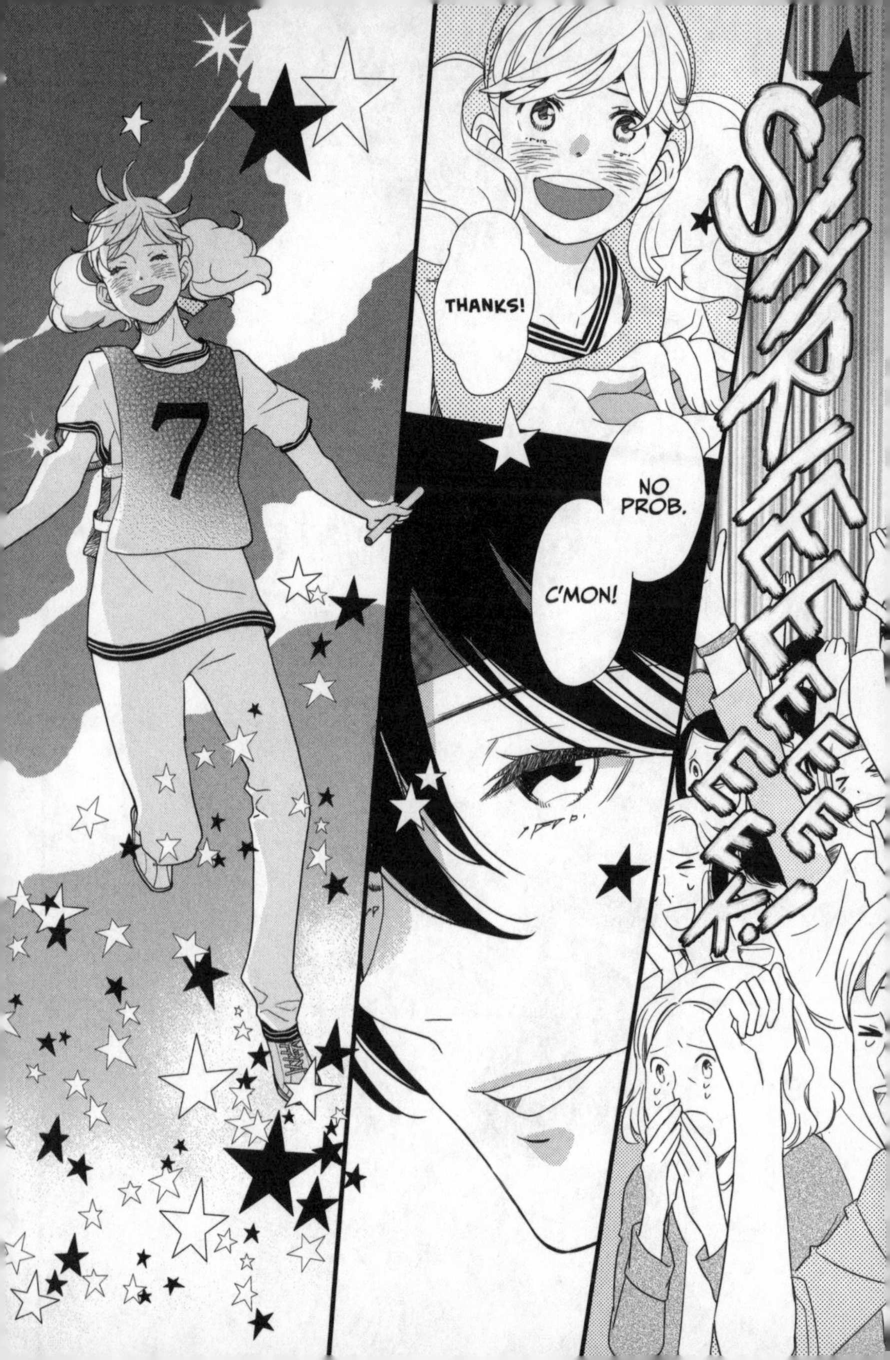
SHRIEEEEEEEEK!
THANKS!
NO PROB.
C'MON!

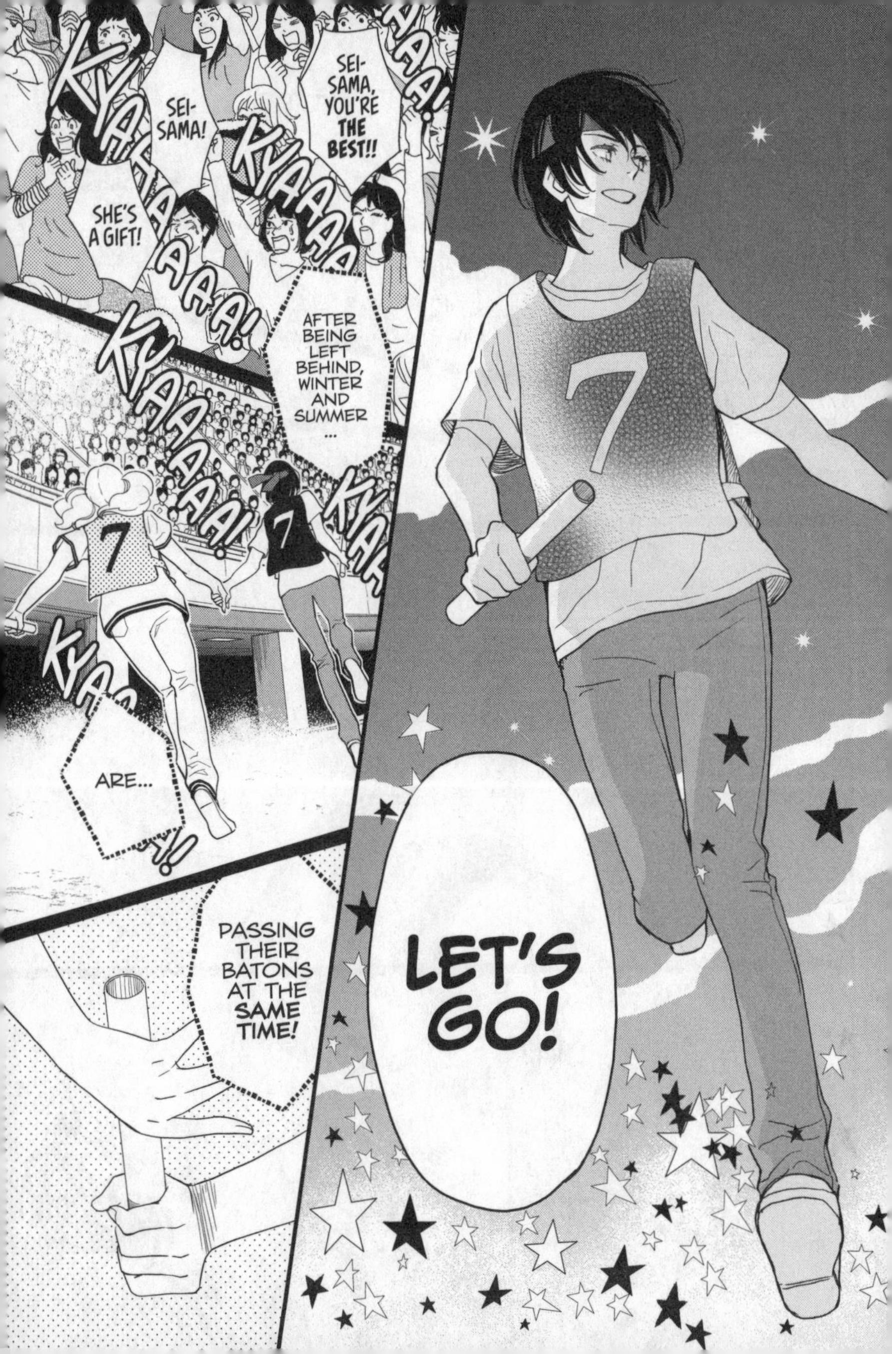

LET'S GO!
SEI-SAMA, YOU'RE THE BEST!!
SEI-SAMA!
KYAAAAA
SHE'S A GIFT!
KYAAAAAAA!
AFTER BEING LEFT BEHIND, WINTER AND SUMMER ...
KYAAAAAAA!
ARE...
PASSING THEIR BATONS AT THE SAME TIME!

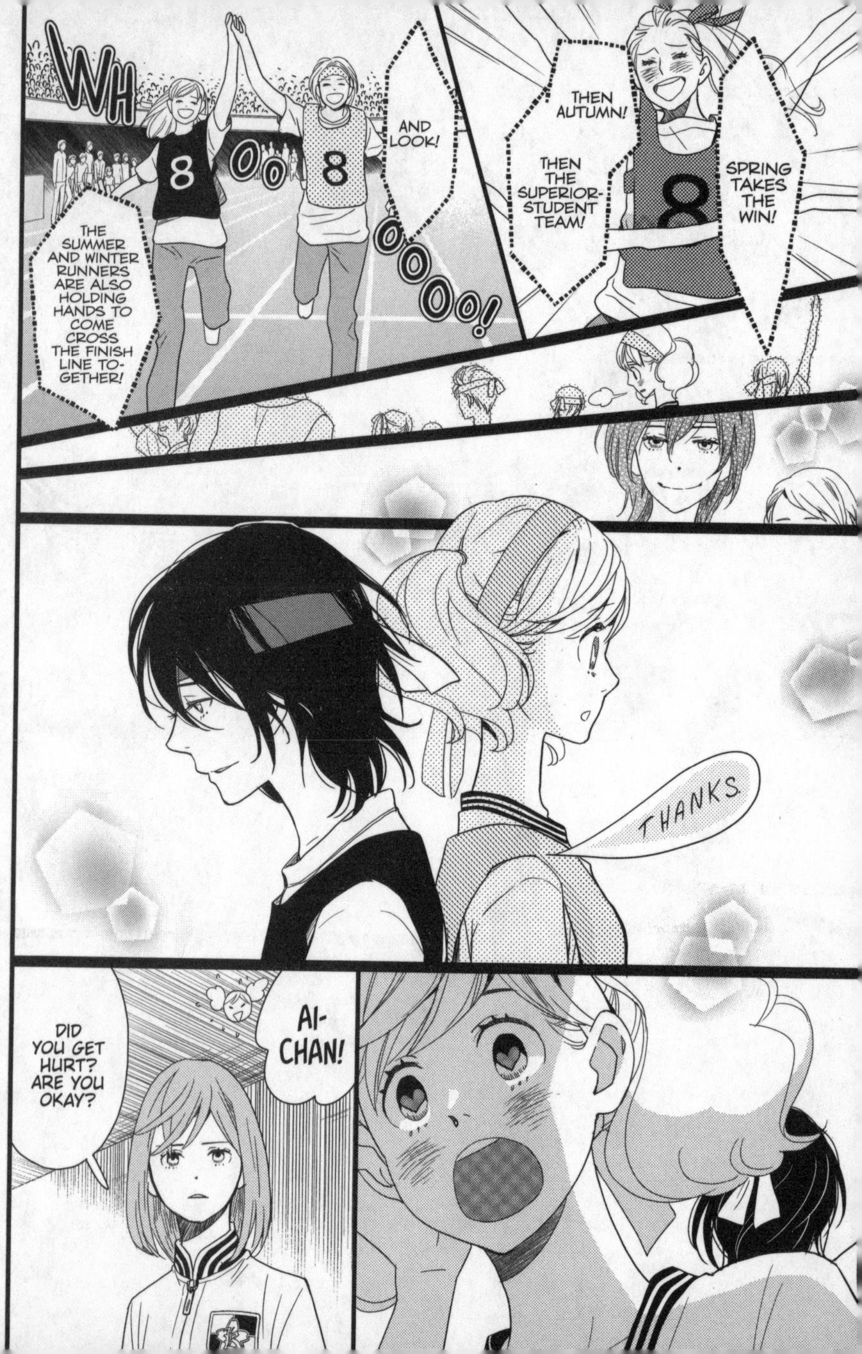

SPRING TAKES THE WIN!
THEN THE SUPERIOR-STUDENT TEAM!
THEN AUTUMN!
AND LOOK!
WHOOOOOOOO!
THE SUMMER AND WINTER RUNNERS ARE ALSO HOLDING HANDS TO COME CROSS THE FINISH LINE TO-GETHER!
THANKS
AI-CHAN!
DID YOU GET HURT? ARE YOU OKAY?

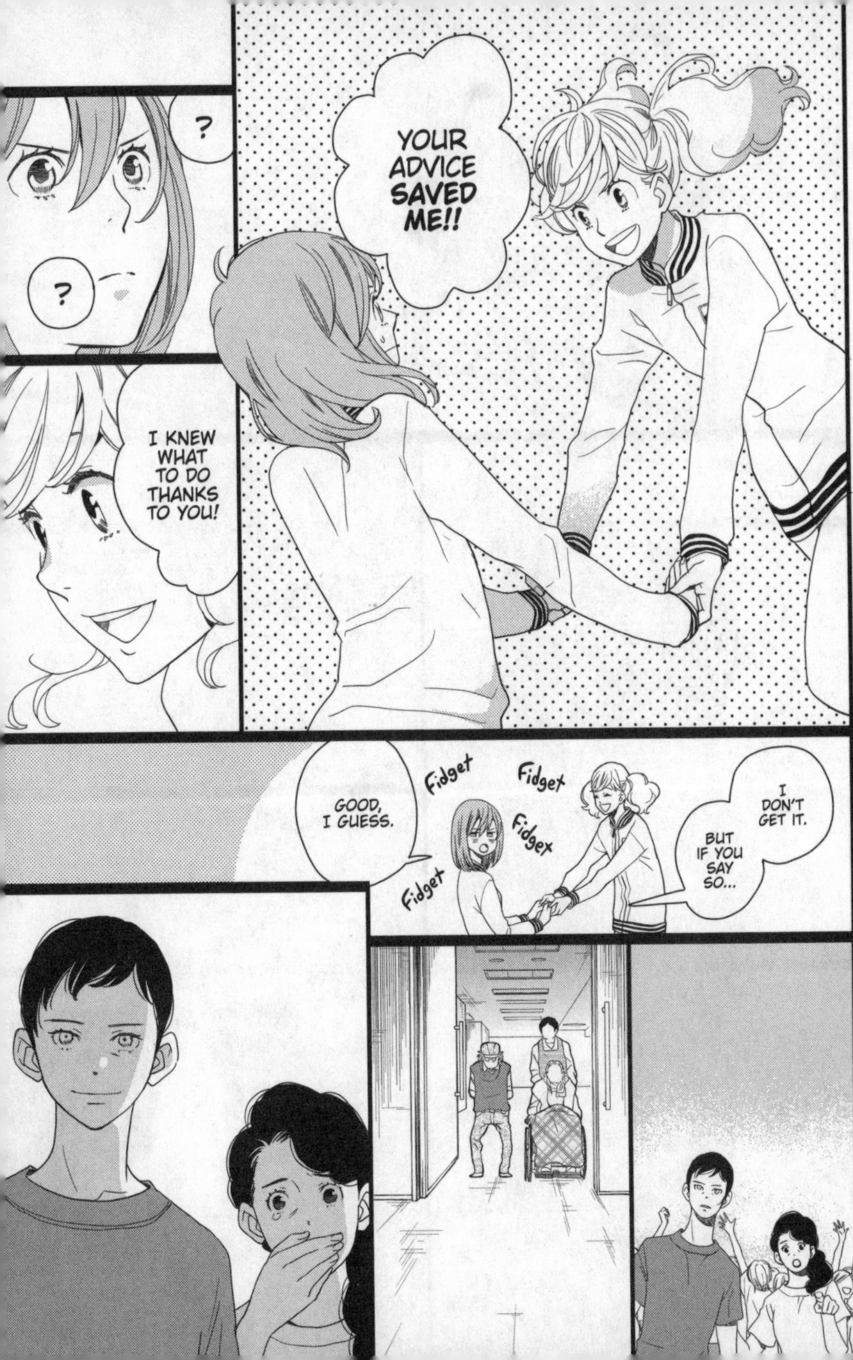
YOUR ADVICE SAVED ME!!
?
?
I KNEW WHAT TO DO THANKS TO YOU!
I DON'T GET IT.
BUT IF YOU SAY SO...
Fidget
Fidget
Fidget
Fidget
GOOD, I GUESS.

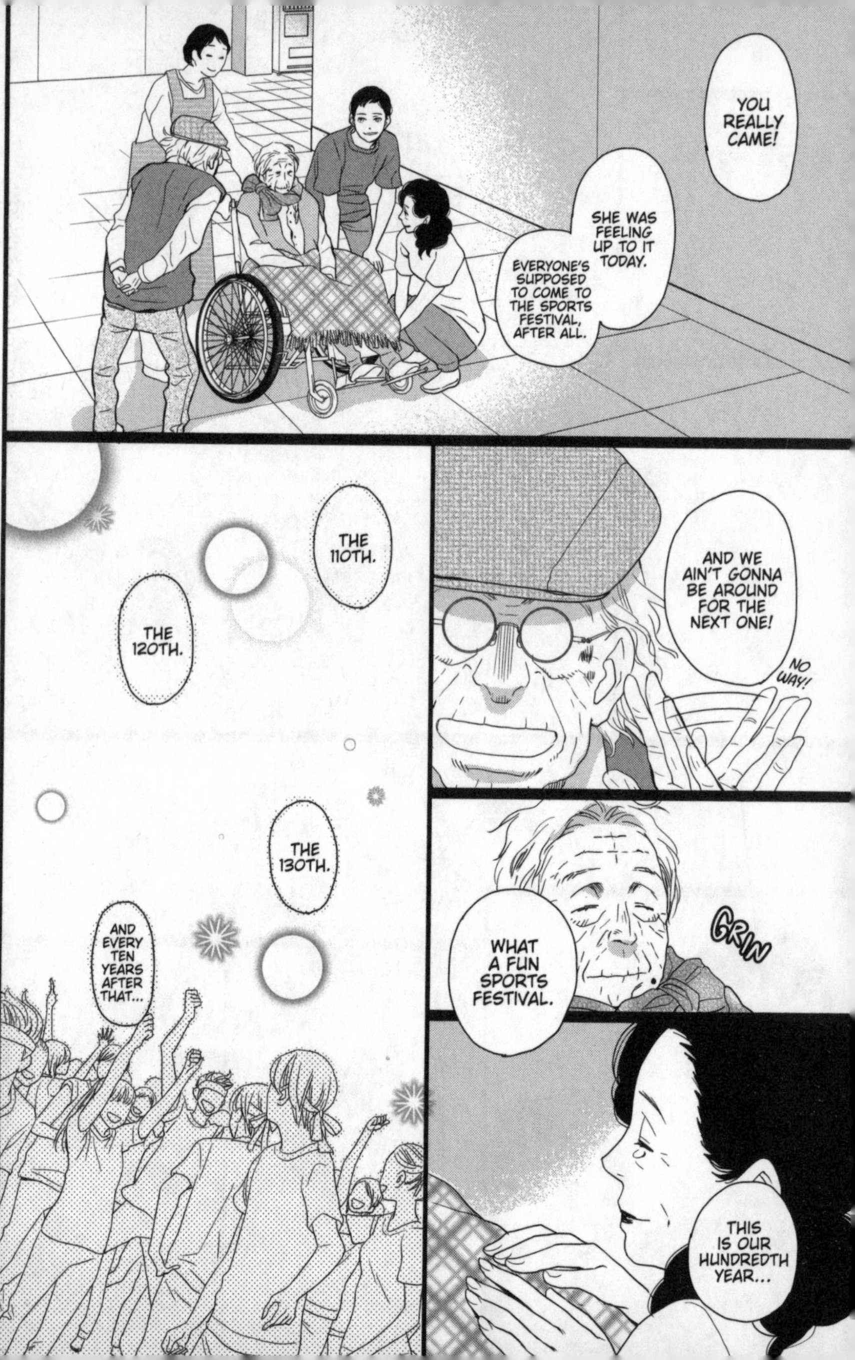
YOU REALLY CAME!
SHE WAS FEELING UP TO IT TODAY.
EVERYONE'S SUPPOSED TO COME TO THE SPORTS FESTIVAL, AFTER ALL.
AND WE AIN'T GONNA BE AROUND FOR THE NEXT ONE!
NO WAY!
GRIN
WHAT A FUN SPORTS FESTIVAL.
THIS IS OUR HUNDREDTH YEAR...
THE 110TH.
THE 120TH.
THE 130TH.
AND EVERY TEN YEARS AFTER THAT...

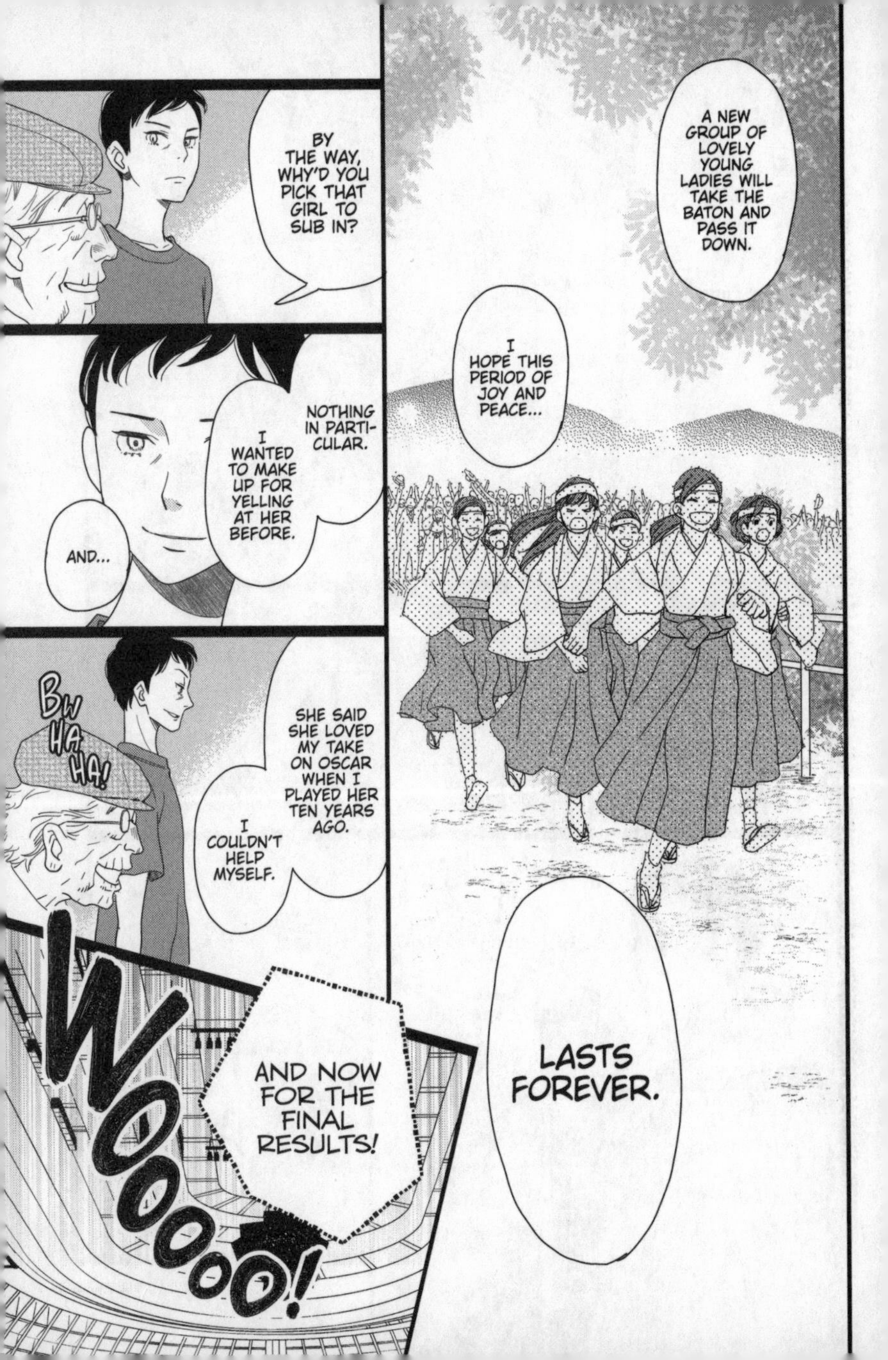
A NEW GROUP OF LOVELY YOUNG LADIES WILL TAKE THE BATON AND PASS IT DOWN.
I HOPE THIS PERIOD OF JOY AND PEACE...
LASTS FOREVER.
BY THE WAY, WHY'D YOU PICK THAT GIRL TO SUB IN?
NOTHING IN PARTICULAR.
I WANTED TO MAKE UP FOR YELLING AT HER BEFORE.
AND...
SHE SAID SHE LOVED MY TAKE ON OSCAR WHEN I PLAYED HER TEN YEARS AGO.
I COULDN'T HELP MYSELF.
BWAHAHA!
AND NOW FOR THE FINAL RESULTS!
WOOOOO!

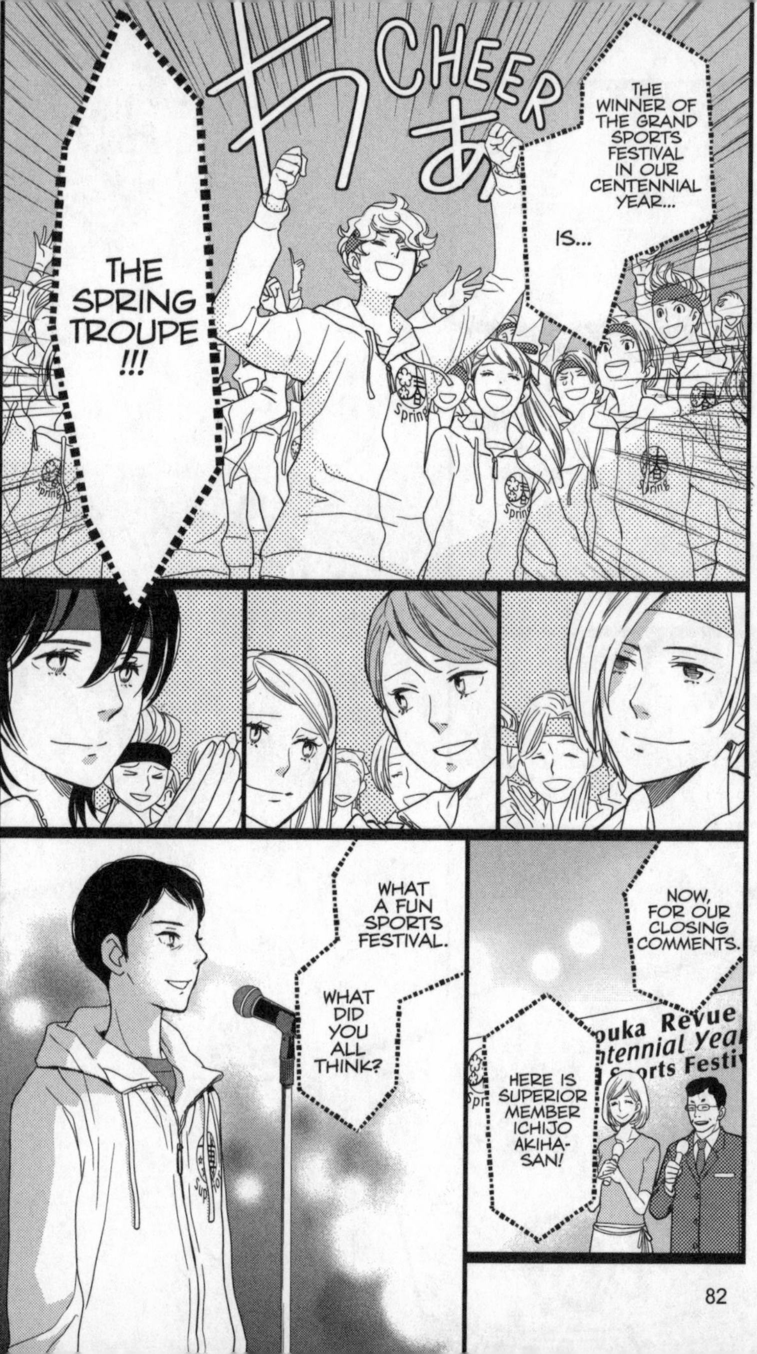
THE WINNER OF THE GRAND SPORTS FESTIVAL IN OUR CENTENNIAL YEAR...
IS...
わ CHEER あ
THE SPRING TROUPE!!!
NOW, FOR OUR CLOSING COMMENTS.
HERE IS SUPERIOR MEMBER ICHIJO AKIHA-SAN!
WHAT A FUN SPORTS FESTIVAL.
WHAT DID YOU ALL THINK?

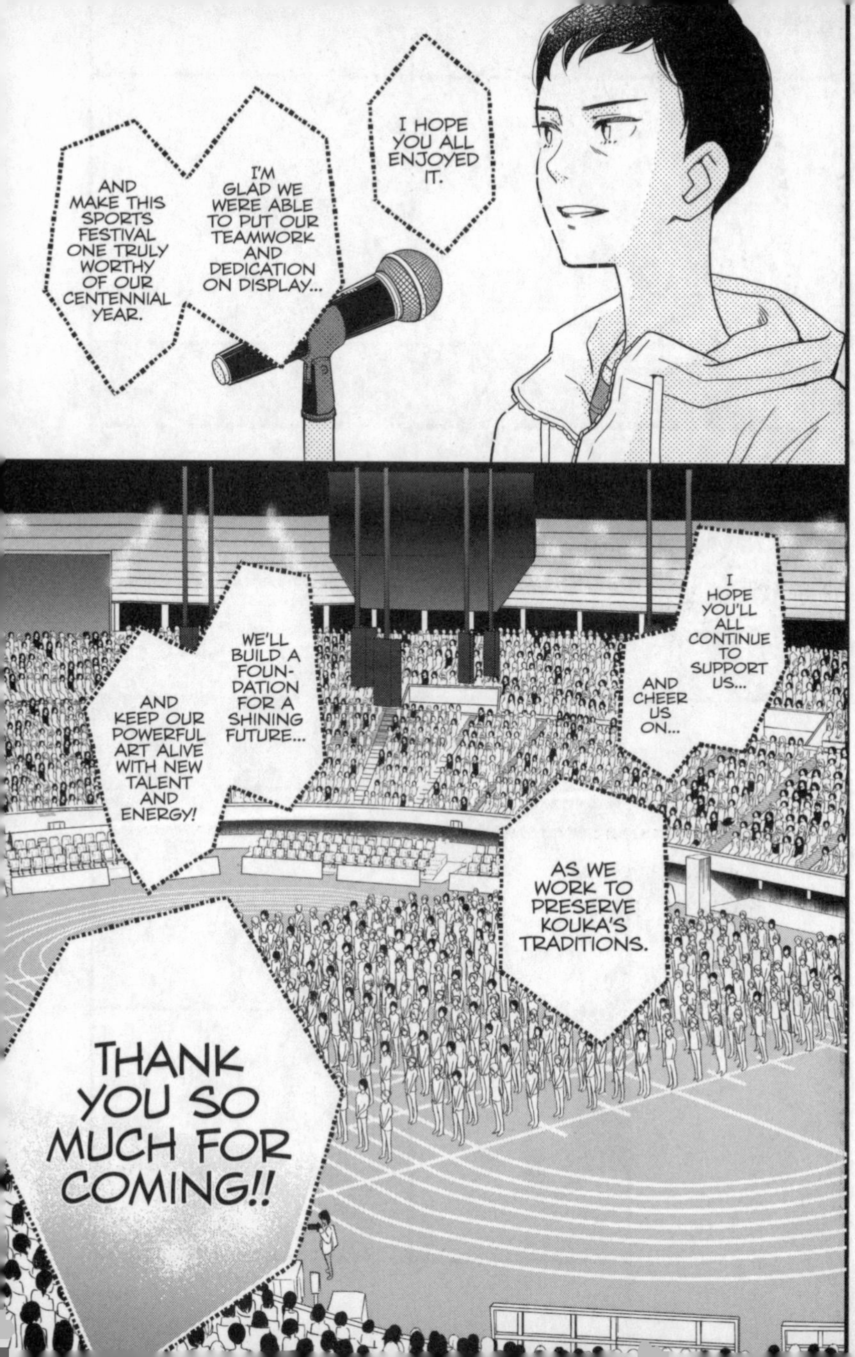
I HOPE YOU ALL ENJOYED IT.
I'M GLAD WE WERE ABLE TO PUT OUR TEAMWORK AND DEDICATION ON DISPLAY...
AND MAKE THIS SPORTS FESTIVAL ONE TRULY WORTHY OF OUR CENTENNIAL YEAR.
I HOPE YOU'LL ALL CONTINUE TO SUPPORT US...
AND CHEER US ON...
AS WE WORK TO PRESERVE KOUKA'S TRADITIONS.
WE'LL BUILD A FOUN-DATION FOR A SHINING FUTURE...
AND KEEP OUR POWERFUL ART ALIVE WITH NEW TALENT AND ENERGY!
THANK YOU SO MUCH FOR COMING!!

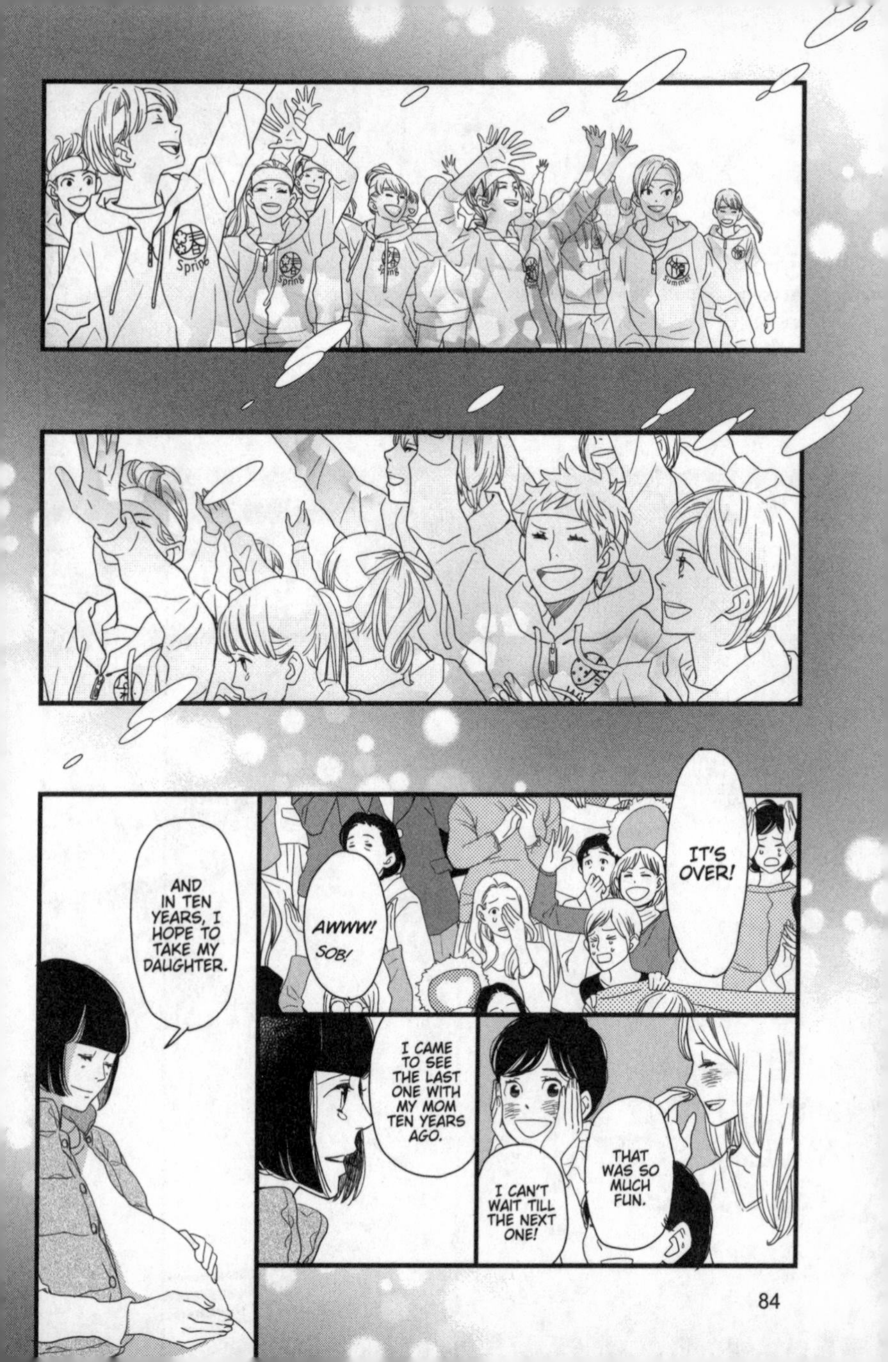
IT'S OVER!
AWWW!
SOB!
THAT WAS SO MUCH FUN.
I CAN'T WAIT TILL THE NEXT ONE!
I CAME TO SEE THE LAST ONE WITH MY MOM TEN YEARS AGO.
AND IN TEN YEARS, I HOPE TO TAKE MY DAUGHTER.

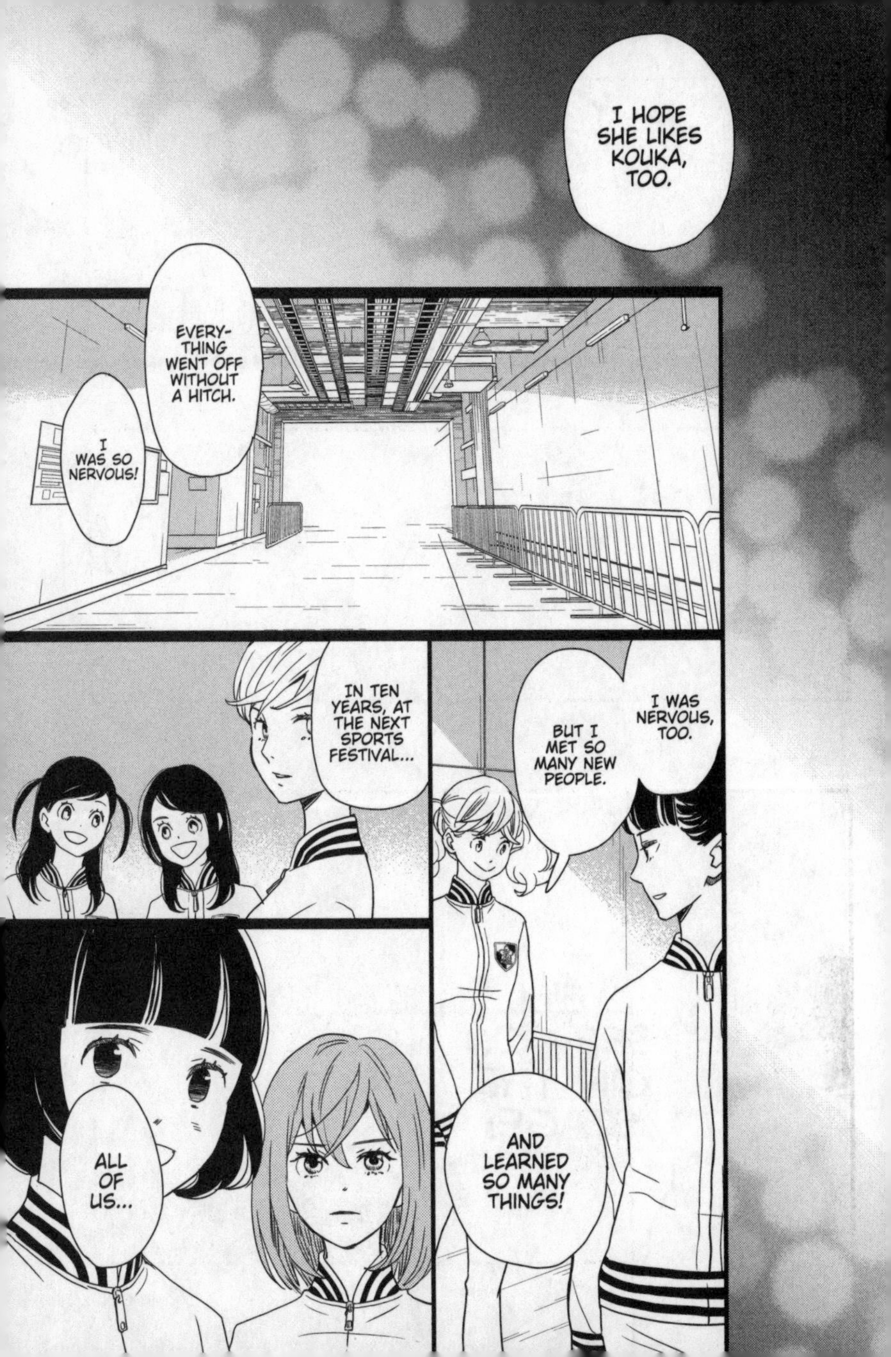
I HOPE SHE LIKES KOUKA, TOO.
EVERY-THING WENT OFF WITHOUT A HITCH.
I WAS SO NERVOUS!
I WAS NERVOUS, TOO.
BUT I MET SO MANY NEW PEOPLE.
AND LEARNED SO MANY THINGS!
IN TEN YEARS, AT THE NEXT SPORTS FESTIVAL...
ALL OF US...

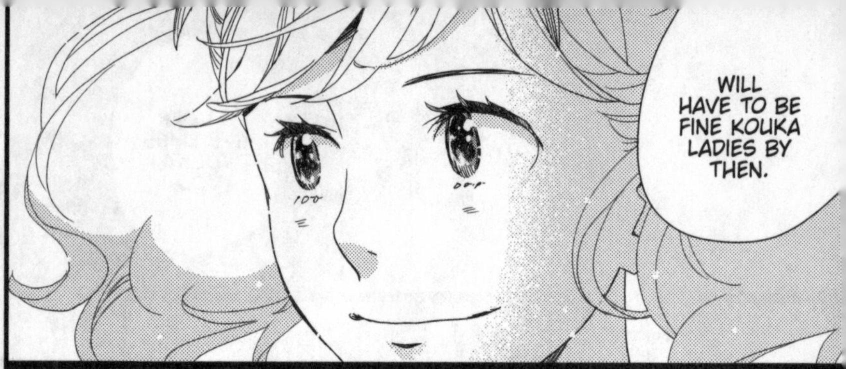
WILL HAVE TO BE FINE KOUKA LADIES BY THEN.
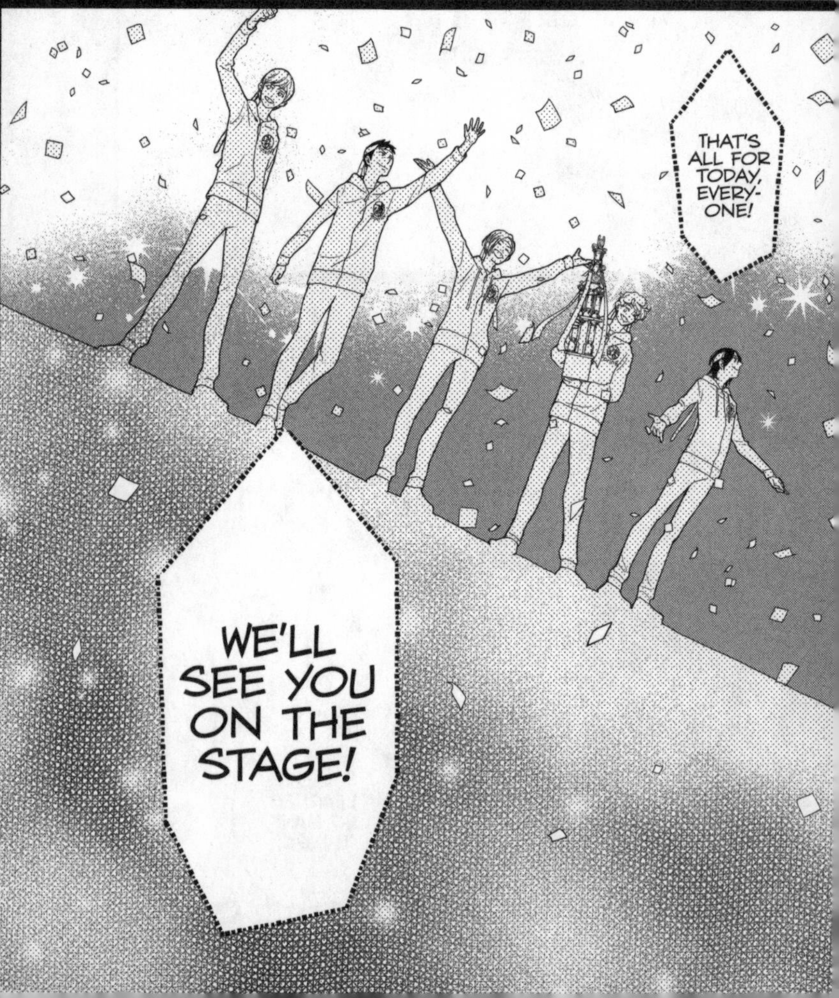
THAT'S ALL FOR TODAY, EVERY-ONE!
WE'LL SEE YOU ON THE STAGE!

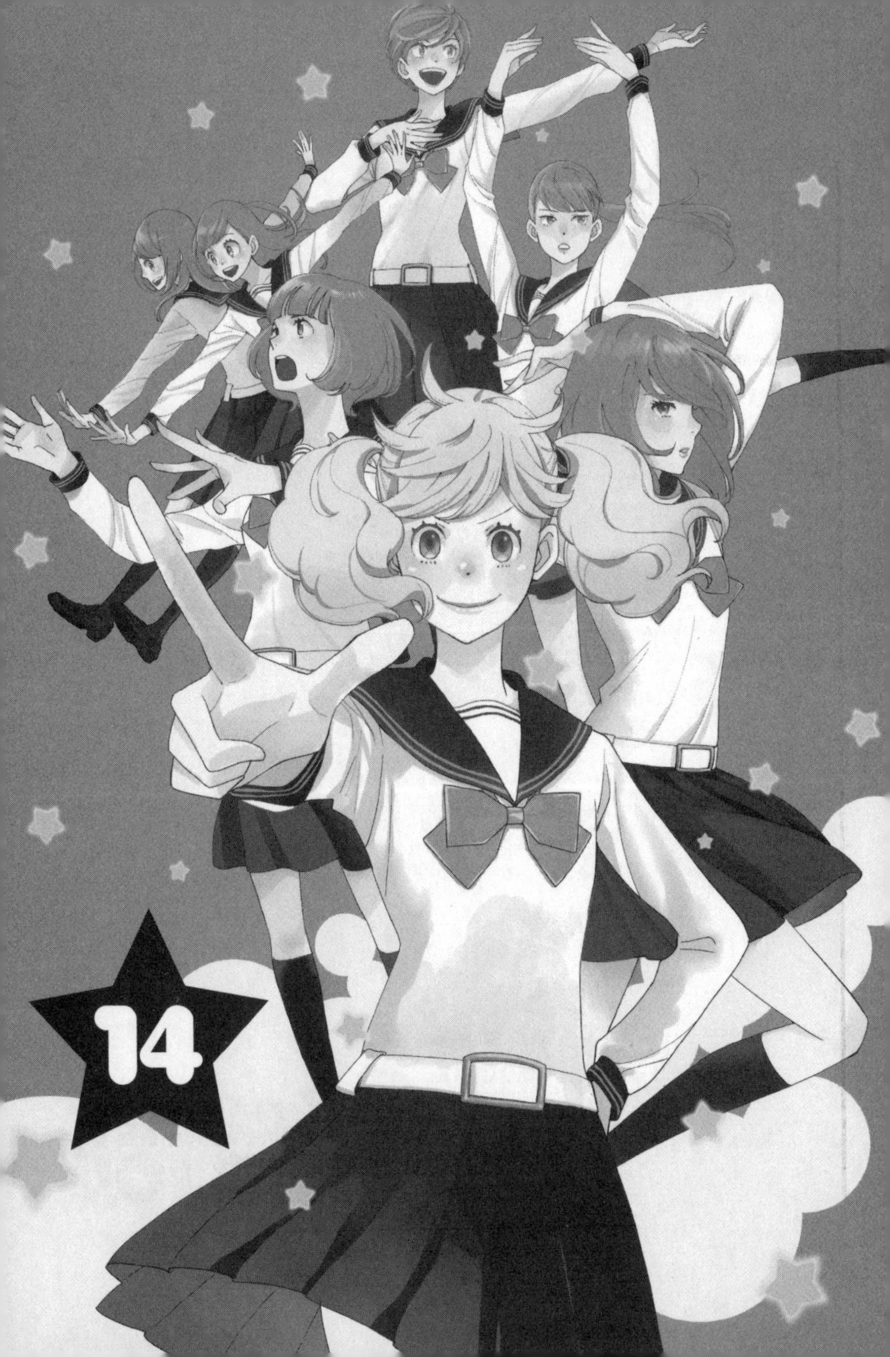
14

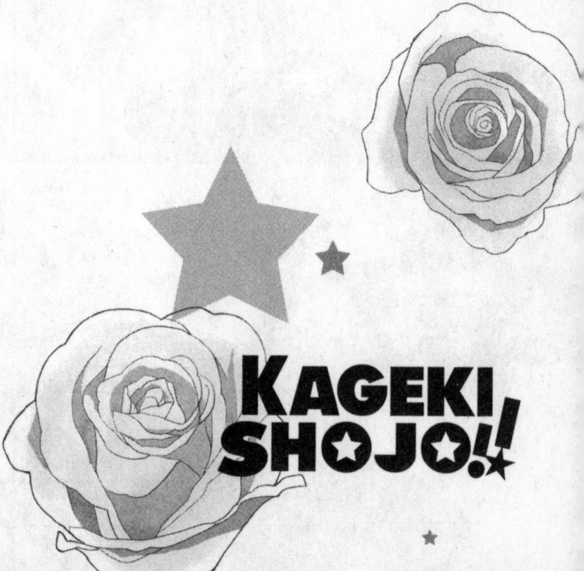
KAGEKI SHOJO!!

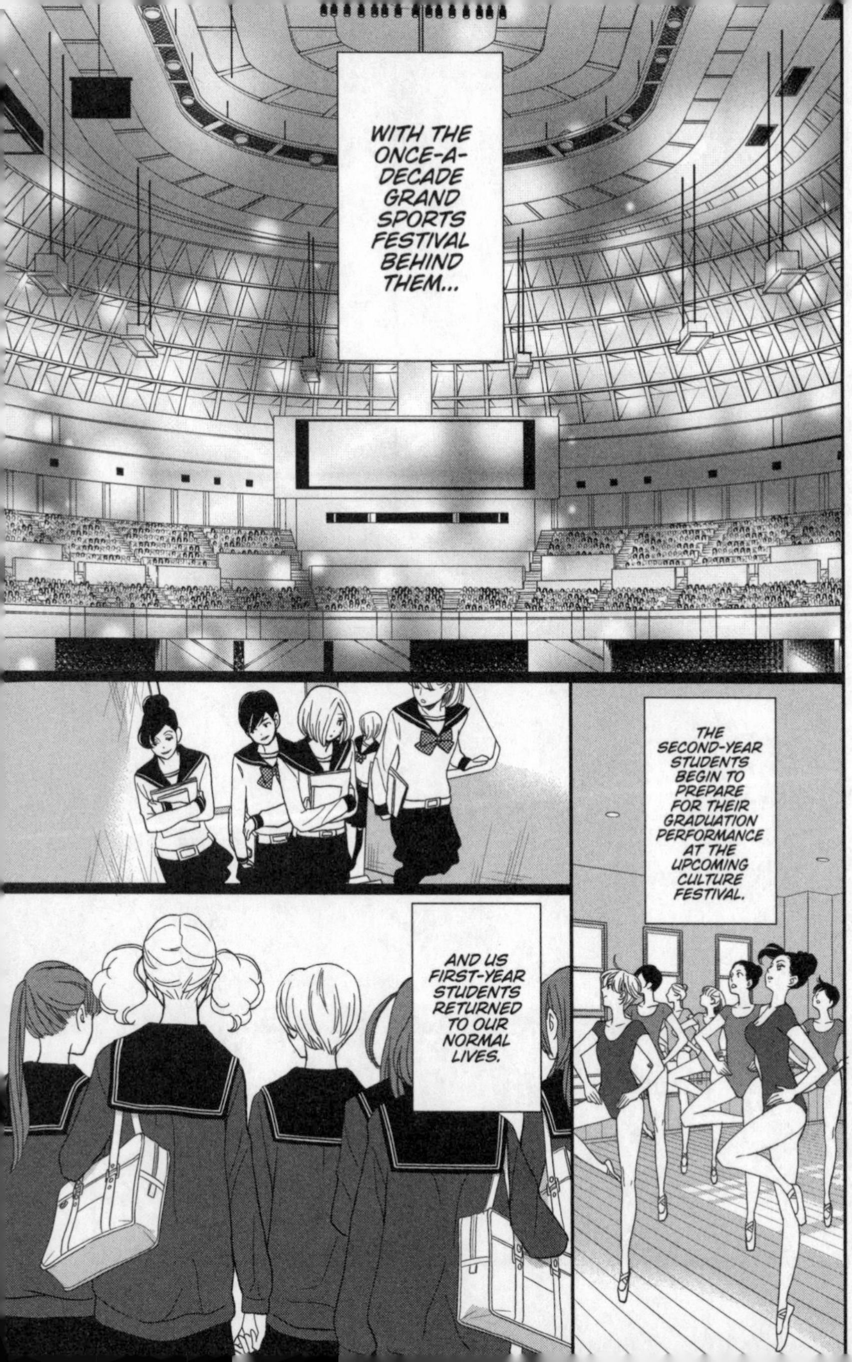
WITH THE ONCE-A-DECADE GRAND SPORTS FESTIVAL BEHIND THEM...
THE SECOND-YEAR STUDENTS BEGIN TO PREPARE FOR THEIR GRADUATION PERFORMANCE AT THE UPCOMING CULTURE FESTIVAL.
AND US FIRST-YEAR STUDENTS RETURNED TO OUR NORMAL LIVES.

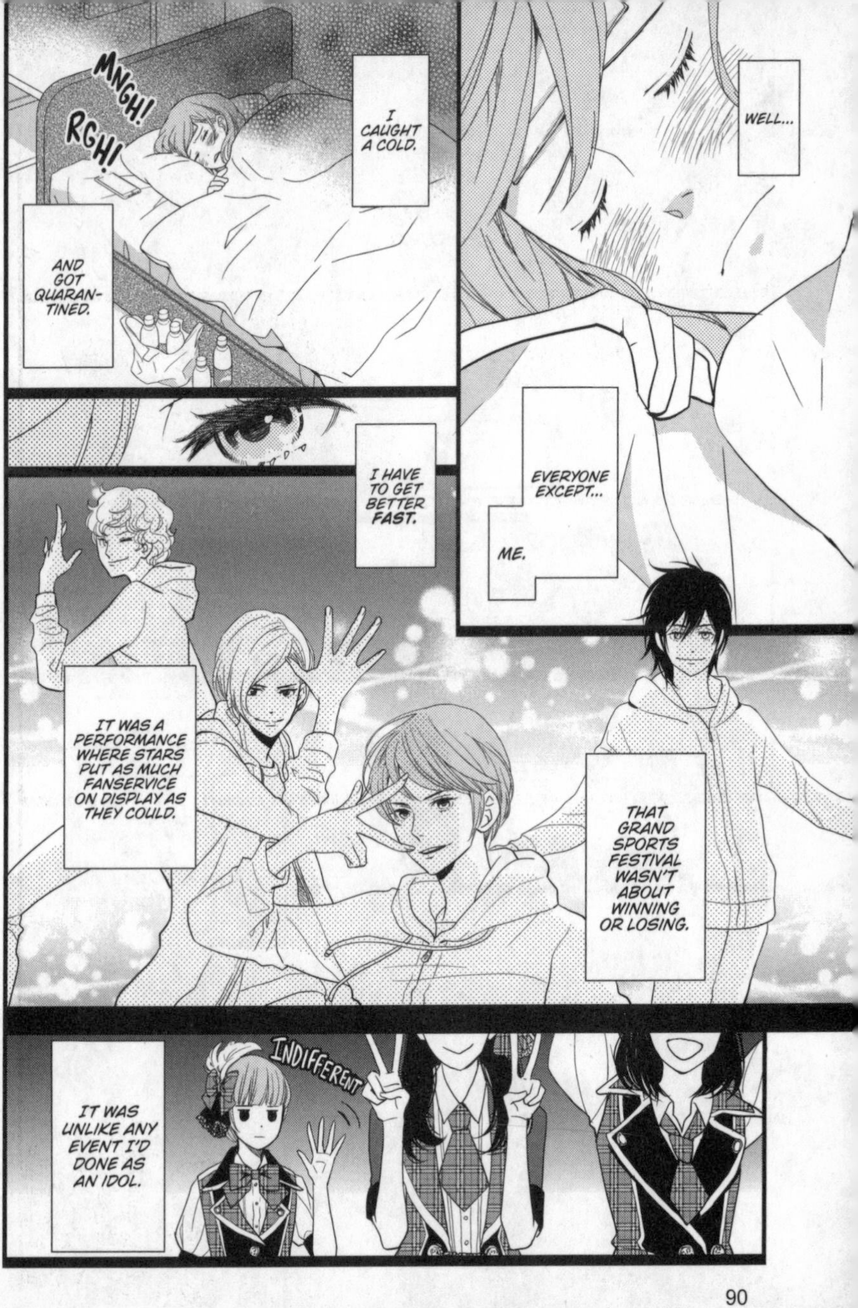
WELL...
EVERYONE EXCEPT...
ME.
I CAUGHT A COLD.
MNGH! RGH!
AND GOT QUARAN-TINED.
I HAVE TO GET BETTER FAST.
THAT GRAND SPORTS FESTIVAL WASN'T ABOUT WINNING OR LOSING.
IT WAS A PERFORMANCE WHERE STARS PUT AS MUCH FANSERVICE ON DISPLAY AS THEY COULD.
INDIFFERENT
IT WAS UNLIKE ANY EVENT I'D DONE AS AN IDOL.

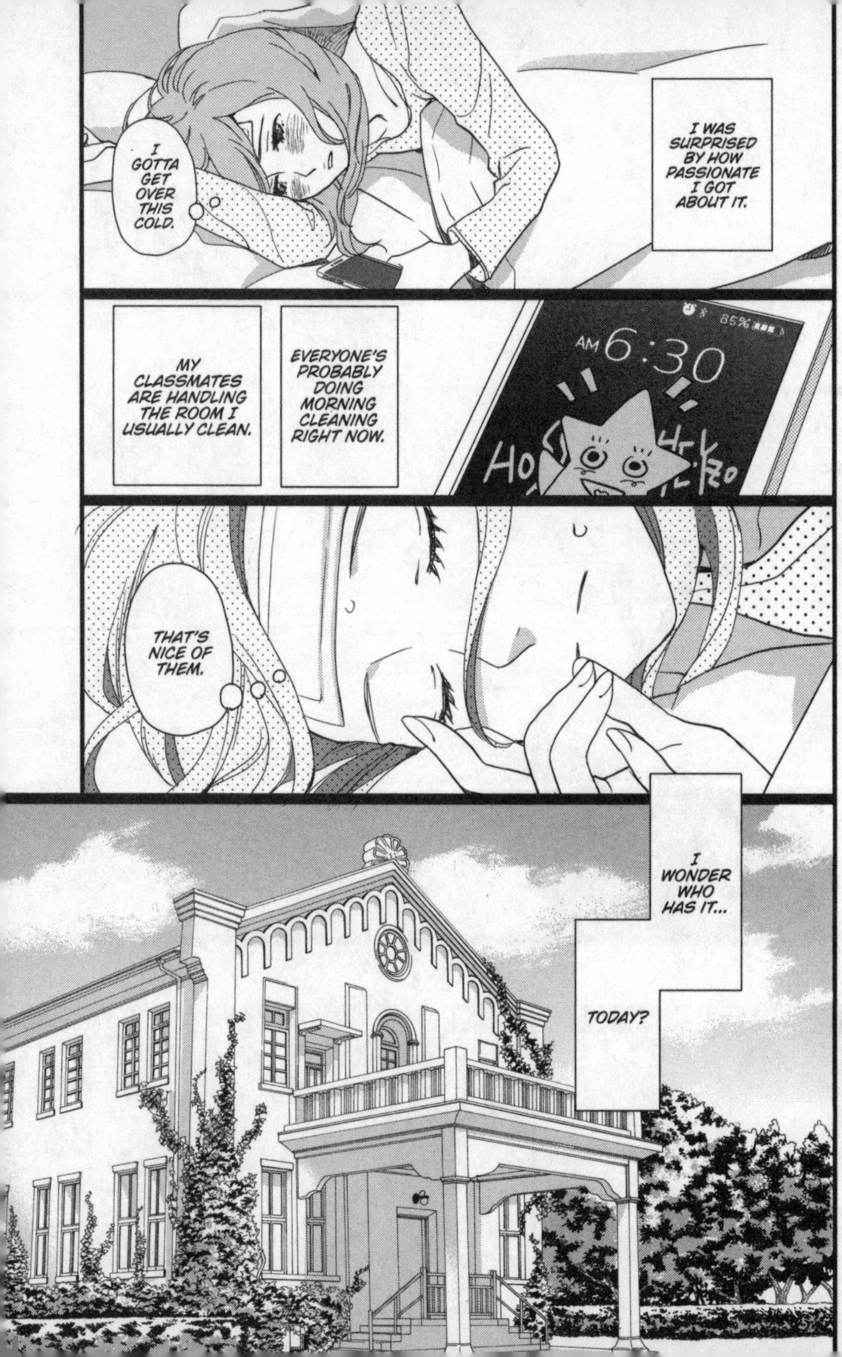
I WAS SURPRISED BY HOW PASSIONATE I GOT ABOUT IT.
I GOTTA GET OVER THIS COLD.
85%
AM 6:30
EVERYONE'S PROBABLY DOING MORNING CLEANING RIGHT NOW.
MY CLASSMATES ARE HANDLING THE ROOM I USUALLY CLEAN.
THAT'S NICE OF THEM.
I WONDER WHO HAS IT...
TODAY?

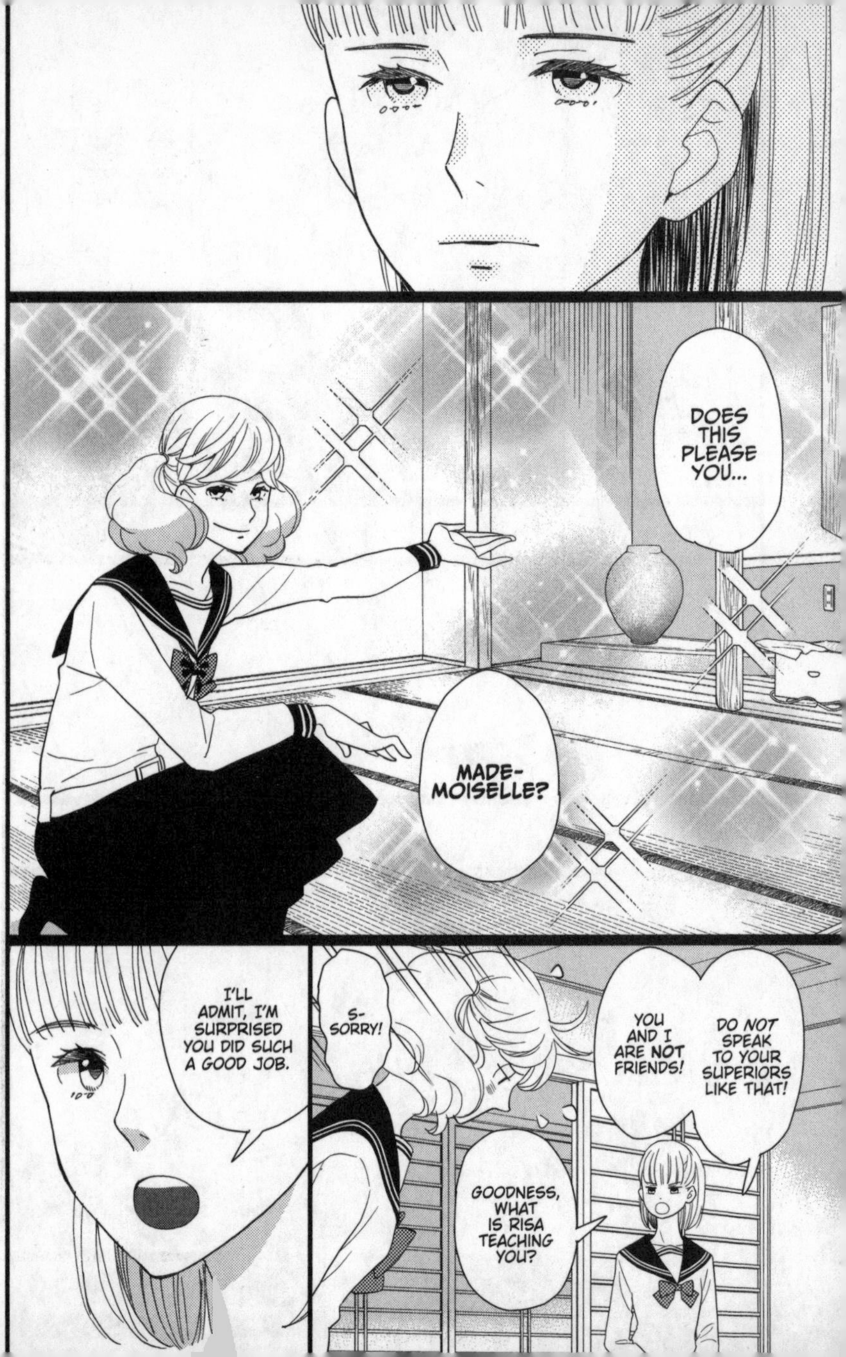
DOES THIS PLEASE YOU...
MADE-MOISELLE?
DO NOT SPEAK TO YOUR SUPERIORS LIKE THAT!
YOU AND I ARE NOT FRIENDS!
S-SORRY!
GOODNESS, WHAT IS RISA TEACHING YOU?
I'LL ADMIT, I'M SURPRISED YOU DID SUCH A GOOD JOB.

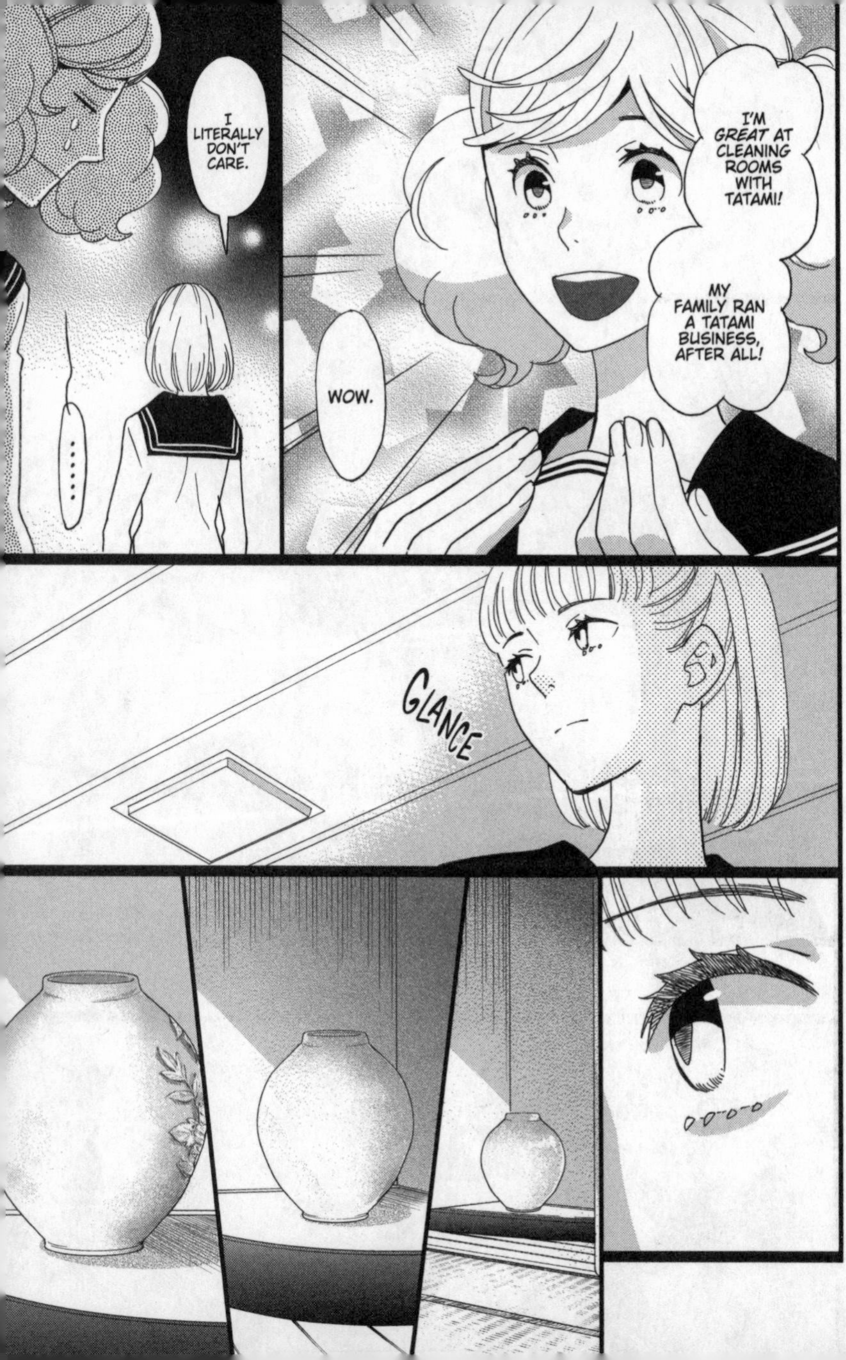
I'M GREAT AT CLEANING ROOMS WITH TATAMI!
MY FAMILY RAN A TATAMI BUSINESS, AFTER ALL!
WOW.
I LITERALLY DON'T CARE.
......
GLANCE

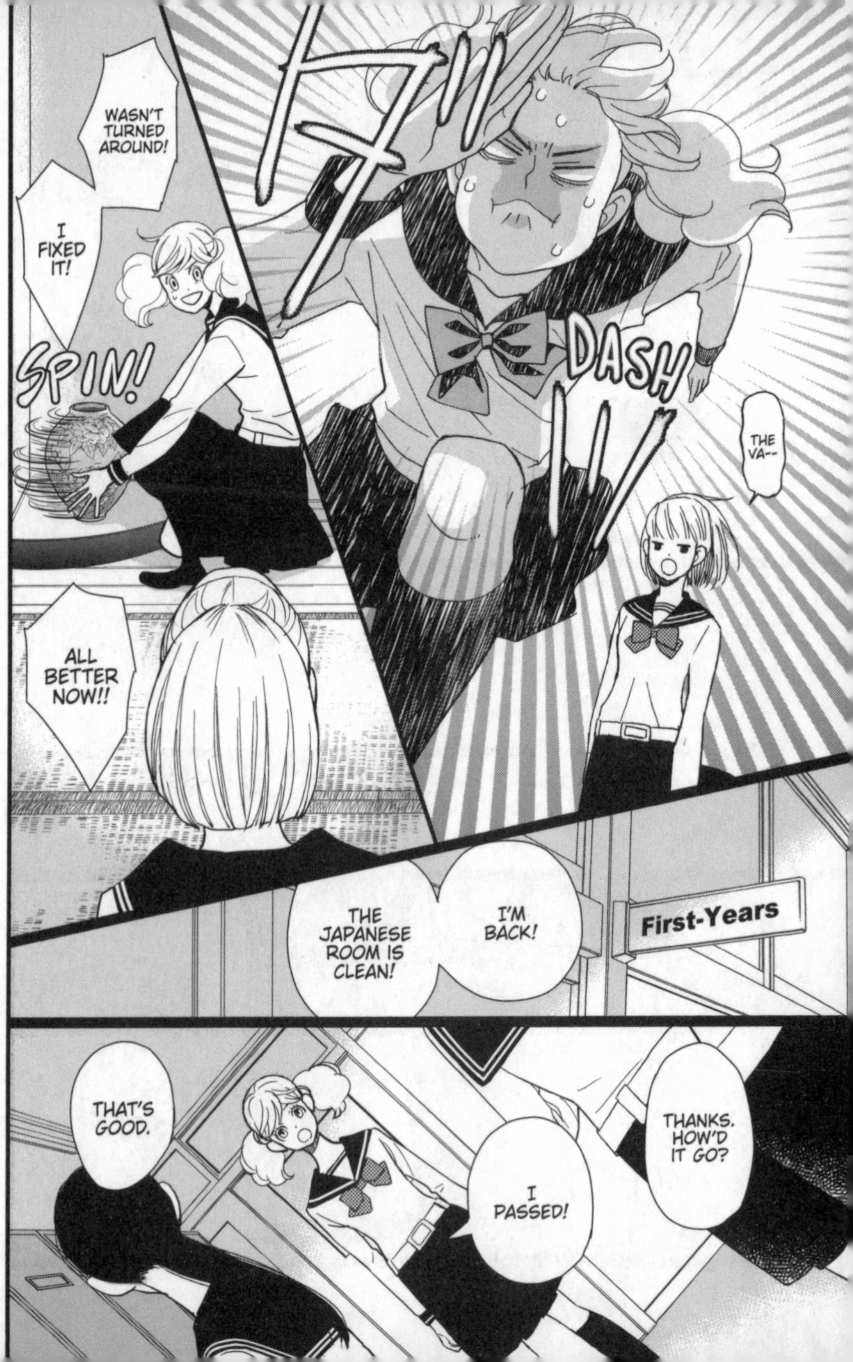
DASH
THE VA--
WASN'T TURNED AROUND!
I FIXED IT!
SPIN!
ALL BETTER NOW!!
First-Years
I'M BACK!
THE JAPANESE ROOM IS CLEAN!
THANKS. HOW'D IT GO?
I PASSED!
THAT'S GOOD.

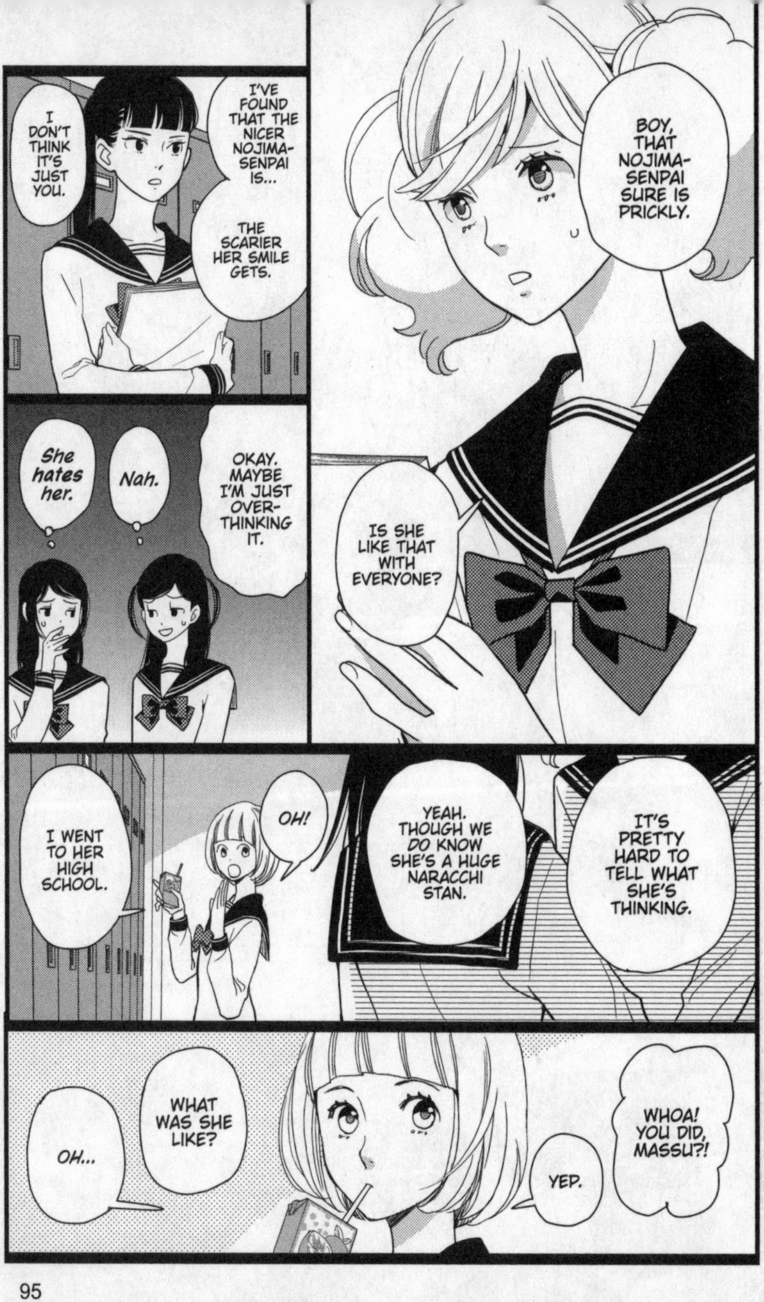
BOY, THAT NOJIMA-SENPAI SURE IS PRICKLY.
IS SHE LIKE THAT WITH EVERYONE?
I'VE FOUND THAT THE NICER NOJIMA-SENPAI IS...
THE SCARIER HER SMILE GETS.
I DON'T THINK IT'S JUST YOU.
OKAY. MAYBE I'M JUST OVER-THINKING IT.
Nah.
She hates her.
IT'S PRETTY HARD TO TELL WHAT SHE'S THINKING.
YEAH. THOUGH WE DO KNOW SHE'S A HUGE NARACCHI STAN.
OH!
I WENT TO HER HIGH SCHOOL.
WHOA! YOU DID, MASSU?!
YEP.
WHAT WAS SHE LIKE?
OH...

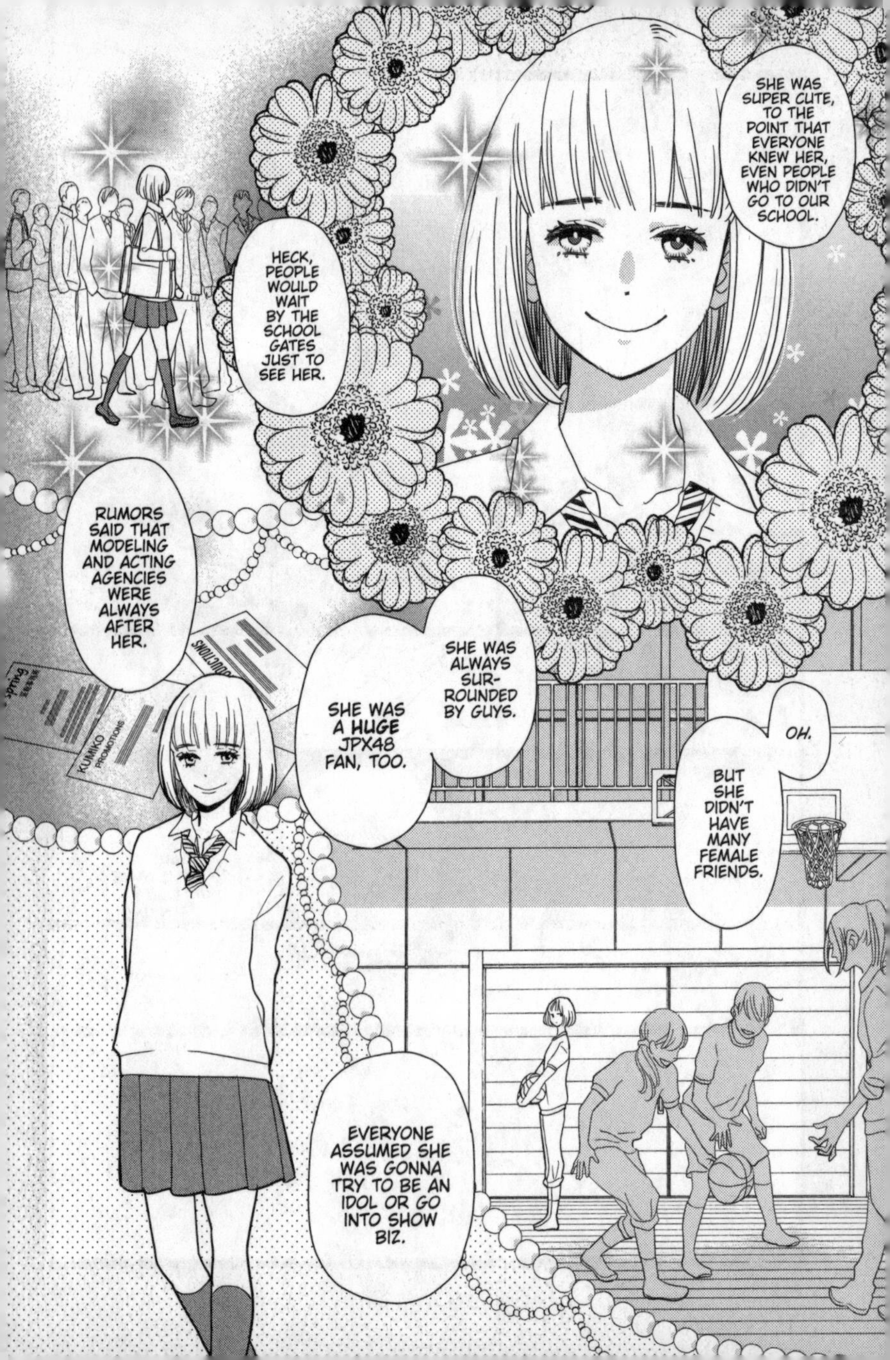
SHE WAS SUPER CUTE, TO THE POINT THAT EVERYONE KNEW HER, EVEN PEOPLE WHO DIDN'T GO TO OUR SCHOOL.
HECK, PEOPLE WOULD WAIT BY THE SCHOOL GATES JUST TO SEE HER.
RUMORS SAID THAT MODELING AND ACTING AGENCIES WERE ALWAYS AFTER HER.
KUMIKO PROMOTIONS
SHE WAS ALWAYS SUR-ROUNDED BY GUYS.
SHE WAS A **HUGE** JPX48 FAN, TOO.
OH.
BUT SHE DIDN'T HAVE MANY FEMALE FRIENDS.
EVERYONE ASSUMED SHE WAS GONNA TRY TO BE AN IDOL OR GO INTO SHOW BIZ.

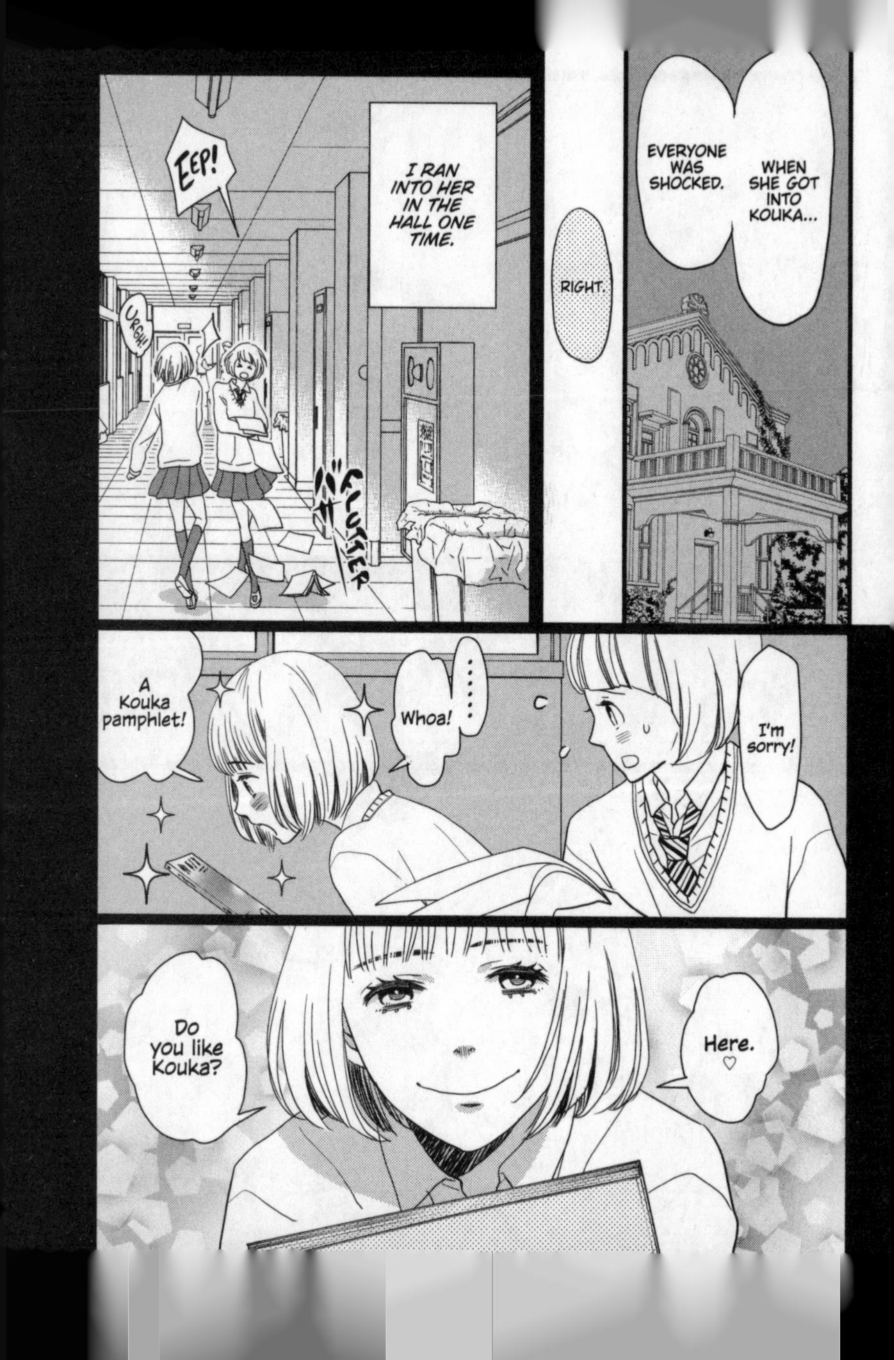
WHEN SHE GOT INTO KOUKA...
EVERYONE WAS SHOCKED.
RIGHT.
I RAN INTO HER IN THE HALL ONE TIME.
EEP!
URGH!
FLUTTER
I'm sorry!
......
Whoa!
A Kouka pamphlet!
Here. ♡
Do you like Kouka?

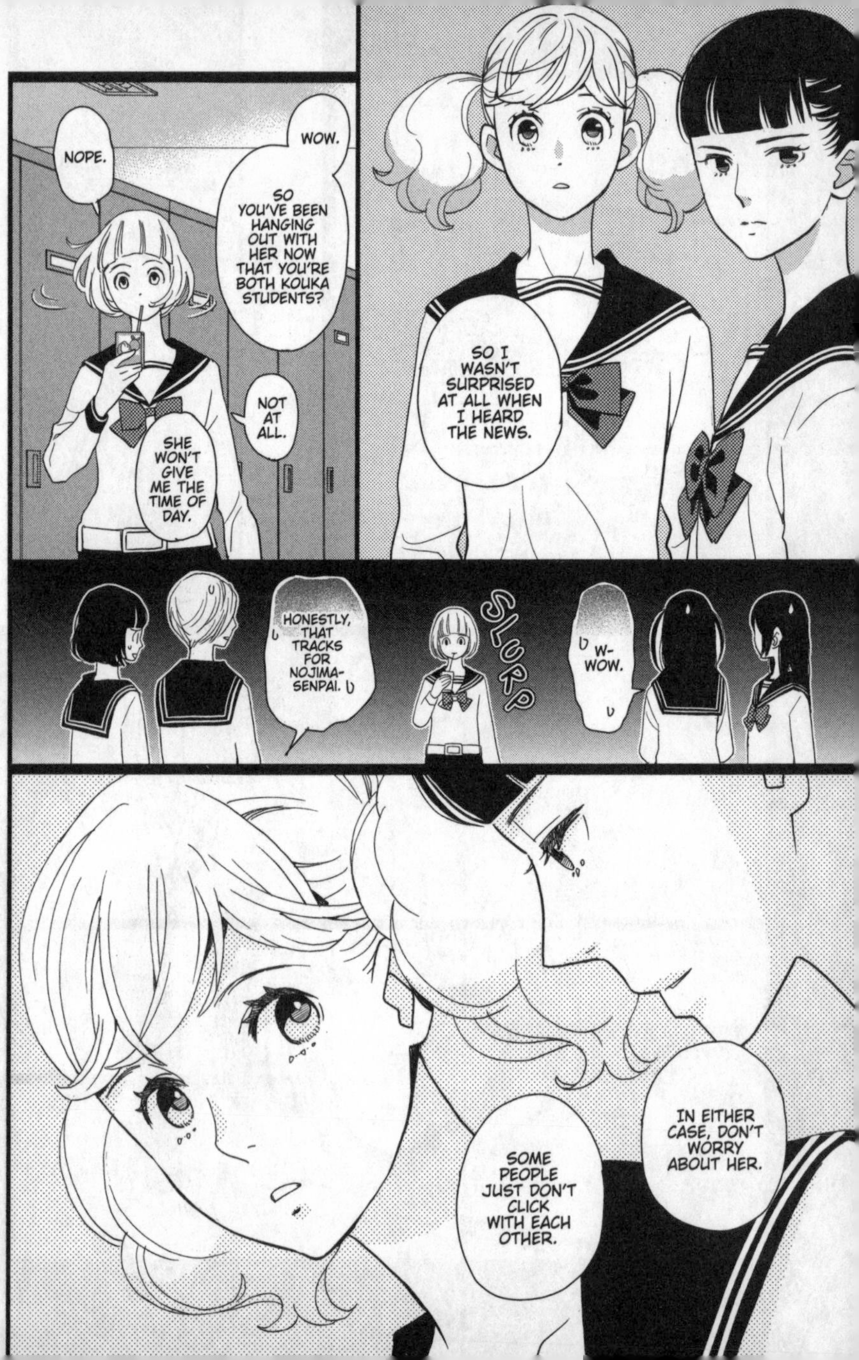
SO I WASN'T SURPRISED AT ALL WHEN I HEARD THE NEWS.
WOW.
SO YOU'VE BEEN HANGING OUT WITH HER NOW THAT YOU'RE BOTH KOUKA STUDENTS?
NOPE.
NOT AT ALL.
SHE WON'T GIVE ME THE TIME OF DAY.
W-WOW.
SLURP
HONESTLY, THAT TRACKS FOR NOJIMA-SENPAI.
IN EITHER CASE, DON'T WORRY ABOUT HER.
SOME PEOPLE JUST DON'T CLICK WITH EACH OTHER.

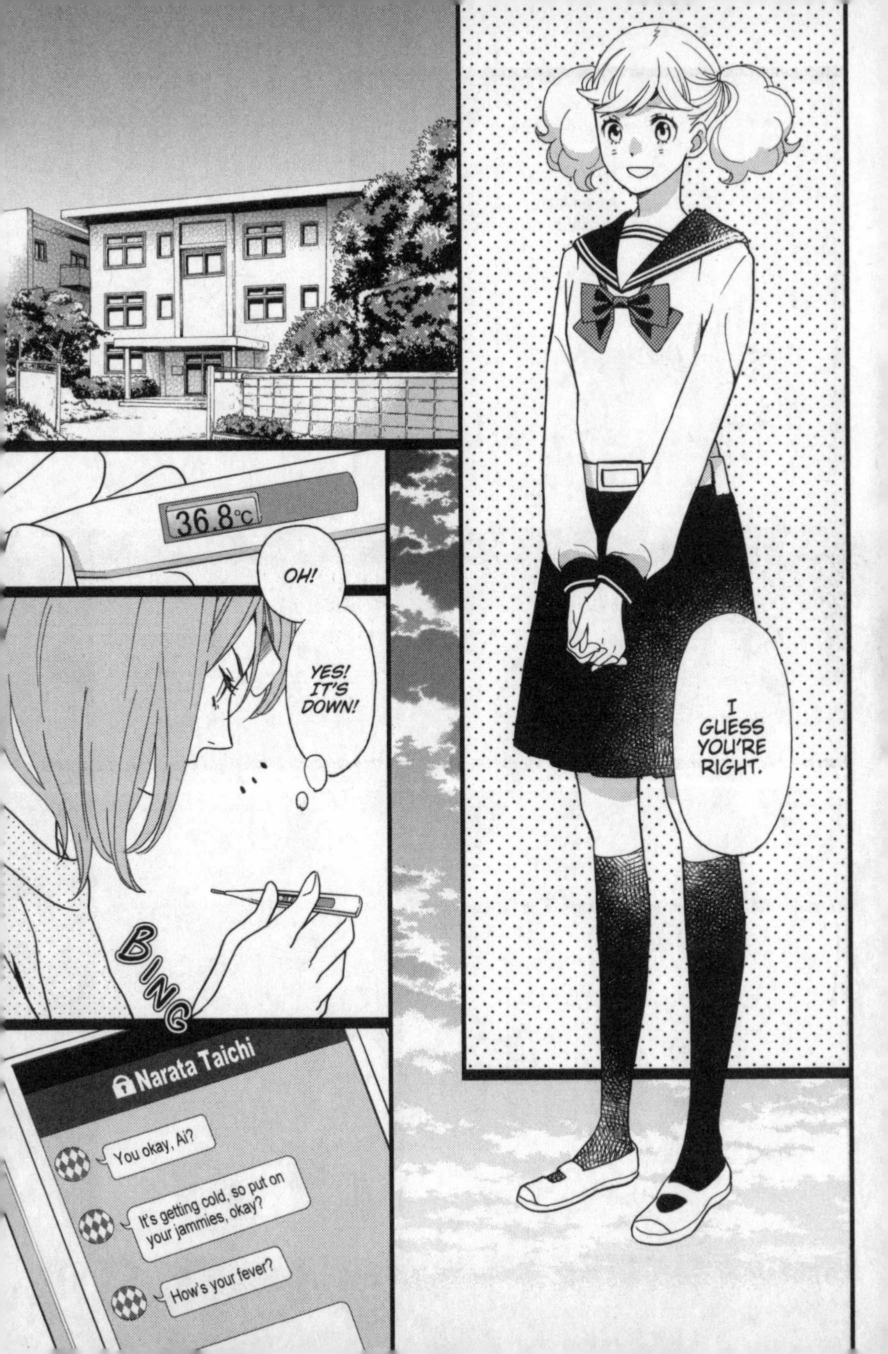
I GUESS YOU'RE RIGHT.
36.8°C
OH!
YES! IT'S DOWN!
BING
Narata Taichi
You okay, Ai?
It's getting cold, so put on your jammies, okay?
How's your fever?

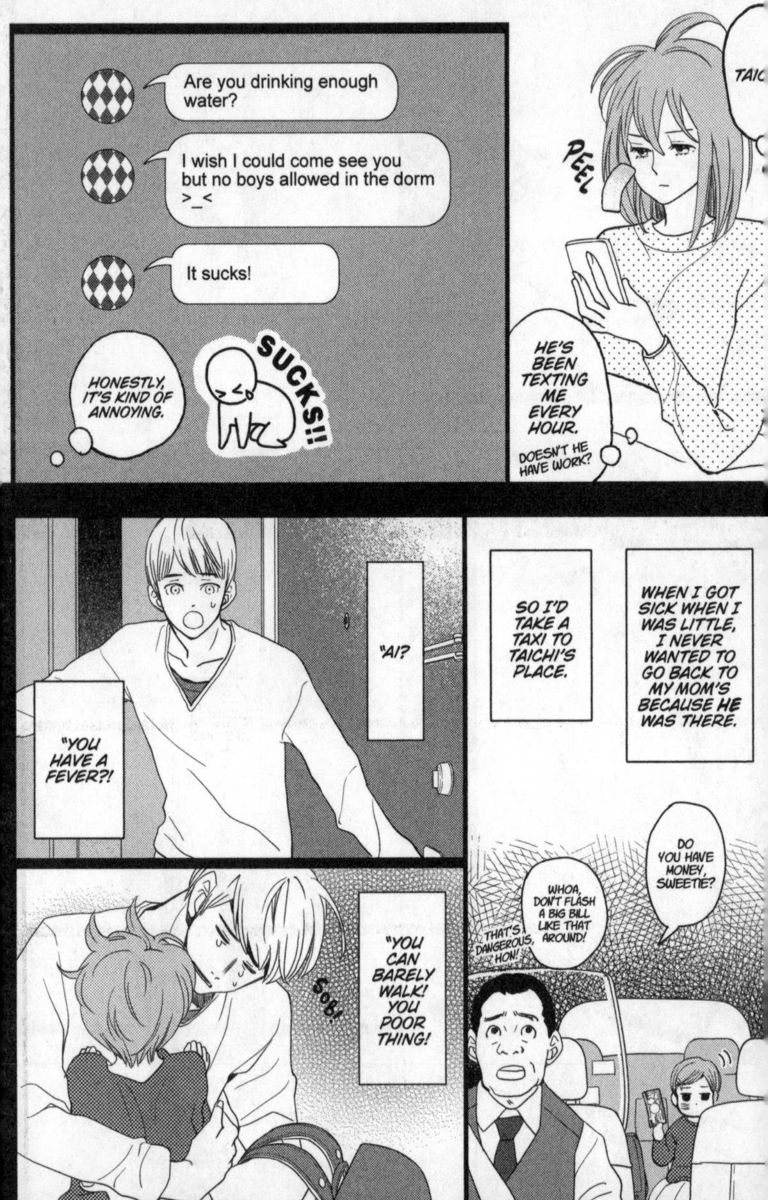

TAIC
PEEL
HE'S BEEN TEXTING ME EVERY HOUR.
DOESN'T HE HAVE WORK?
Are you drinking enough water?
I wish I could come see you but no boys allowed in the dorm >_<
It sucks!
HONESTLY, IT'S KIND OF ANNOYING.
SUCKS!!
WHEN I GOT SICK WHEN I WAS LITTLE, I NEVER WANTED TO GO BACK TO MY MOM'S BECAUSE HE WAS THERE.
SO I'D TAKE A TAXI TO TAICHI'S PLACE.
DO YOU HAVE MONEY, SWEETIE?
WHOA, DON'T FLASH A BIG BILL LIKE THAT AROUND!
THAT'S DANGEROUS, HON!
"AI?
"YOU HAVE A FEVER?!
"YOU CAN BARELY WALK! YOU POOR THING!
SOB!

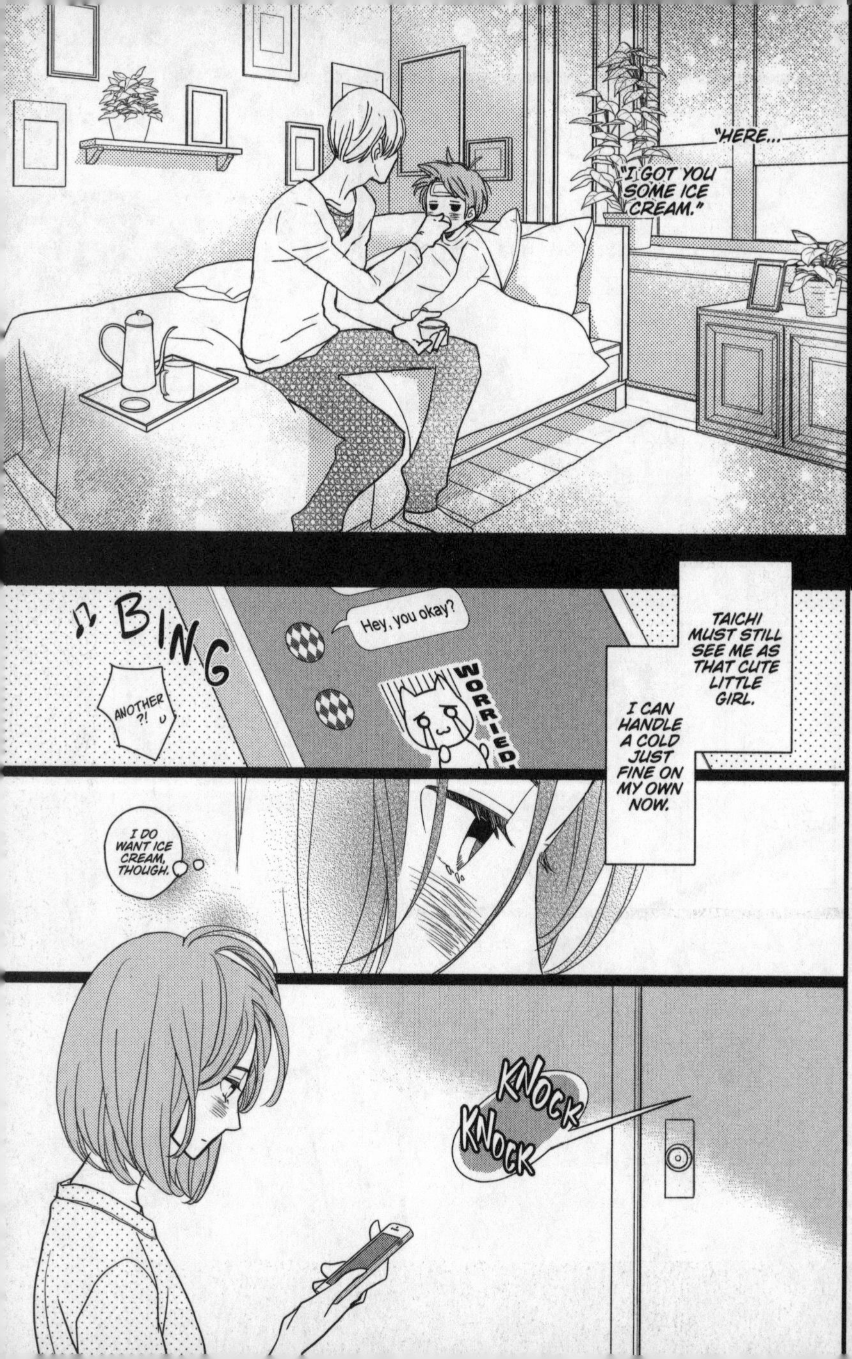
"HERE...
"I GOT YOU SOME ICE CREAM."
TAICHI MUST STILL SEE ME AS THAT CUTE LITTLE GIRL.
I CAN HANDLE A COLD JUST FINE ON MY OWN NOW.
Hey, you okay?
WORRIED
BING
ANOTHER ?!
I DO WANT ICE CREAM, THOUGH.
KNOCK KNOCK

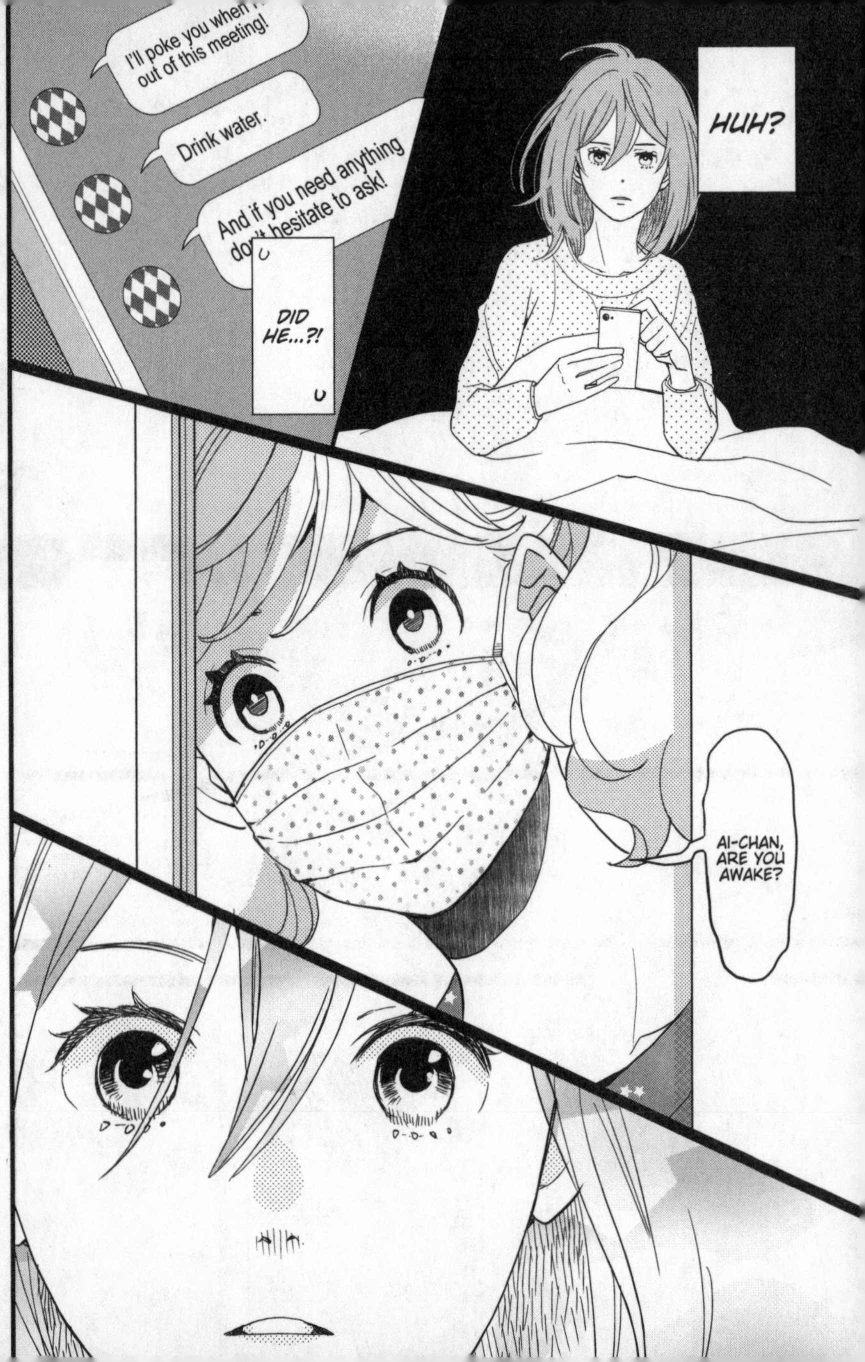
HUH?
I'll poke you when I'm out of this meeting!
Drink water.
And if you need anything don't hesitate to ask!
DID HE...?!
AI-CHAN, ARE YOU AWAKE?

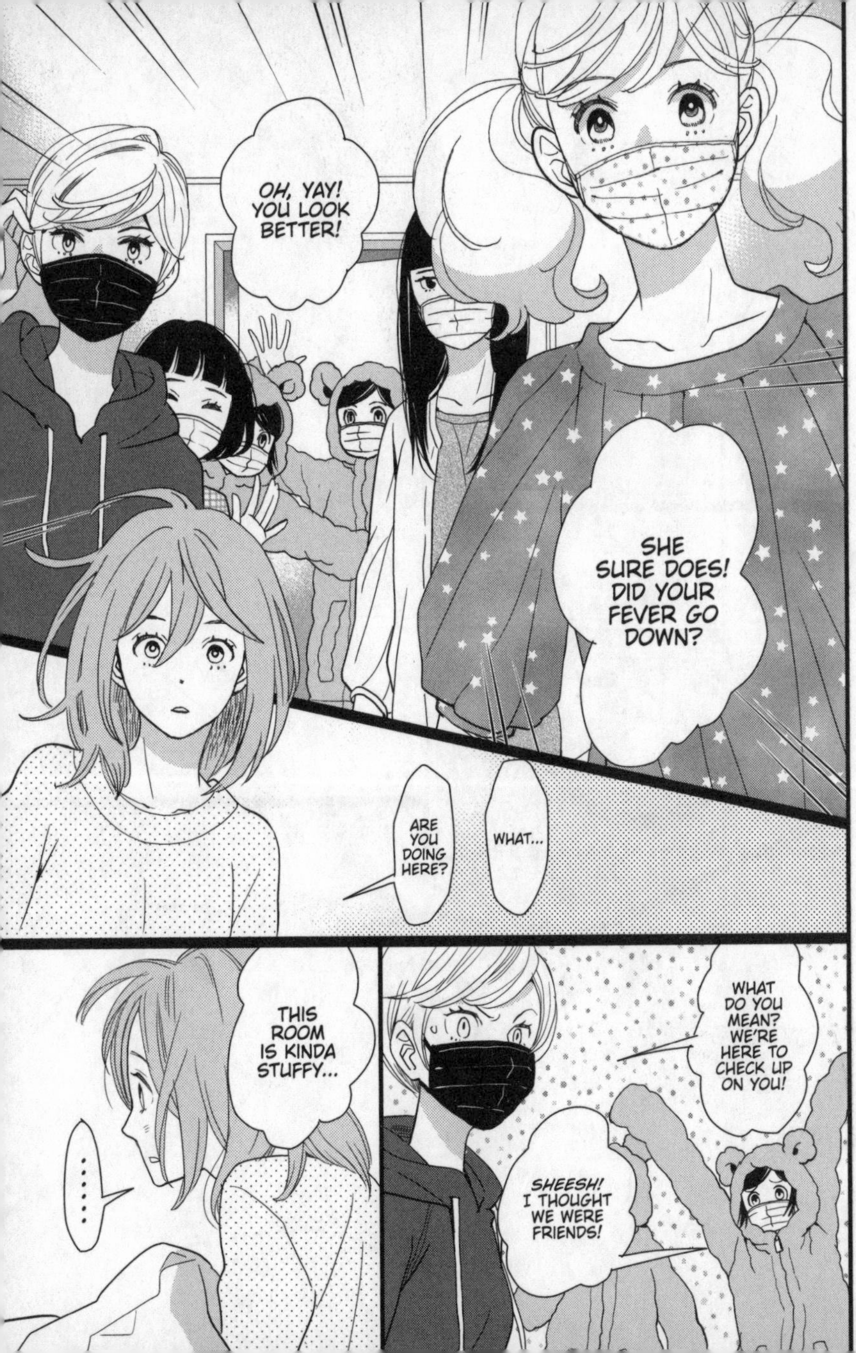
OH, YAY! YOU LOOK BETTER!
SHE SURE DOES! DID YOUR FEVER GO DOWN?
WHAT...
ARE YOU DOING HERE?
WHAT DO YOU MEAN? WE'RE HERE TO CHECK UP ON YOU!
SHEESH! I THOUGHT WE WERE FRIENDS!
THIS ROOM IS KINDA STUFFY...
......

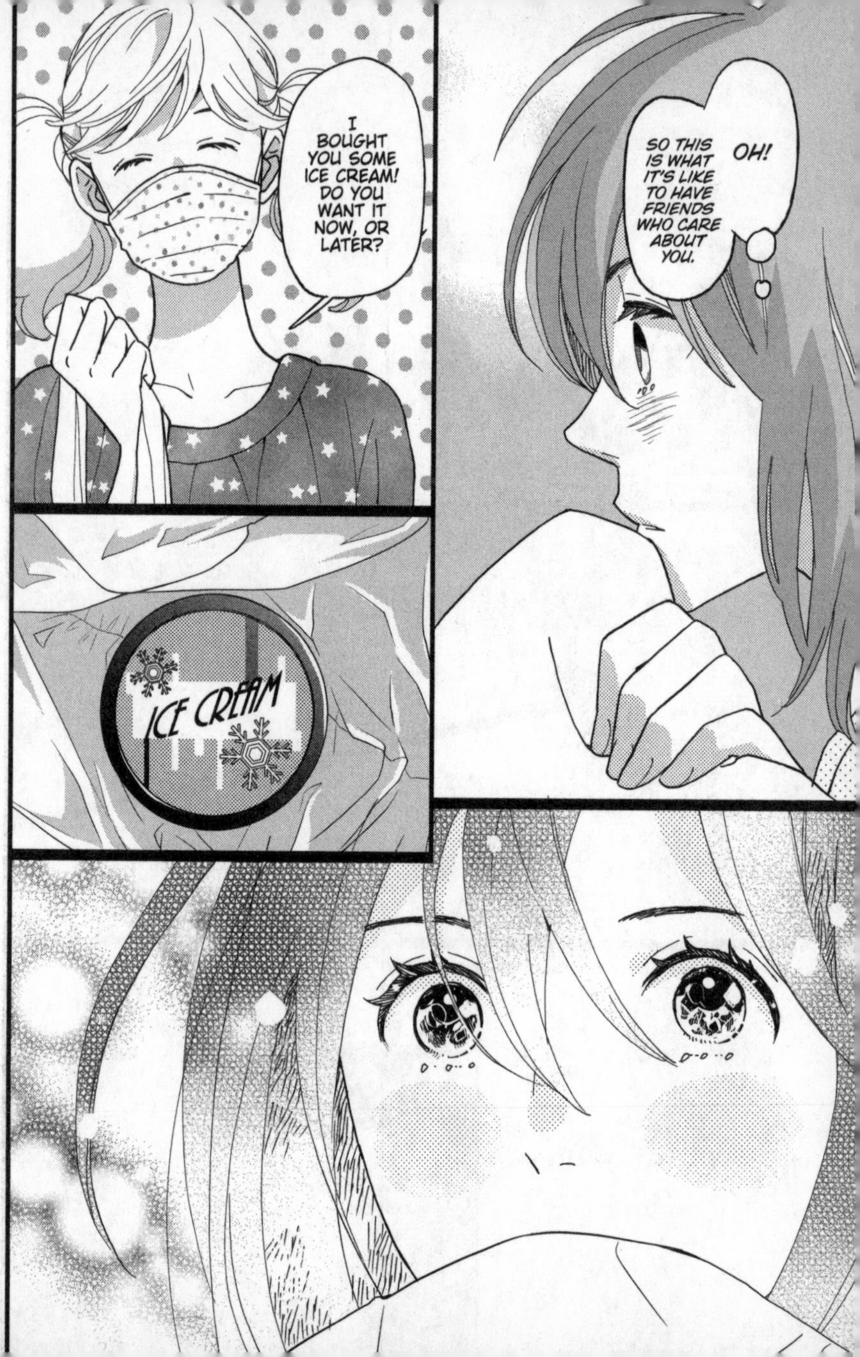
OH!
SO THIS IS WHAT IT'S LIKE TO HAVE FRIENDS WHO CARE ABOUT YOU.
I BOUGHT YOU SOME ICE CREAM! DO YOU WANT IT NOW, OR LATER?
ICE CREAM

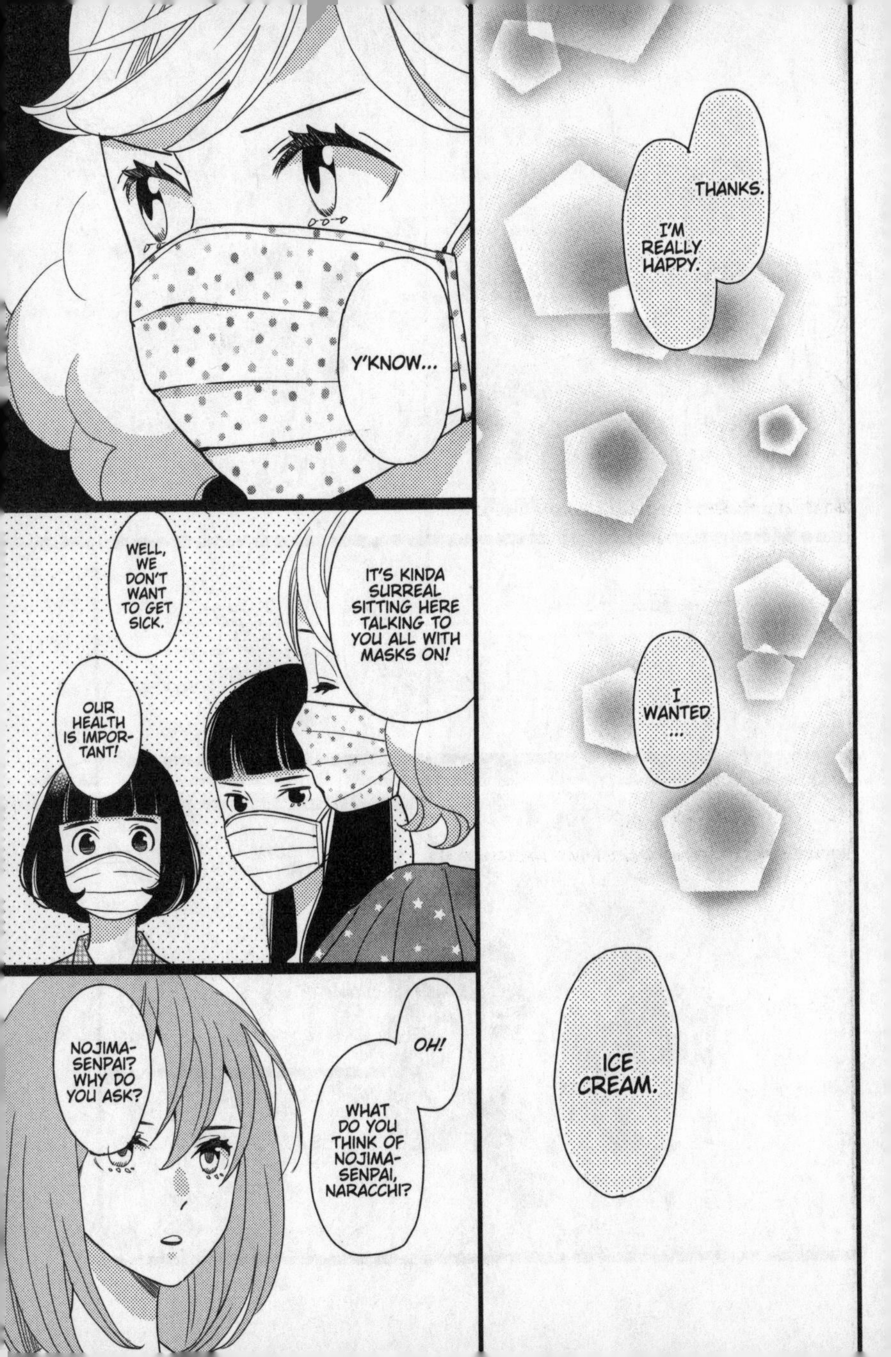
THANKS.
I'M REALLY HAPPY.
I WANTED ...
ICE CREAM.
Y'KNOW...
IT'S KINDA SURREAL SITTING HERE TALKING TO YOU ALL WITH MASKS ON!
WELL, WE DON'T WANT TO GET SICK.
OUR HEALTH IS IMPOR-TANT!
OH!
WHAT DO YOU THINK OF NOJIMA-SENPAI, NARACCHI?
NOJIMA-SENPAI? WHY DO YOU ASK?

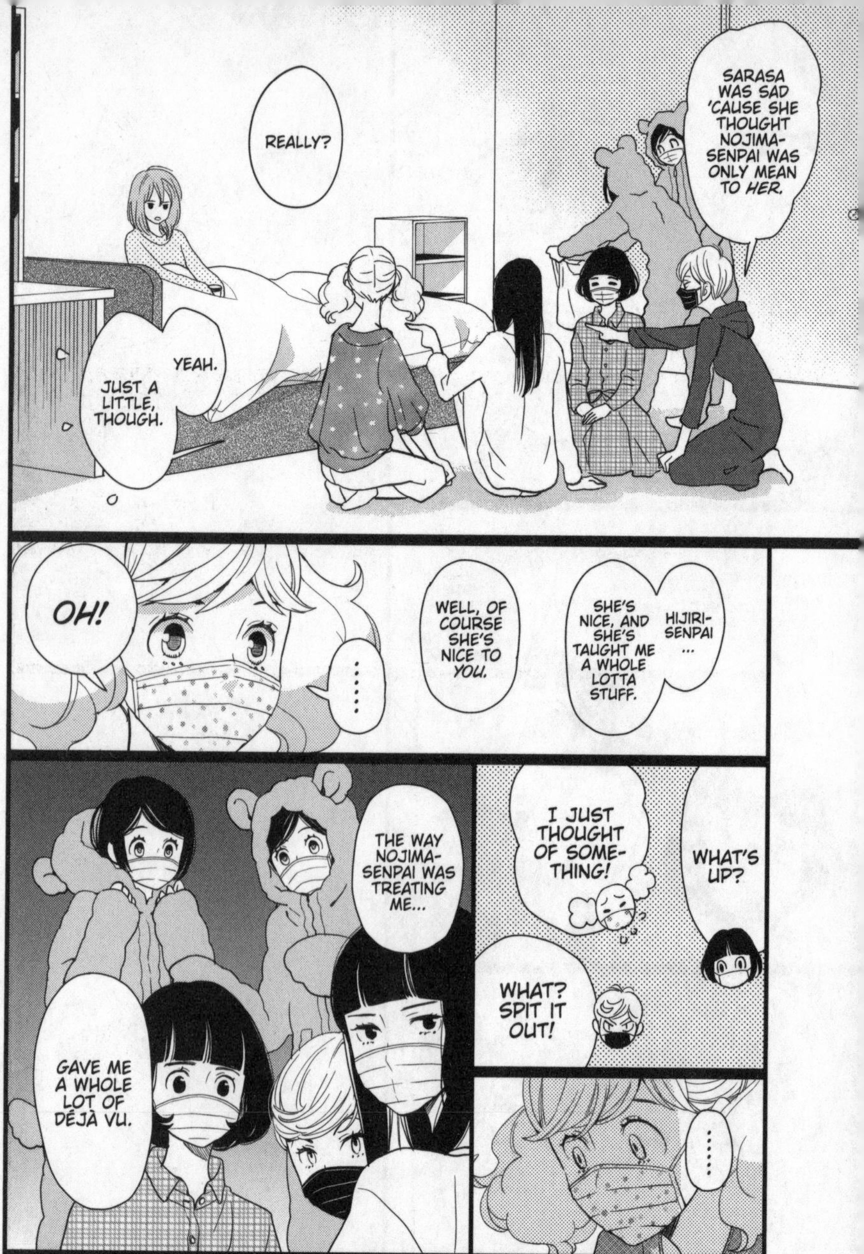
SARASA WAS SAD 'CAUSE SHE THOUGHT NOJIMA-SENPAI WAS ONLY MEAN TO *HER.*
REALLY?
YEAH.
JUST A LITTLE, THOUGH.
HIJIRI-SENPAI ...
SHE'S NICE, AND SHE'S TAUGHT ME A WHOLE LOTTA STUFF.
WELL, OF COURSE SHE'S NICE TO *YOU.*
......
OH!
WHAT'S UP?
I JUST THOUGHT OF SOME-THING!
WHAT? SPIT IT OUT!
......
THE WAY NOJIMA-SENPAI WAS TREATING ME...
GAVE ME A WHOLE LOT OF DÉJÀ VU.

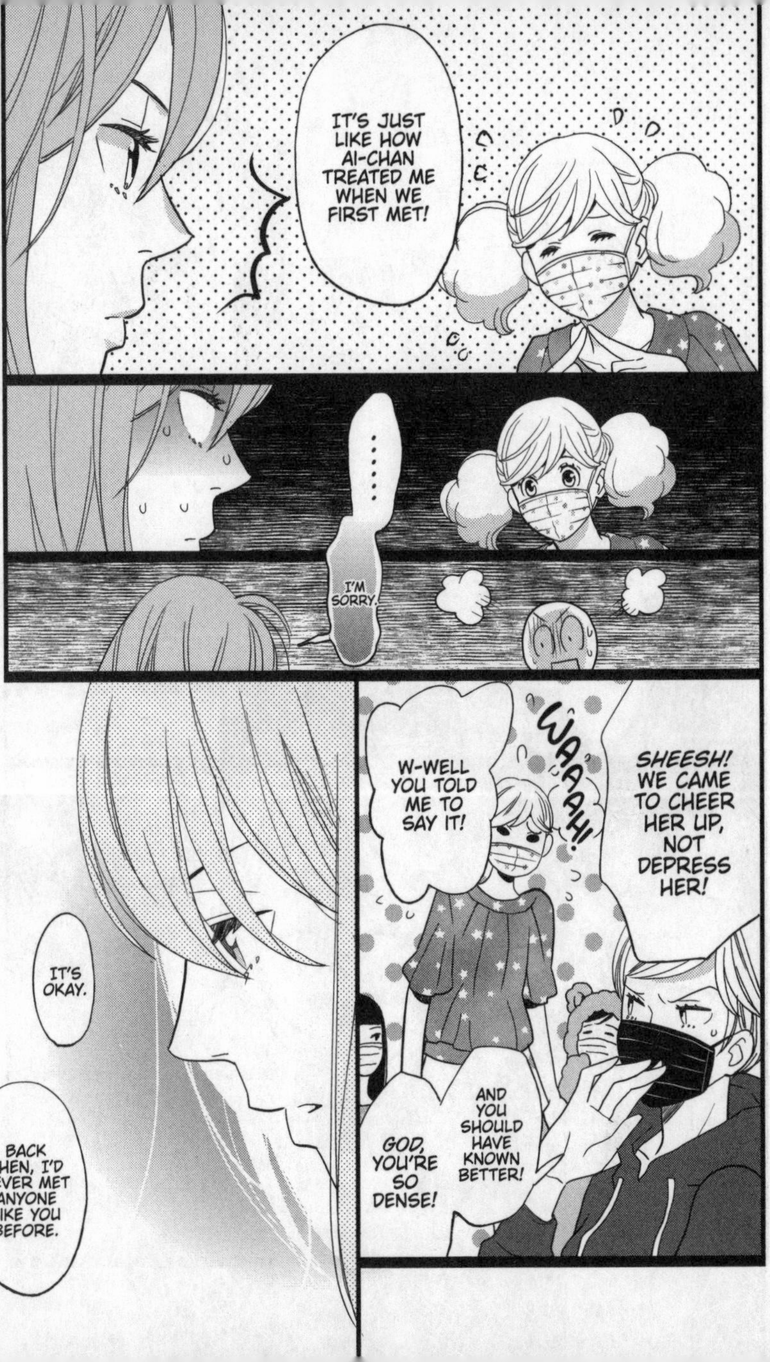
IT'S JUST LIKE HOW AI-CHAN TREATED ME WHEN WE FIRST MET!
.....
I'M SORRY.
SHEESH! WE CAME TO CHEER HER UP, NOT DEPRESS HER!
WAAAH!
W-WELL YOU TOLD ME TO SAY IT!
AND YOU SHOULD HAVE KNOWN BETTER!
GOD, YOU'RE SO DENSE!
IT'S OKAY.
BACK THEN, I'D NEVER MET ANYONE LIKE YOU BEFORE.

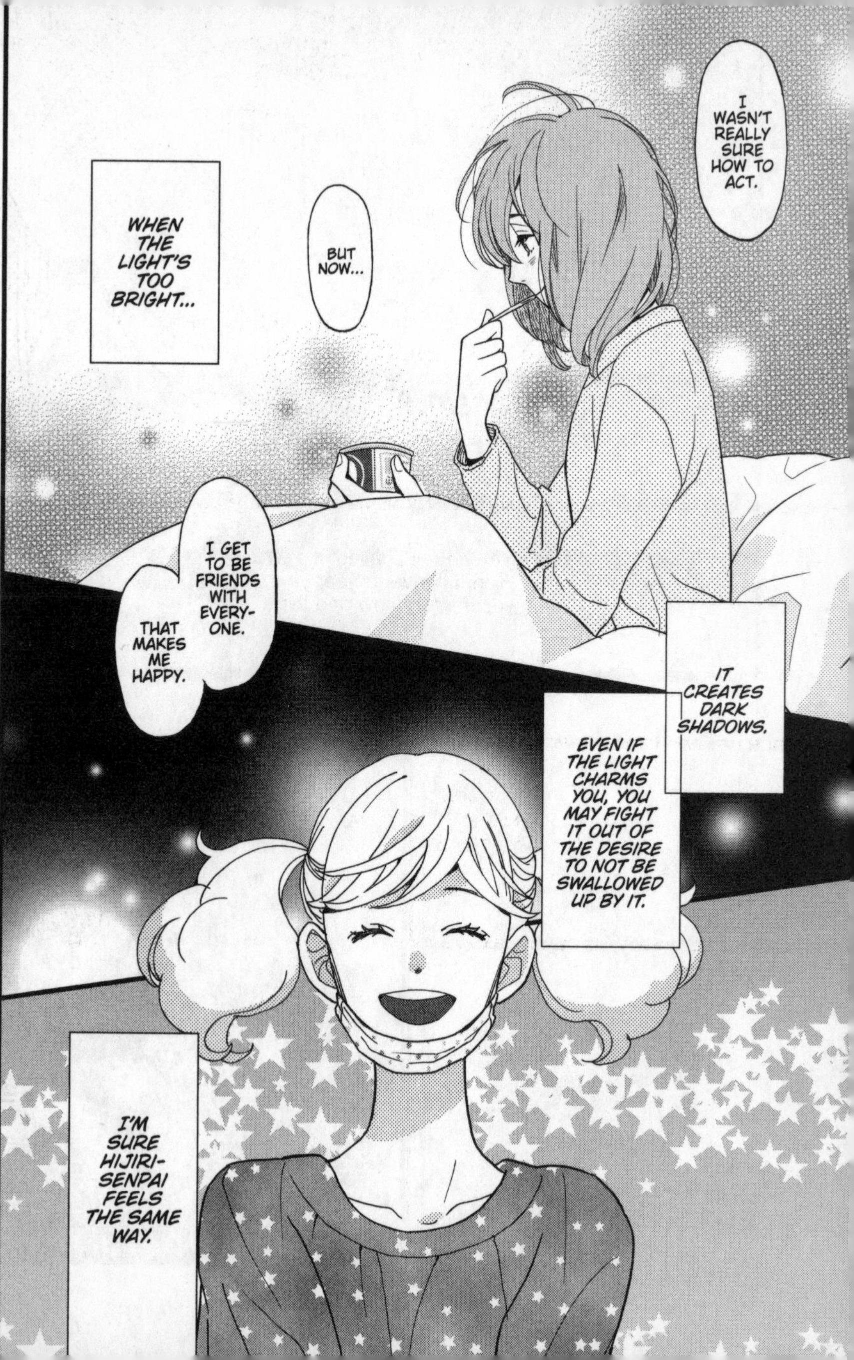
I WASN'T REALLY SURE HOW TO ACT.
BUT NOW...
WHEN THE LIGHT'S TOO BRIGHT...
I GET TO BE FRIENDS WITH EVERY-ONE.
THAT MAKES ME HAPPY.
IT CREATES DARK SHADOWS.
EVEN IF THE LIGHT CHARMS YOU, YOU MAY FIGHT IT OUT OF THE DESIRE TO NOT BE SWALLOWED UP BY IT.
I'M SURE HIJIRI-SENPAI FEELS THE SAME WAY.

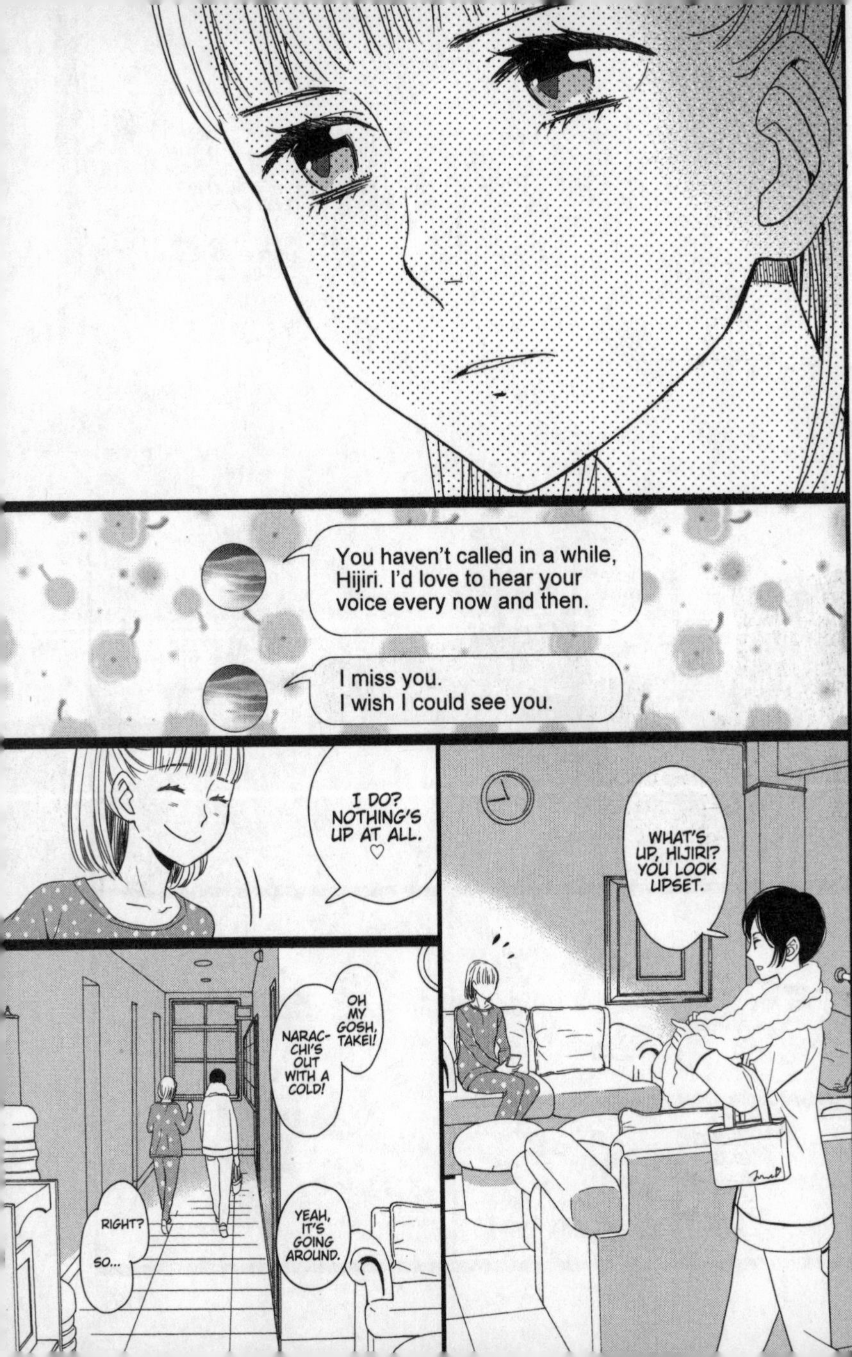
You haven't called in a while, Hijiri. I'd love to hear your voice every now and then.
I miss you. I wish I could see you.
WHAT'S UP, HIJIRI? YOU LOOK UPSET.
I DO? NOTHING'S UP AT ALL. ♡
OH MY GOSH, TAKEI!
NARAC-CHI'S OUT WITH A COLD!
YEAH, IT'S GOING AROUND.
RIGHT?
SO...

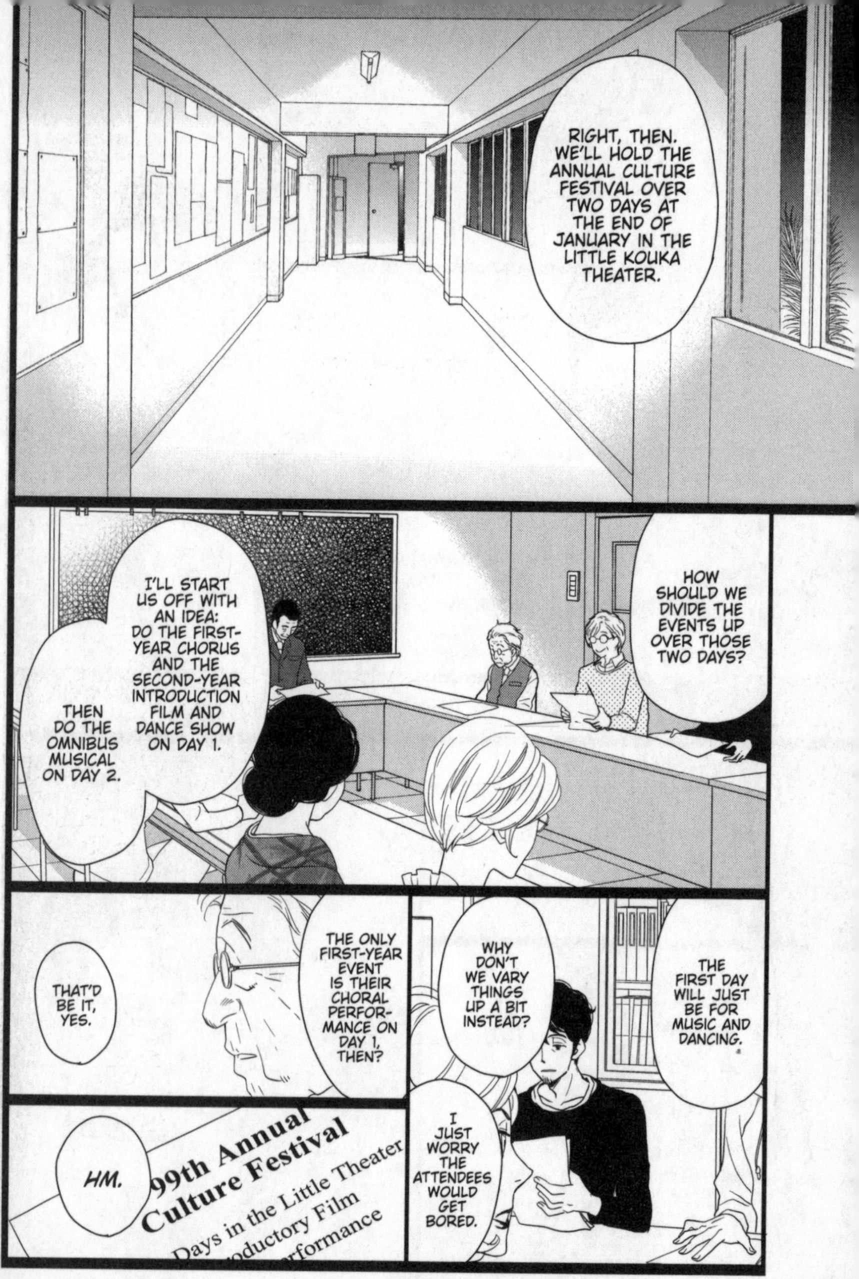

RIGHT, THEN. WE'LL HOLD THE ANNUAL CULTURE FESTIVAL OVER TWO DAYS AT THE END OF JANUARY IN THE LITTLE KOUKA THEATER.
HOW SHOULD WE DIVIDE THE EVENTS UP OVER THOSE TWO DAYS?
I'LL START US OFF WITH AN IDEA: DO THE FIRST-YEAR CHORUS AND THE SECOND-YEAR INTRODUCTION FILM AND DANCE SHOW ON DAY 1.
THEN DO THE OMNIBUS MUSICAL ON DAY 2.
THE FIRST DAY WILL JUST BE FOR MUSIC AND DANCING.
WHY DON'T WE VARY THINGS UP A BIT INSTEAD?
I JUST WORRY THE ATTENDEES WOULD GET BORED.
THE ONLY FIRST-YEAR EVENT IS THEIR CHORAL PERFORMANCE ON DAY 1, THEN?
THAT'D BE IT, YES.
HM.
99th Annual
Culture Festival
Days in the Little Theater

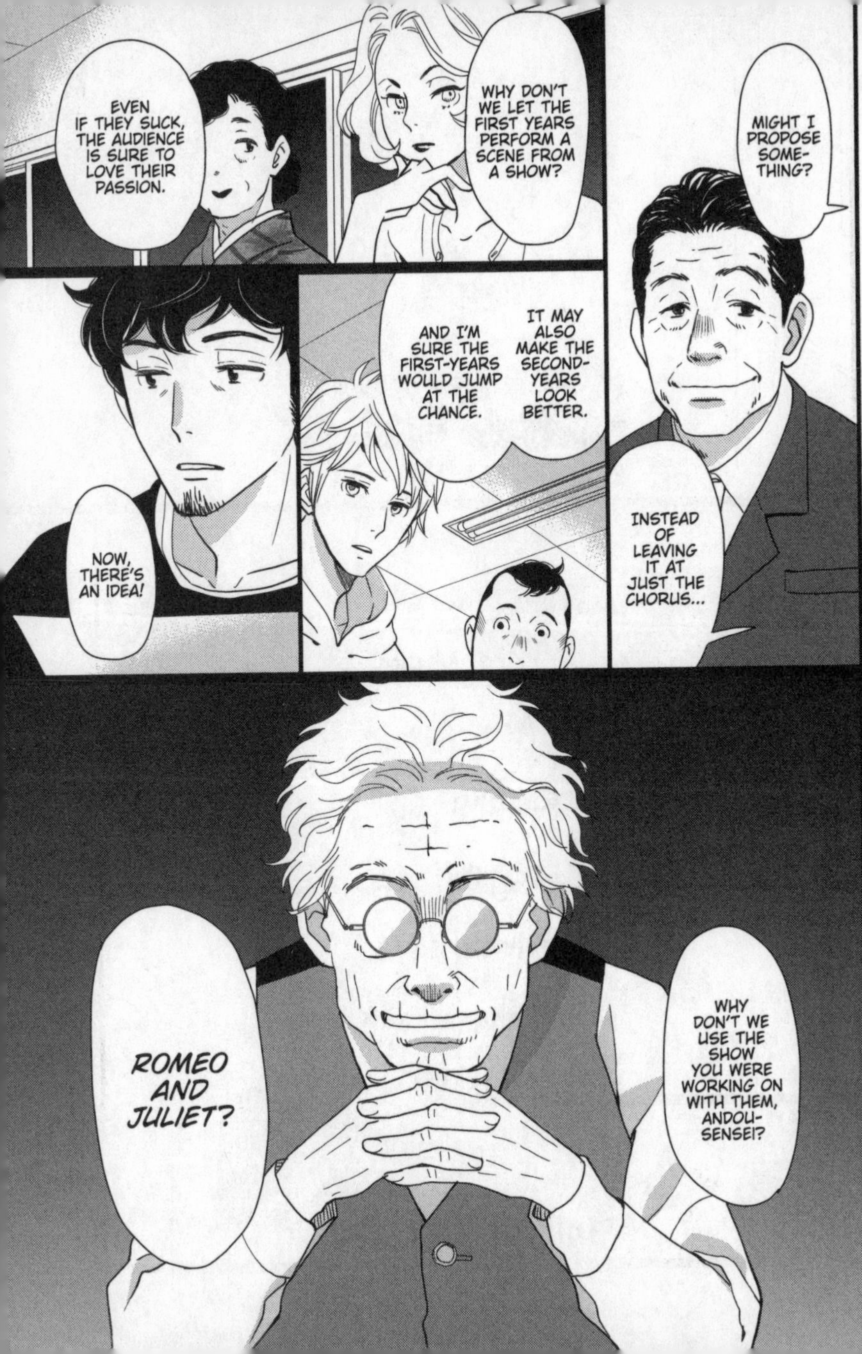
MIGHT I PROPOSE SOME-THING?
INSTEAD OF LEAVING IT AT JUST THE CHORUS...
WHY DON'T WE LET THE FIRST YEARS PERFORM A SCENE FROM A SHOW?
EVEN IF THEY SUCK, THE AUDIENCE IS SURE TO LOVE THEIR PASSION.
IT MAY ALSO MAKE THE SECOND-YEARS LOOK BETTER.
AND I'M SURE THE FIRST-YEARS WOULD JUMP AT THE CHANCE.
NOW, THERE'S AN IDEA!
WHY DON'T WE USE THE SHOW YOU WERE WORKING ON WITH THEM, ANDOU-SENSEI?
ROMEO AND JULIET?

Special Thanks

Tara-chan

Asai-san

Kazami-san

Ishigaki-san

Kuroki-san

Takahashi-san

Nono Jill

&

♡all my readers♡

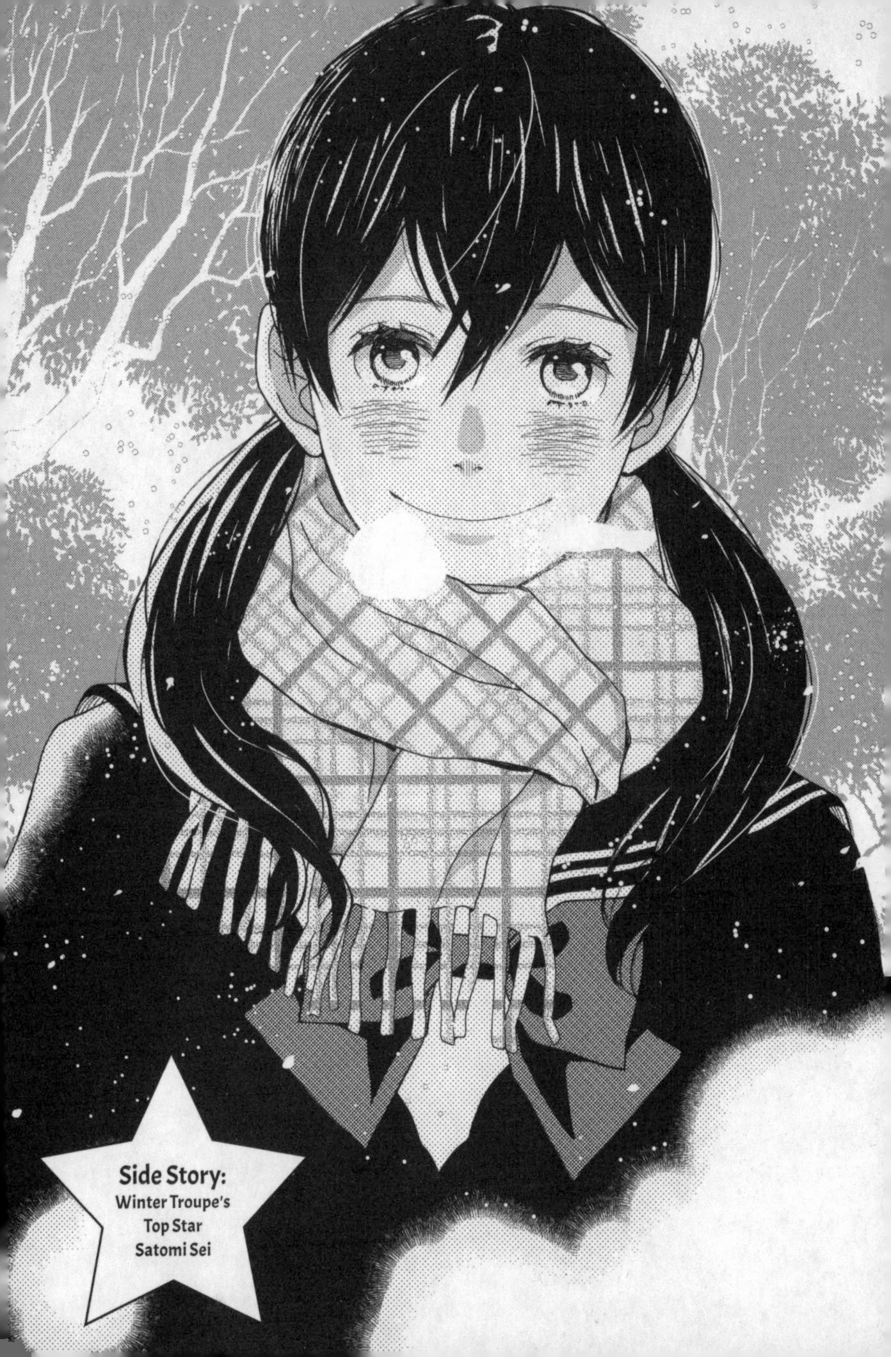
Side Story:
Winter Troupe's
Top Star
Satomi Sei

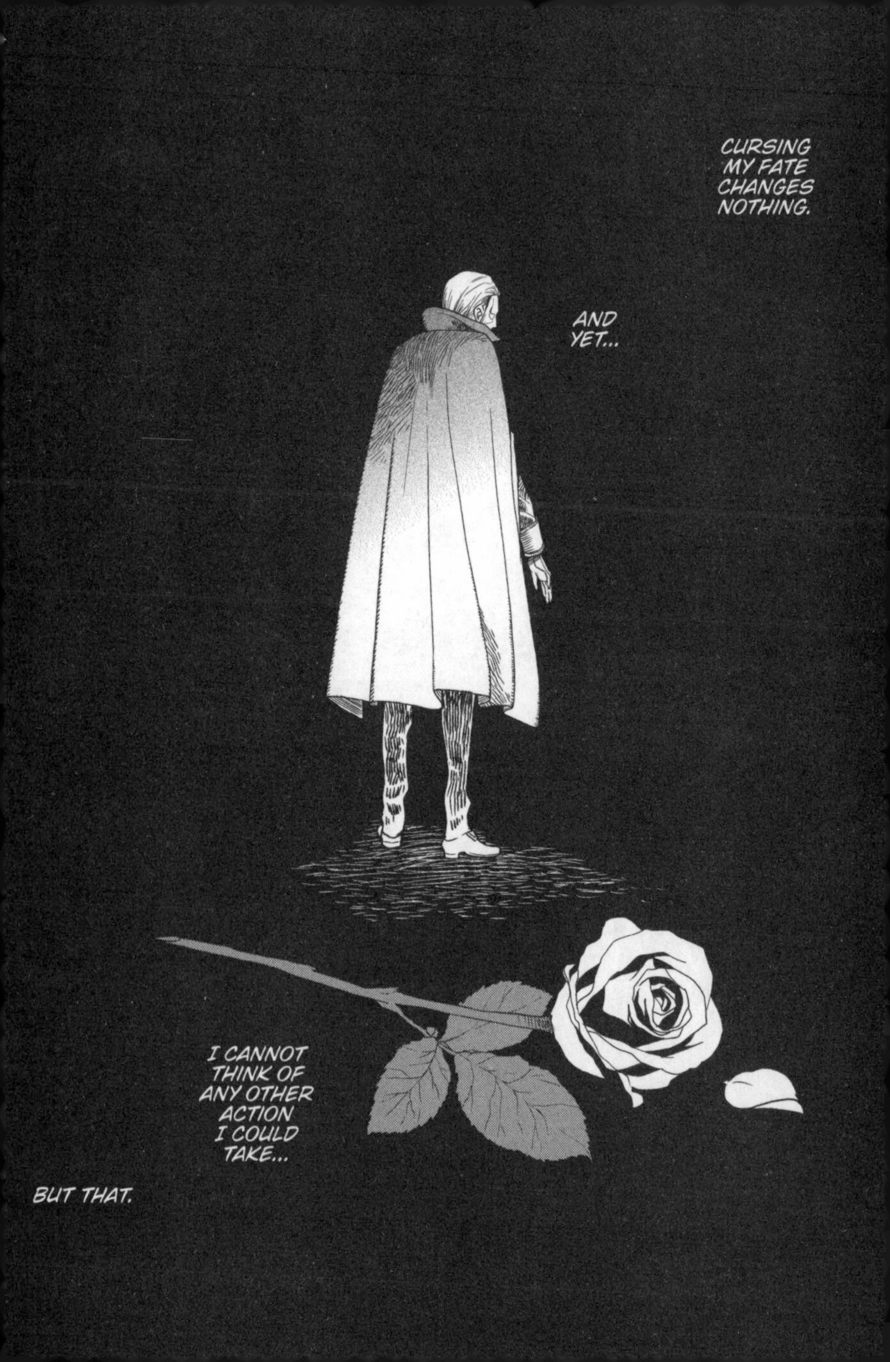
CURSING MY FATE CHANGES NOTHING.
AND YET...
I CANNOT THINK OF ANY OTHER ACTION I COULD TAKE...
BUT THAT.

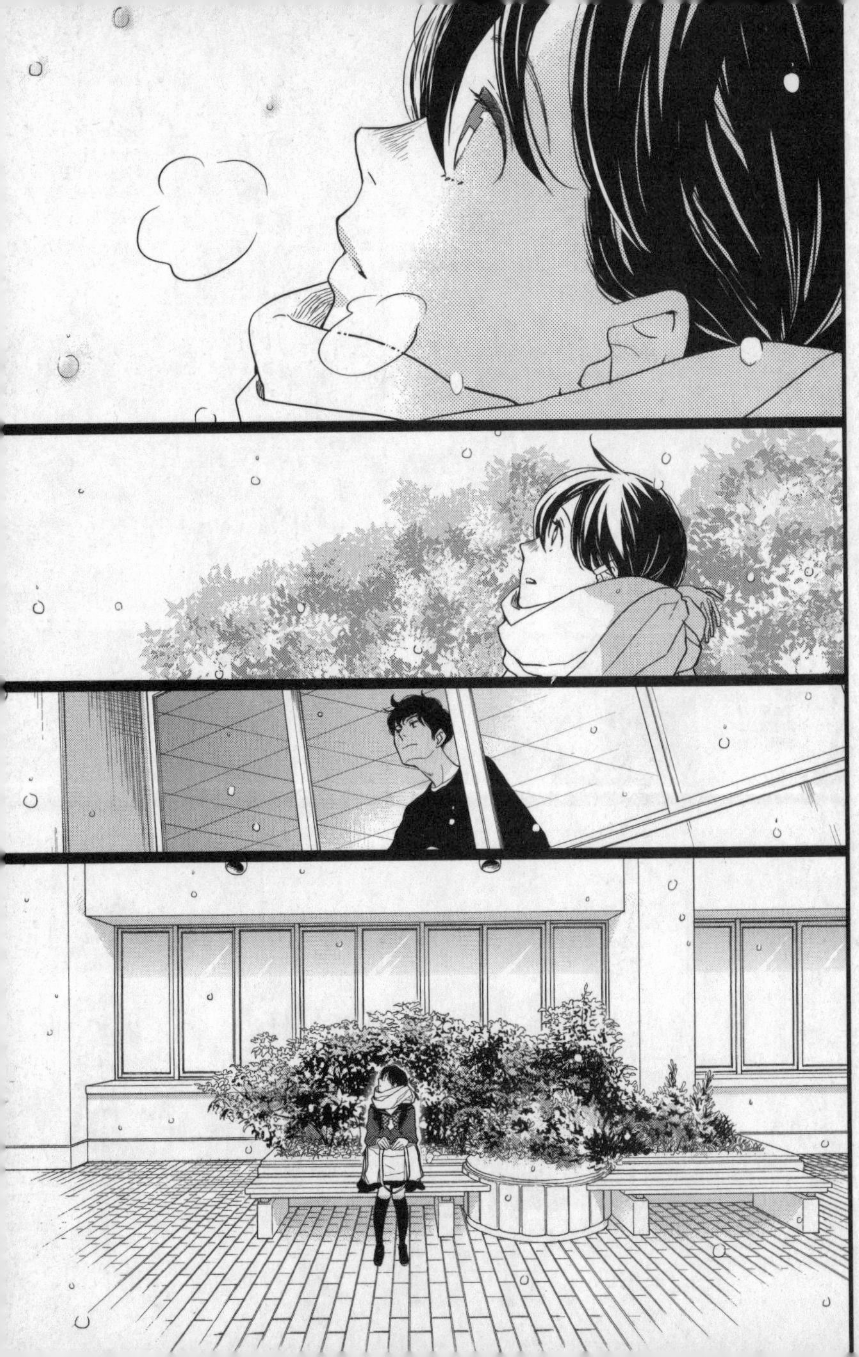

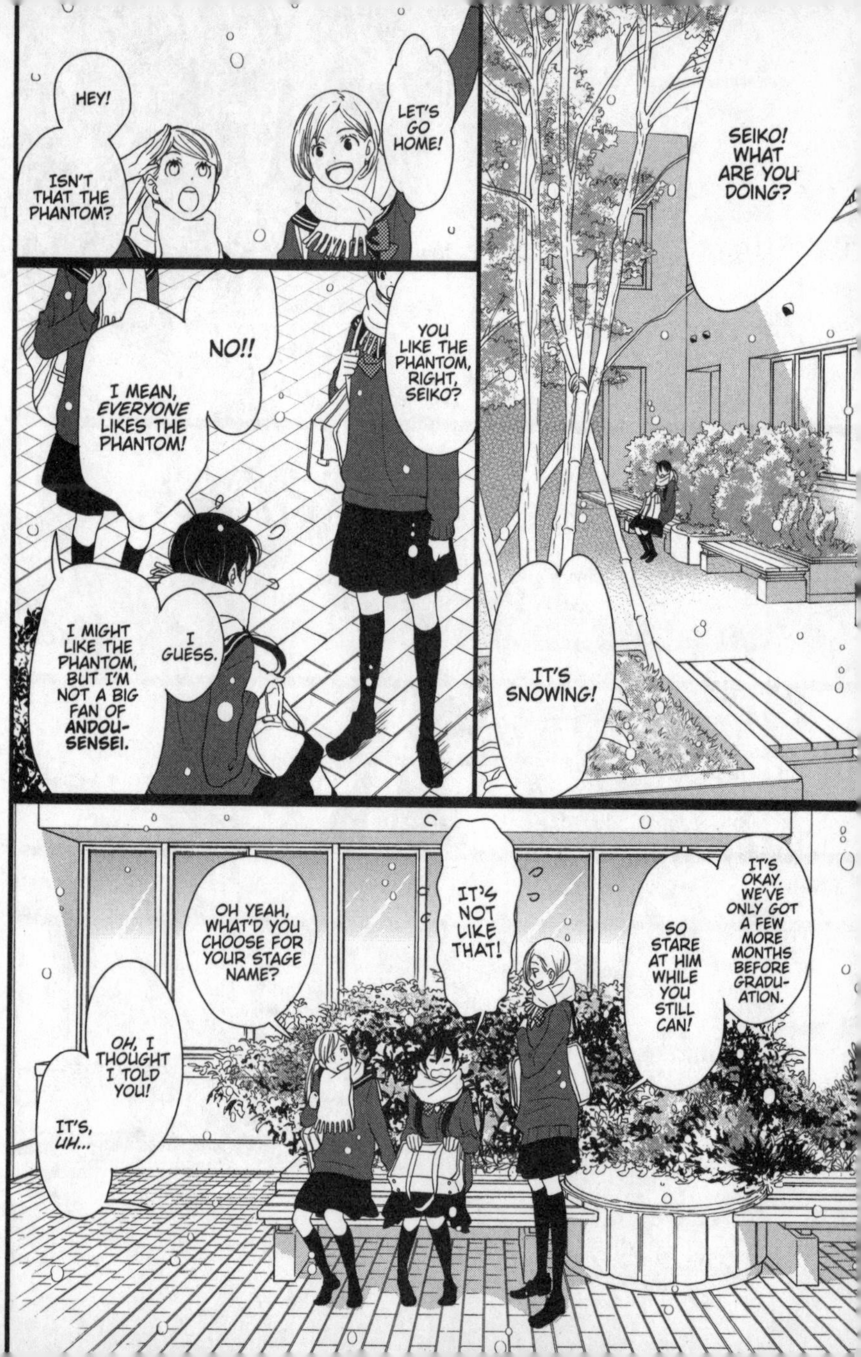
SEIKO! WHAT ARE YOU DOING?
IT'S SNOWING!
LET'S GO HOME!
HEY!
ISN'T THAT THE PHANTOM?
YOU LIKE THE PHANTOM, RIGHT, SEIKO?
NO!!
I MEAN, *EVERYONE* LIKES THE PHANTOM!
I GUESS.
I MIGHT LIKE THE PHANTOM, BUT I'M NOT A BIG FAN OF ANDOU-SENSEI.
IT'S OKAY. WE'VE ONLY GOT A FEW MORE MONTHS BEFORE GRADUATION.
SO STARE AT HIM WHILE YOU STILL CAN!
IT'S NOT LIKE THAT!
OH YEAH, WHAT'D YOU CHOOSE FOR YOUR STAGE NAME?
OH, I THOUGHT I TOLD YOU!
IT'S, UH...

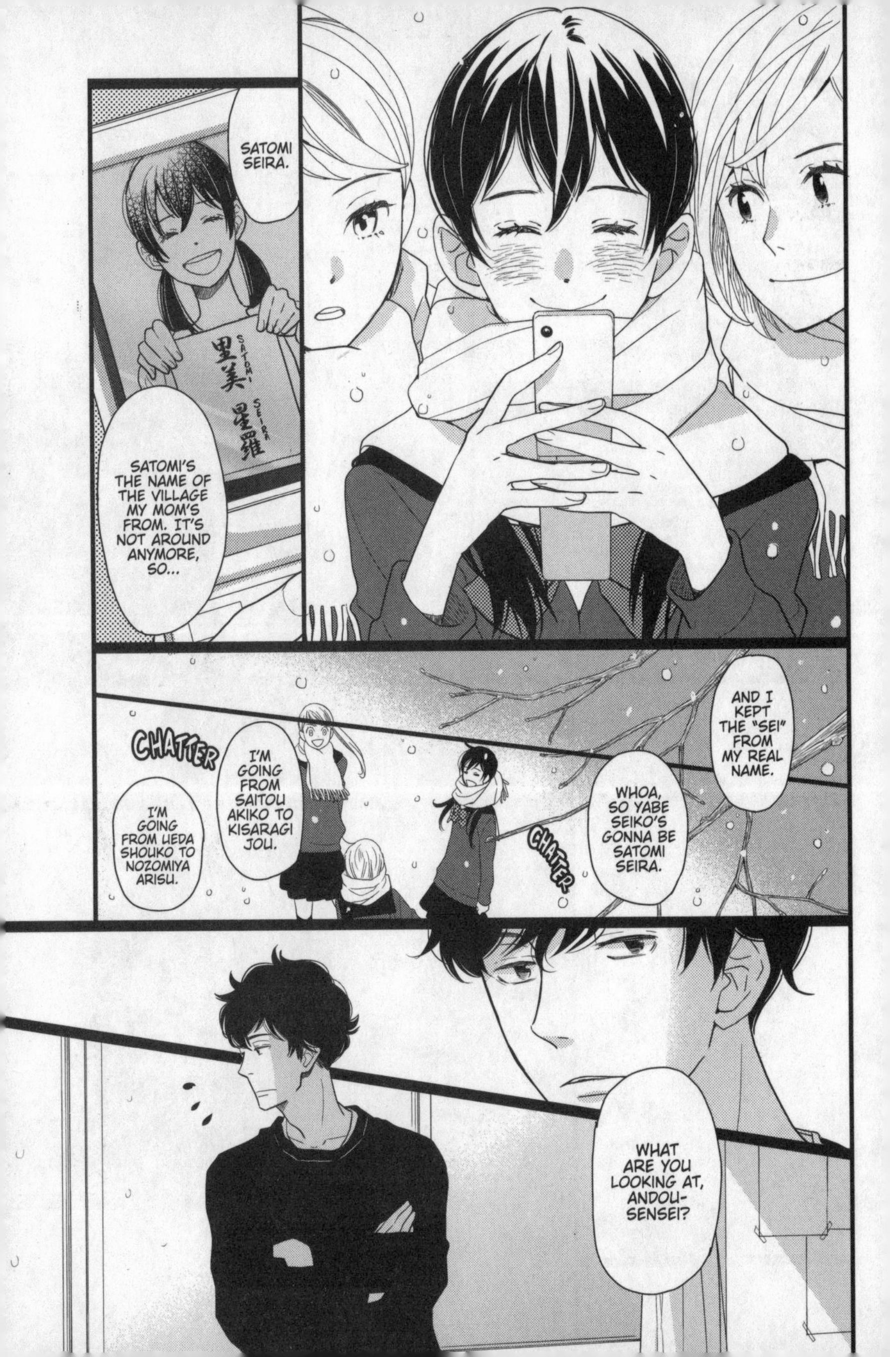
SATOMI SEIRA.
里美 星羅
SATOMI SEIRA
SATOMI'S THE NAME OF THE VILLAGE MY MOM'S FROM. IT'S NOT AROUND ANYMORE, SO...
AND I KEPT THE "SEI" FROM MY REAL NAME.
WHOA, SO YABE SEIKO'S GONNA BE SATOMI SEIRA.
CHATTER
I'M GOING FROM SAITOU AKIKO TO KISARAGI JOU.
CHATTER
I'M GOING FROM UEDA SHOUKO TO NOZOMIYA ARISU.
WHAT ARE YOU LOOKING AT, ANDOU-SENSEI?

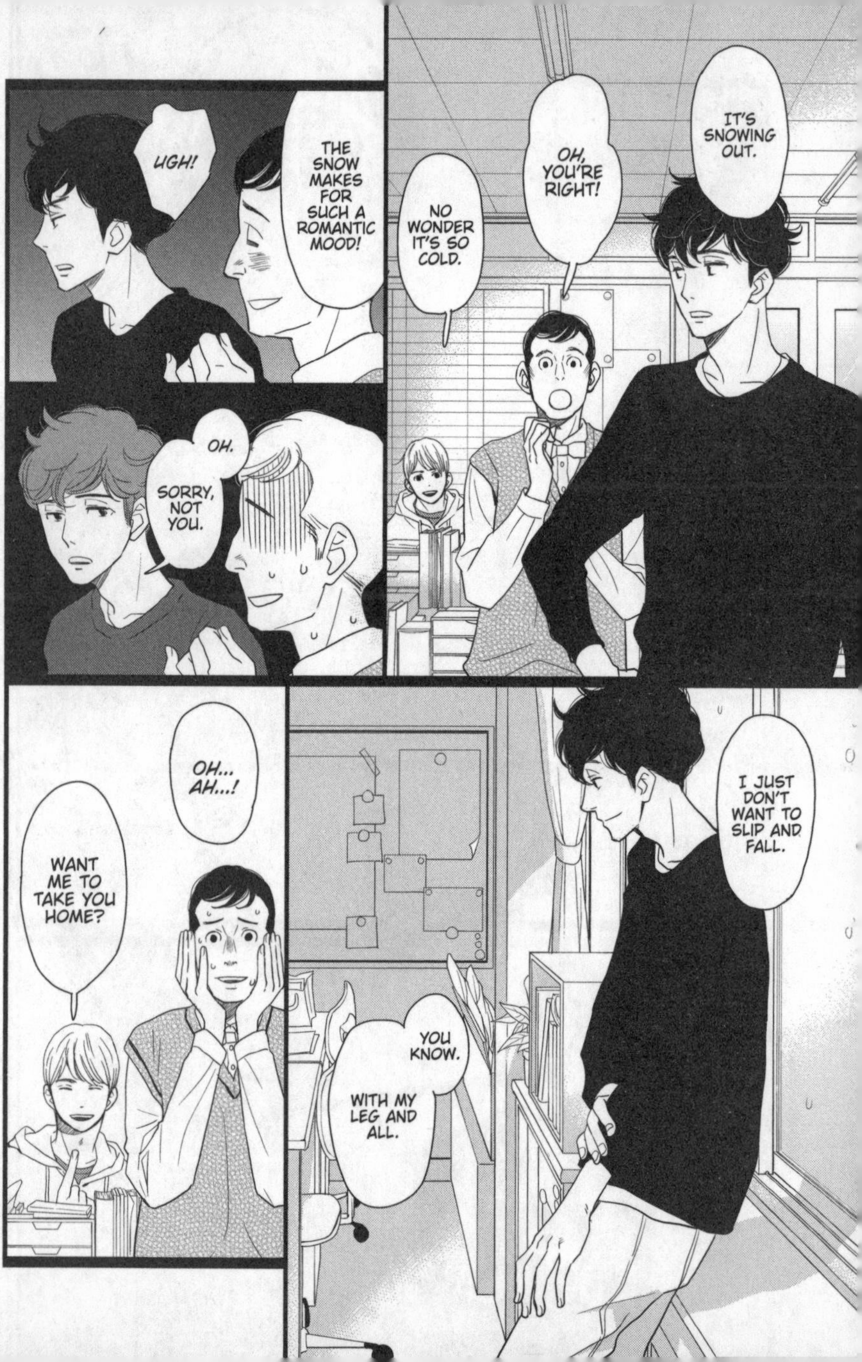
IT'S SNOWING OUT.
OH, YOU'RE RIGHT!
NO WONDER IT'S SO COLD.
THE SNOW MAKES FOR SUCH A ROMANTIC MOOD!
UGH!
OH.
SORRY, NOT YOU.
I JUST DON'T WANT TO SLIP AND FALL.
YOU KNOW.
WITH MY LEG AND ALL.
OH... AH...!
WANT ME TO TAKE YOU HOME?

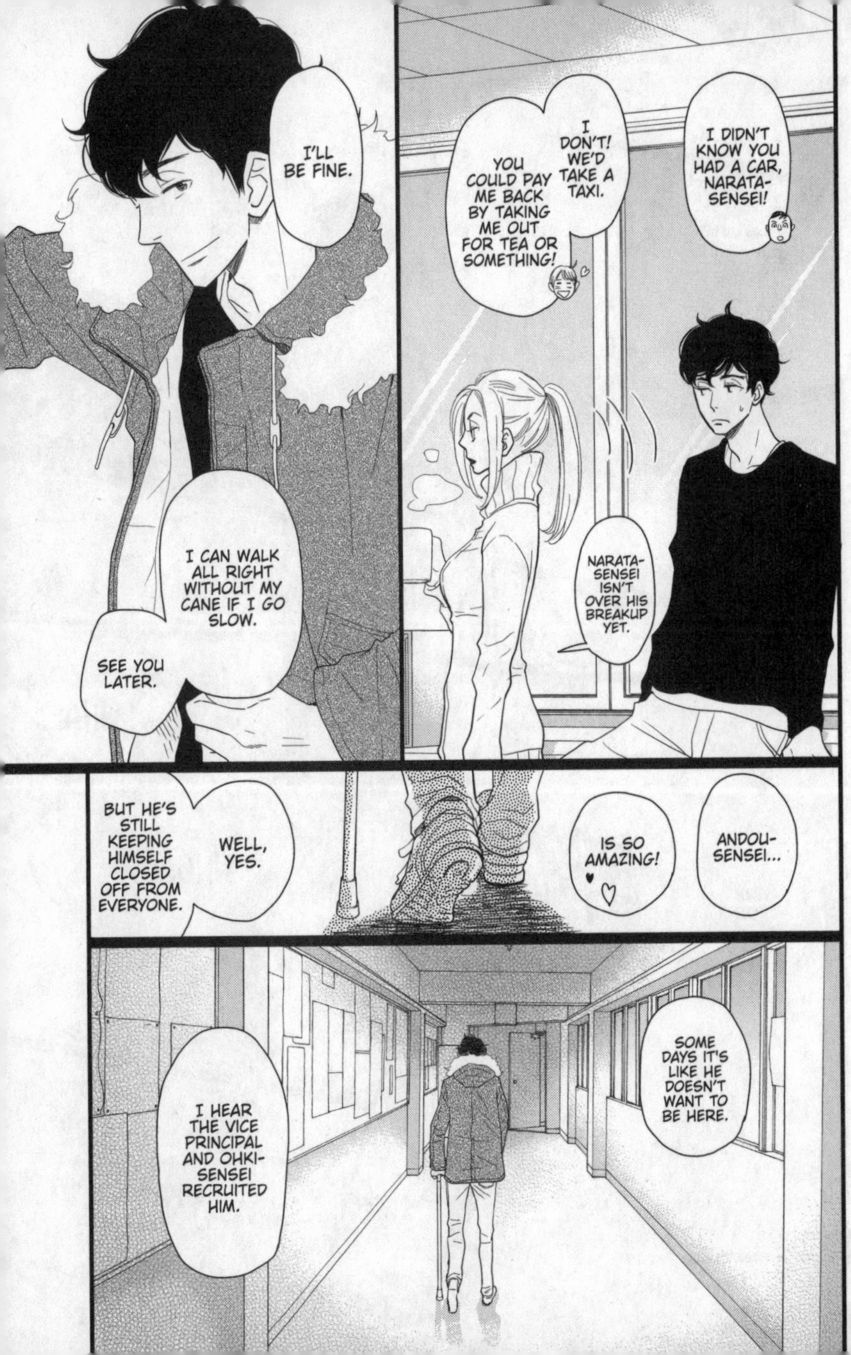
I DIDN'T KNOW YOU HAD A CAR, NARATA-SENSEI!
I DON'T! WE'D TAKE A TAXI.
YOU COULD PAY ME BACK BY TAKING ME OUT FOR TEA OR SOMETHING!
NARATA-SENSEI ISN'T OVER HIS BREAKUP YET.
I'LL BE FINE.
I CAN WALK ALL RIGHT WITHOUT MY CANE IF I GO SLOW.
SEE YOU LATER.
ANDOU-SENSEI...
IS SO AMAZING!
WELL, YES.
BUT HE'S STILL KEEPING HIMSELF CLOSED OFF FROM EVERYONE.
SOME DAYS IT'S LIKE HE DOESN'T WANT TO BE HERE.
I HEAR THE VICE PRINCIPAL AND OHKI-SENSEI RECRUITED HIM.

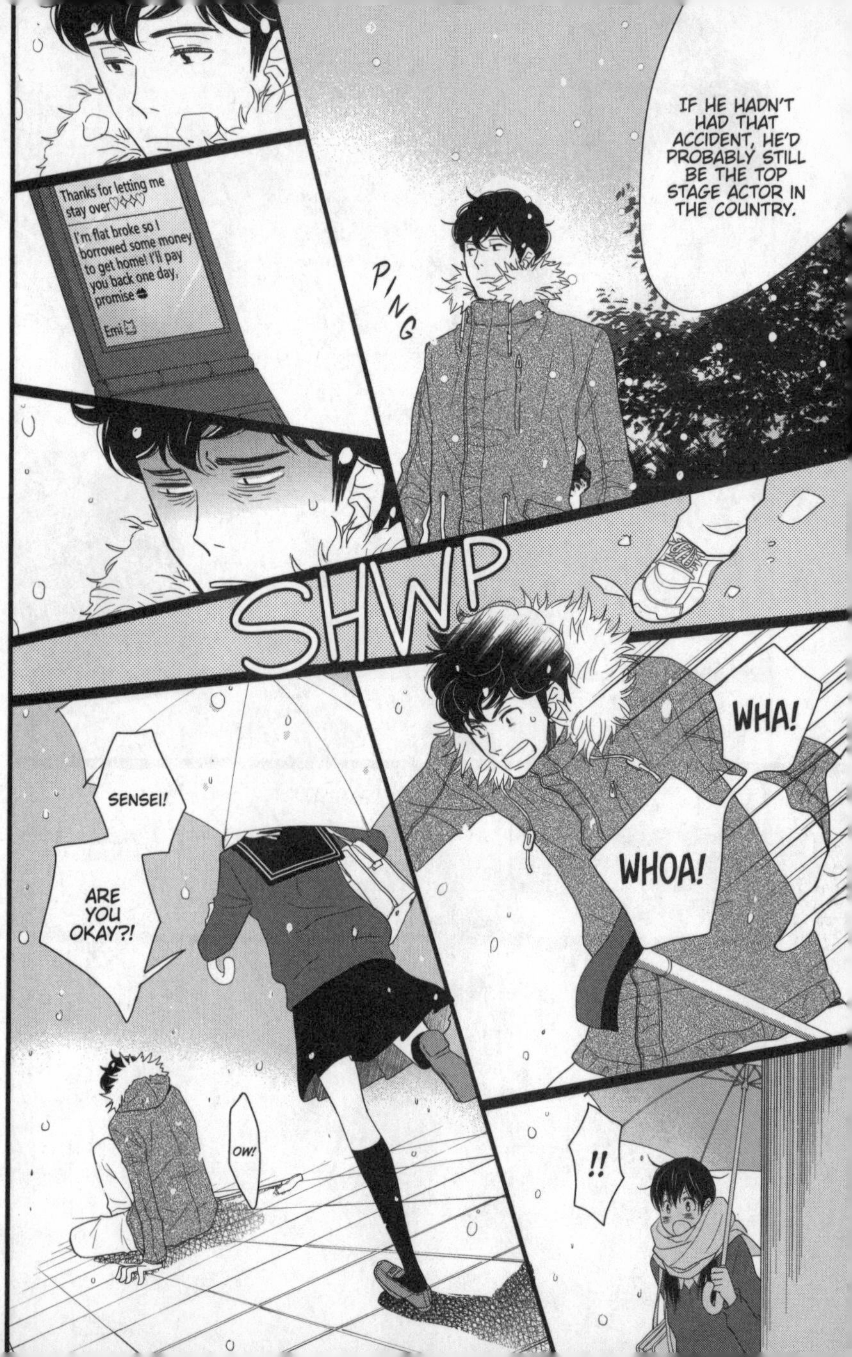
IF HE HADN'T HAD THAT ACCIDENT, HE'D PROBABLY STILL BE THE TOP STAGE ACTOR IN THE COUNTRY.
PING
Thanks for letting me stay over♡♡♡
I'm flat broke so I borrowed some money to get home! I'll pay you back one day, promise
Emi
SHWP
WHA!
WHOA!
!!
SENSEI!
ARE YOU OKAY?!
OW!

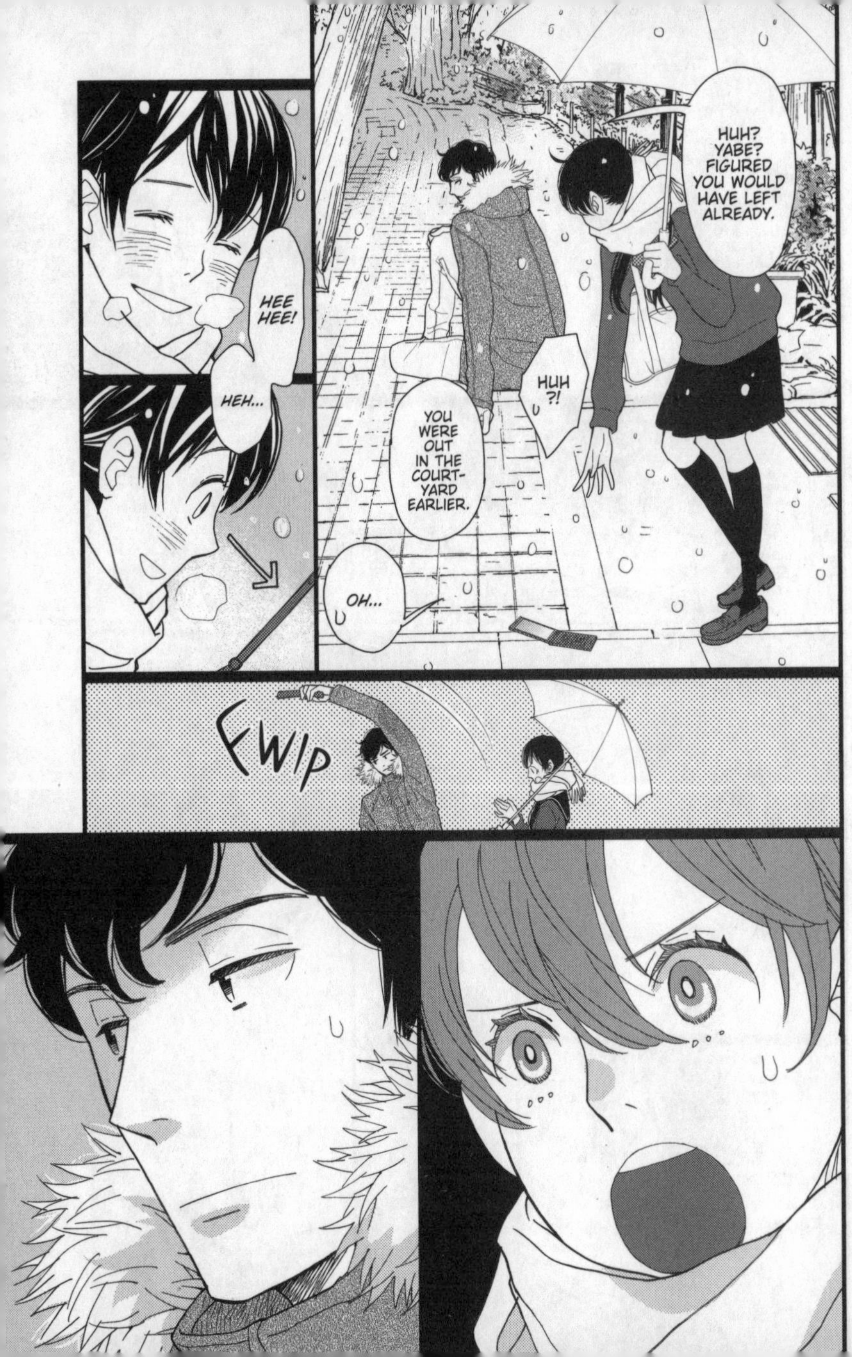
HUH? YABE? FIGURED YOU WOULD HAVE LEFT ALREADY.
HUH ?!
YOU WERE OUT IN THE COURT-YARD EARLIER.
OH...
HEE HEE!
HEH...
FWIP

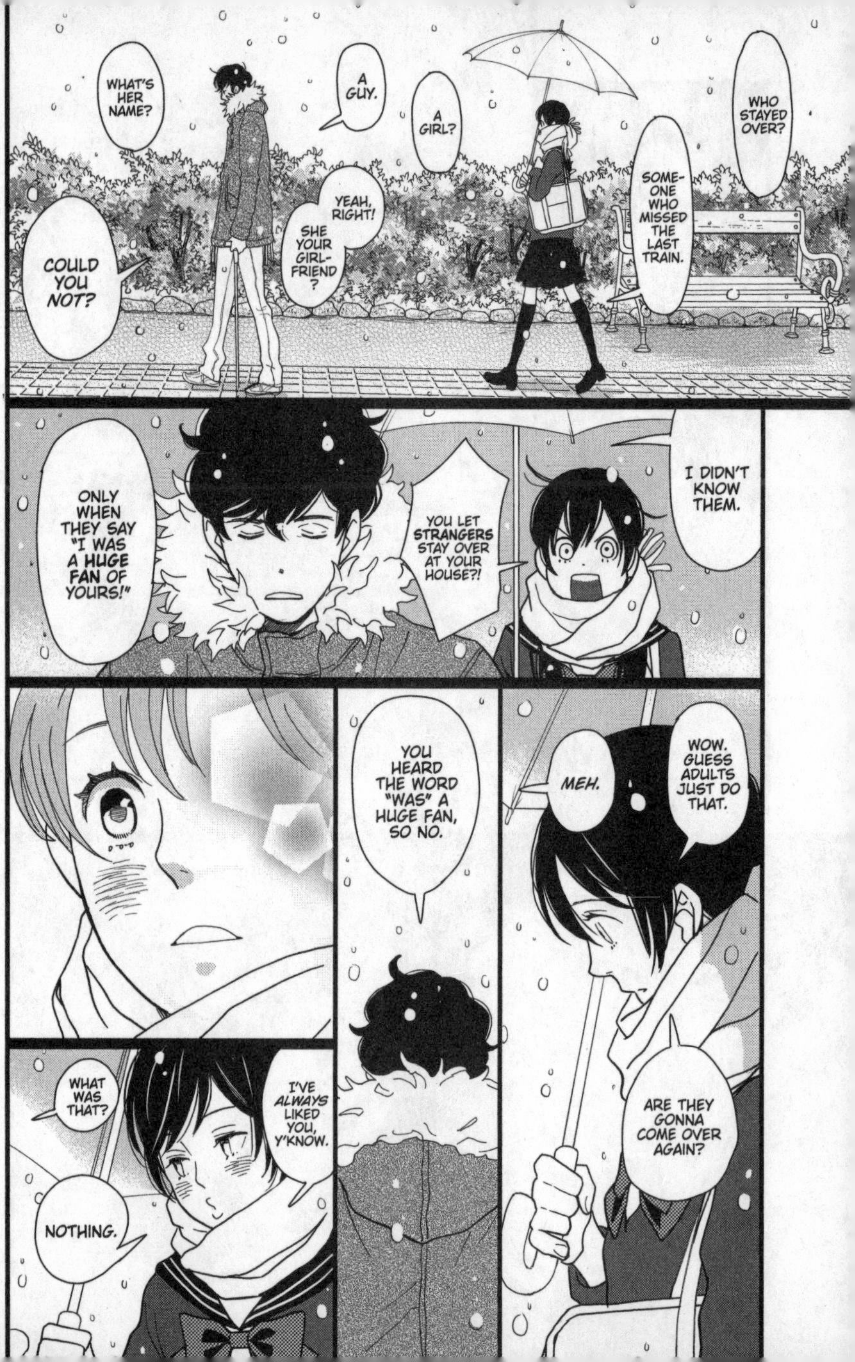
WHO STAYED OVER?
SOME-ONE WHO MISSED THE LAST TRAIN.
A GIRL?
A GUY.
YEAH, RIGHT! SHE YOUR GIRL-FRIEND?
WHAT'S HER NAME?
COULD YOU NOT?
I DIDN'T KNOW THEM.
YOU LET STRANGERS STAY OVER AT YOUR HOUSE?!
ONLY WHEN THEY SAY "I WAS A HUGE FAN OF YOURS!"
WOW. GUESS ADULTS JUST DO THAT.
MEH.
ARE THEY GONNA COME OVER AGAIN?
YOU HEARD THE WORD "WAS" A HUGE FAN, SO NO.
I'VE *ALWAYS* LIKED YOU, Y'KNOW.
WHAT WAS THAT?
NOTHING.

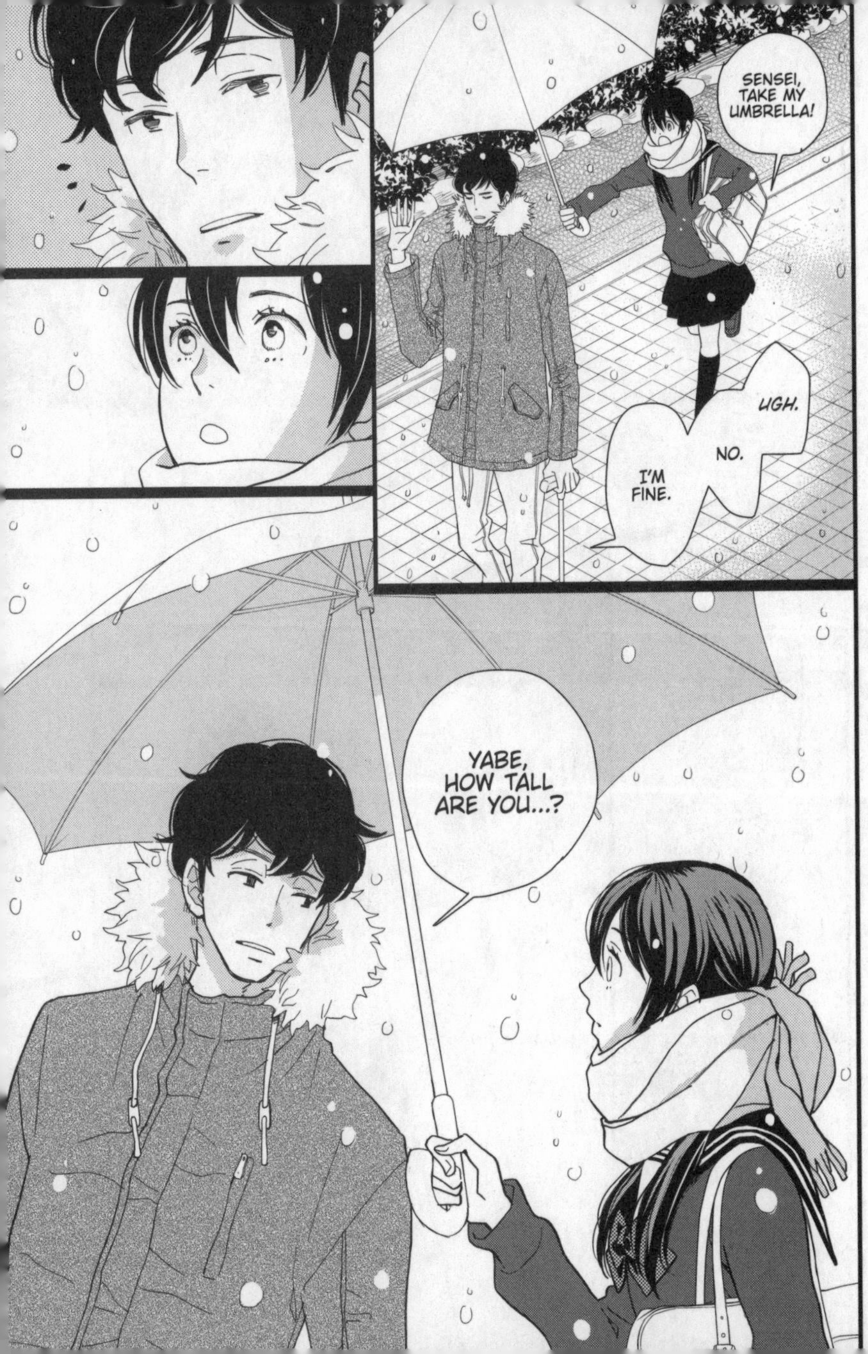
SENSEI, TAKE MY UMBRELLA!
UGH. NO. I'M FINE.
YABE, HOW TALL ARE YOU...?

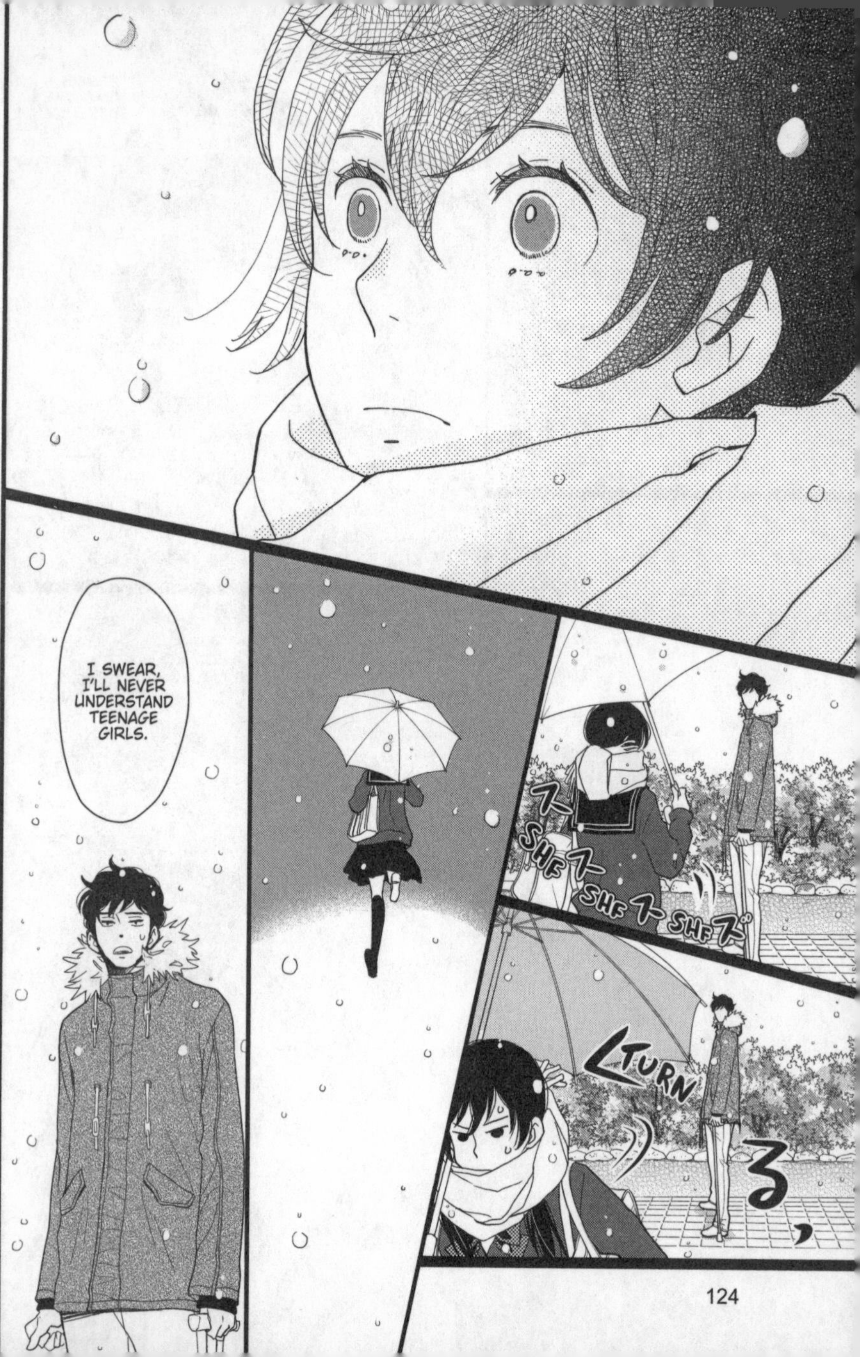
SHF SHF SHF
TURN
I SWEAR, I'LL NEVER UNDERSTAND TEENAGE GIRLS.

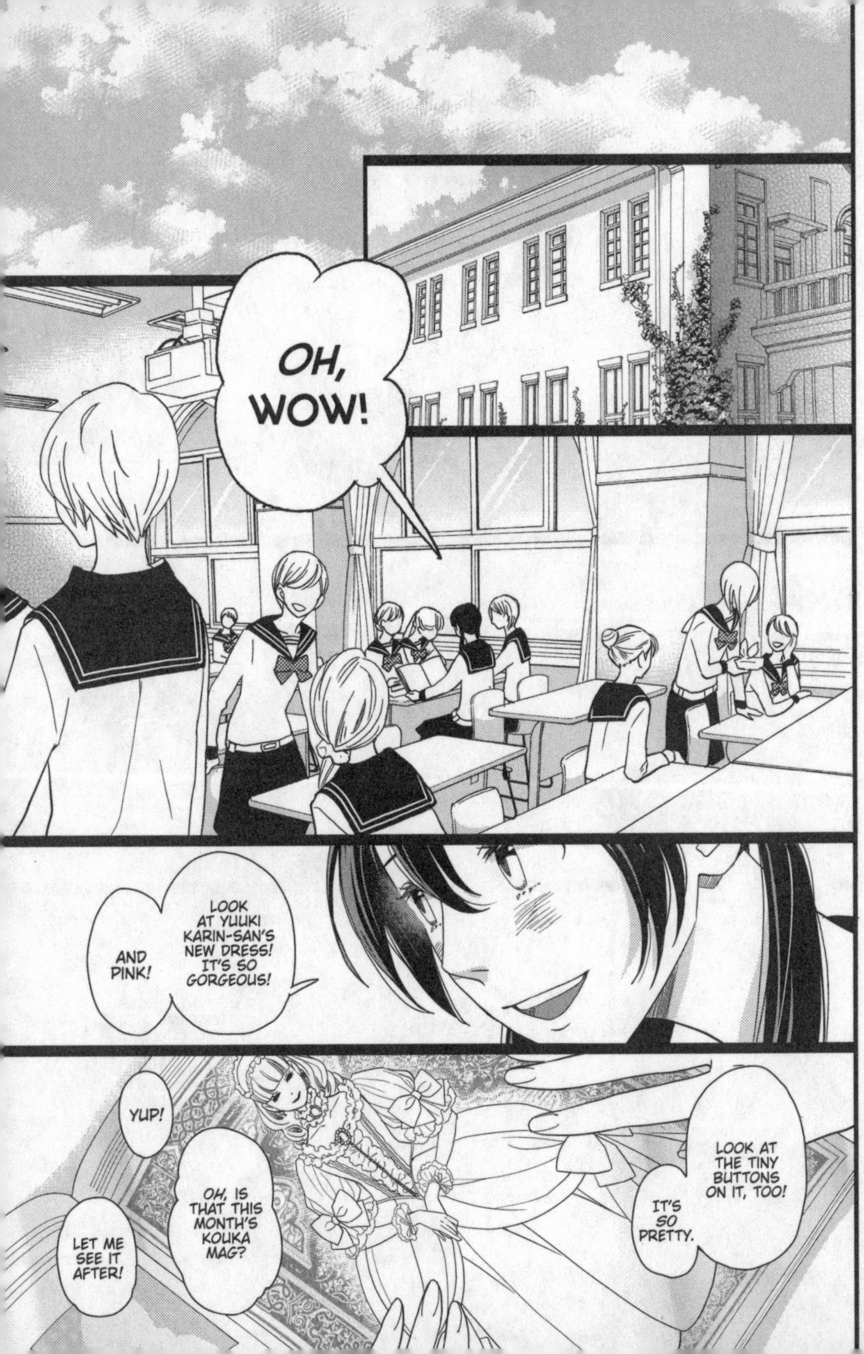
OH, WOW!
LOOK AT YUUKI KARIN-SAN'S NEW DRESS! IT'S SO GORGEOUS!
AND PINK!
LOOK AT THE TINY BUTTONS ON IT, TOO!
IT'S SO PRETTY.
OH, IS THAT THIS MONTH'S KOUKA MAG?
YUP!
LET ME SEE IT AFTER!

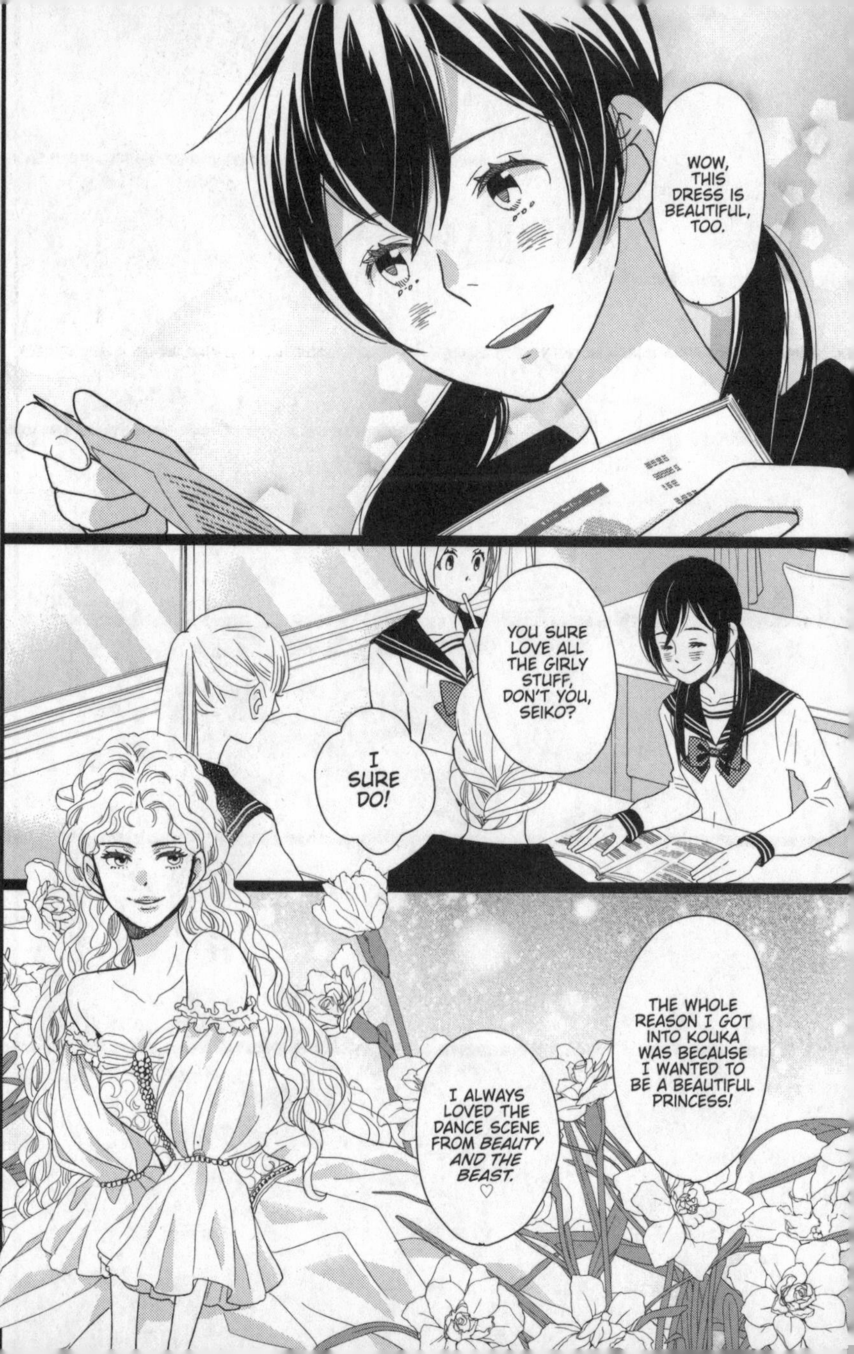
WOW, THIS DRESS IS BEAUTIFUL, TOO.
YOU SURE LOVE ALL THE GIRLY STUFF, DON'T YOU, SEIKO?
I SURE DO!
THE WHOLE REASON I GOT INTO KOUKA WAS BECAUSE I WANTED TO BE A BEAUTIFUL PRINCESS!
I ALWAYS LOVED THE DANCE SCENE FROM *BEAUTY AND THE BEAST.* ♡

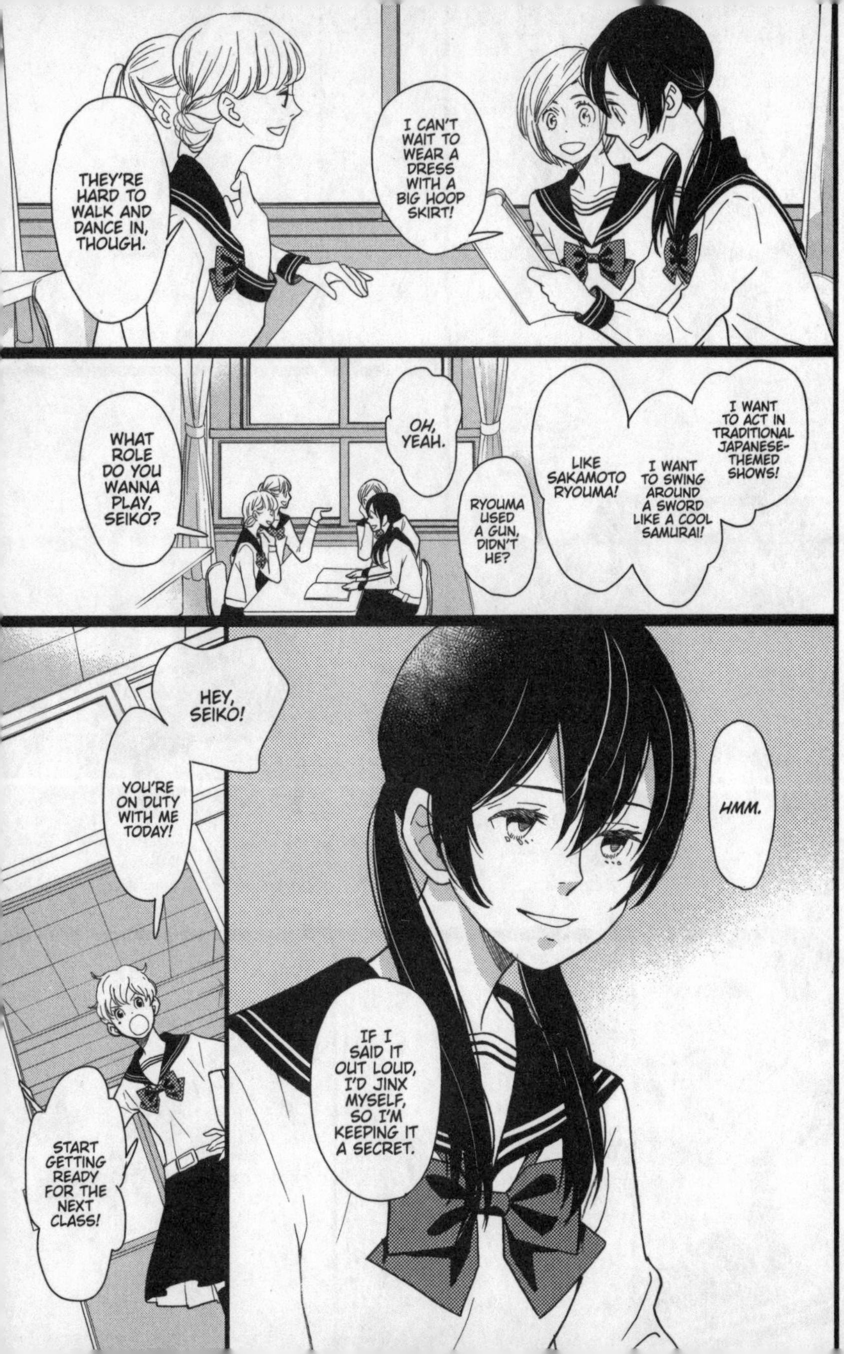
I CAN'T WAIT TO WEAR A DRESS WITH A BIG HOOP SKIRT!
THEY'RE HARD TO WALK AND DANCE IN, THOUGH.
I WANT TO ACT IN TRADITIONAL JAPANESE-THEMED SHOWS!
I WANT TO SWING AROUND A SWORD LIKE A COOL SAMURAI!
LIKE SAKAMOTO RYOUMA!
OH, YEAH.
RYOUMA USED A GUN, DIDN'T HE?
WHAT ROLE DO YOU WANNA PLAY, SEIKO?
HMM.
IF I SAID IT OUT LOUD, I'D JINX MYSELF, SO I'M KEEPING IT A SECRET.
HEY, SEIKO!
YOU'RE ON DUTY WITH ME TODAY!
START GETTING READY FOR THE NEXT CLASS!

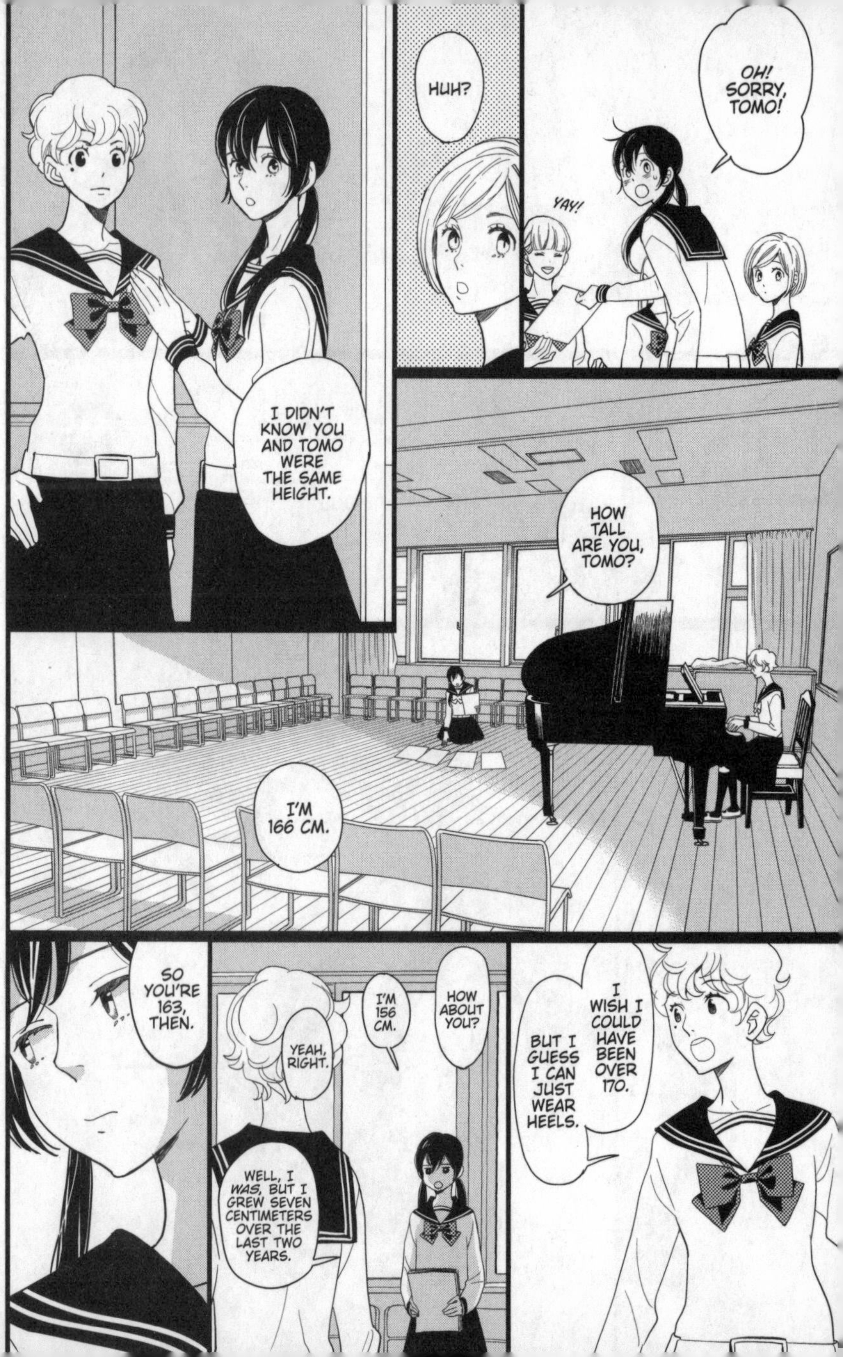
OH! SORRY, TOMO!
YAY!
HUH?
HOW TALL ARE YOU, TOMO?
I'M 166 CM.
I DIDN'T KNOW YOU AND TOMO WERE THE SAME HEIGHT.
I WISH I COULD HAVE BEEN OVER 170.
BUT I GUESS I CAN JUST WEAR HEELS.
HOW ABOUT YOU?
I'M 156 CM.
YEAH, RIGHT.
WELL, I *WAS*, BUT I GREW SEVEN CENTIMETERS OVER THE LAST TWO YEARS.
SO YOU'RE 163, THEN.

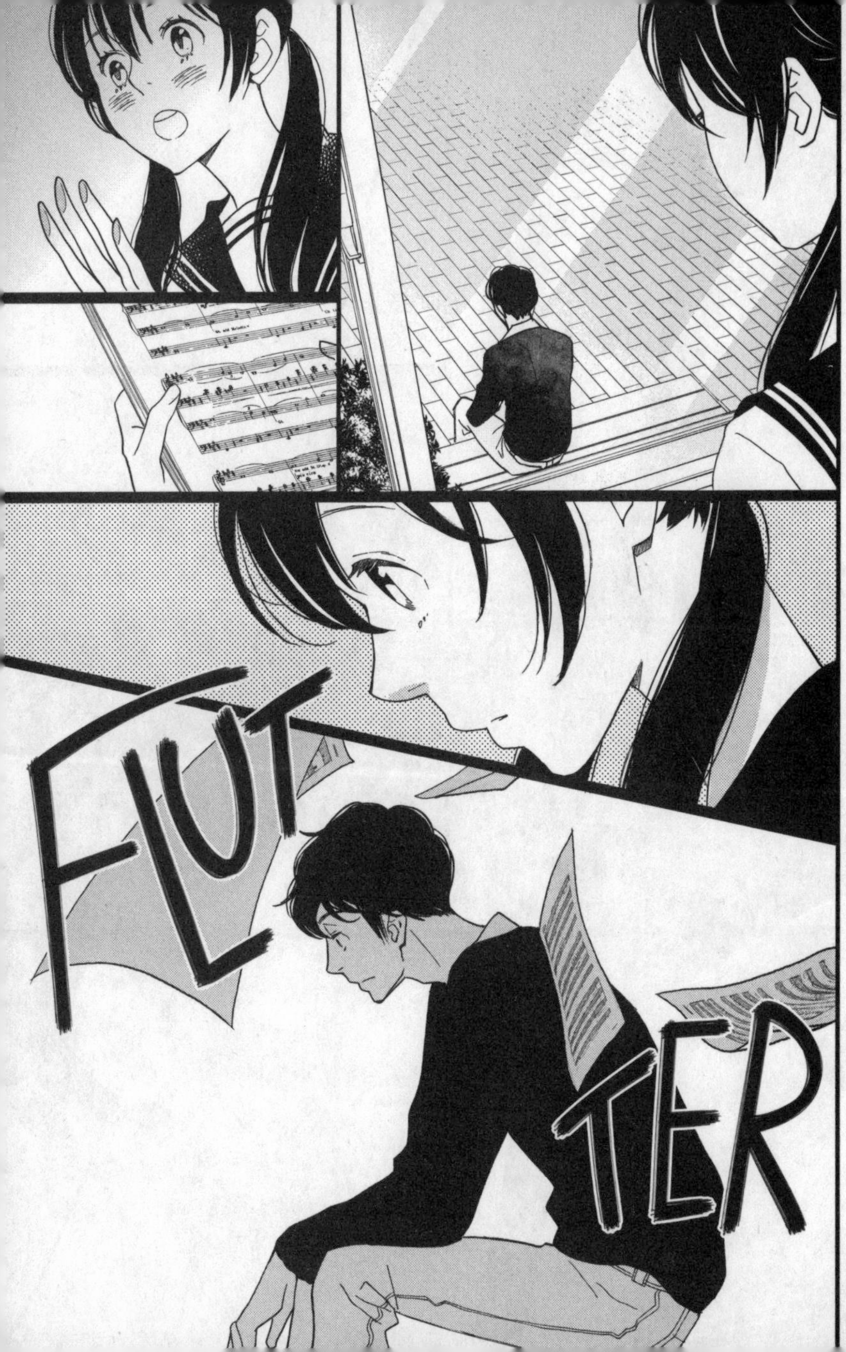
FLUTTER

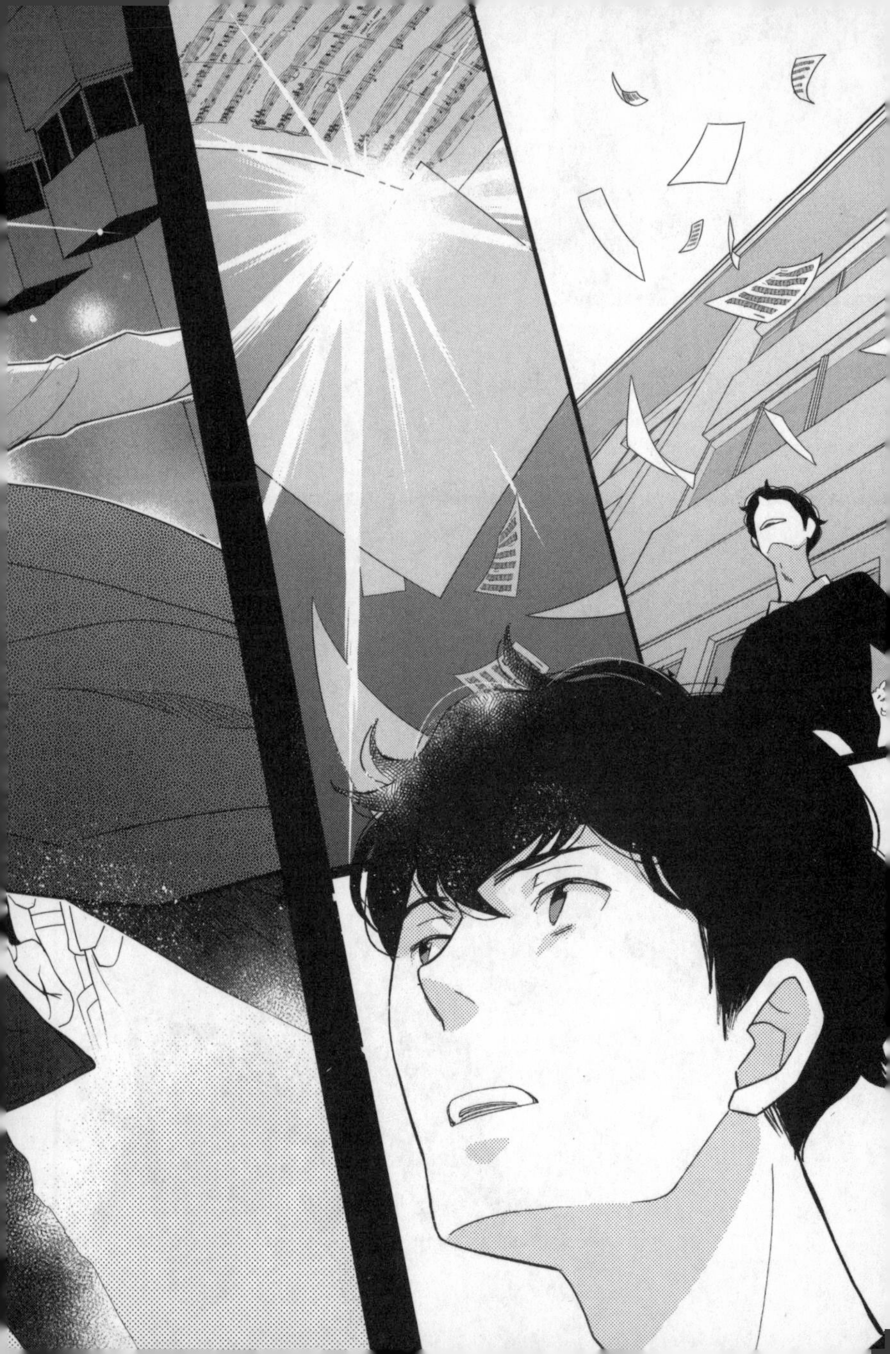

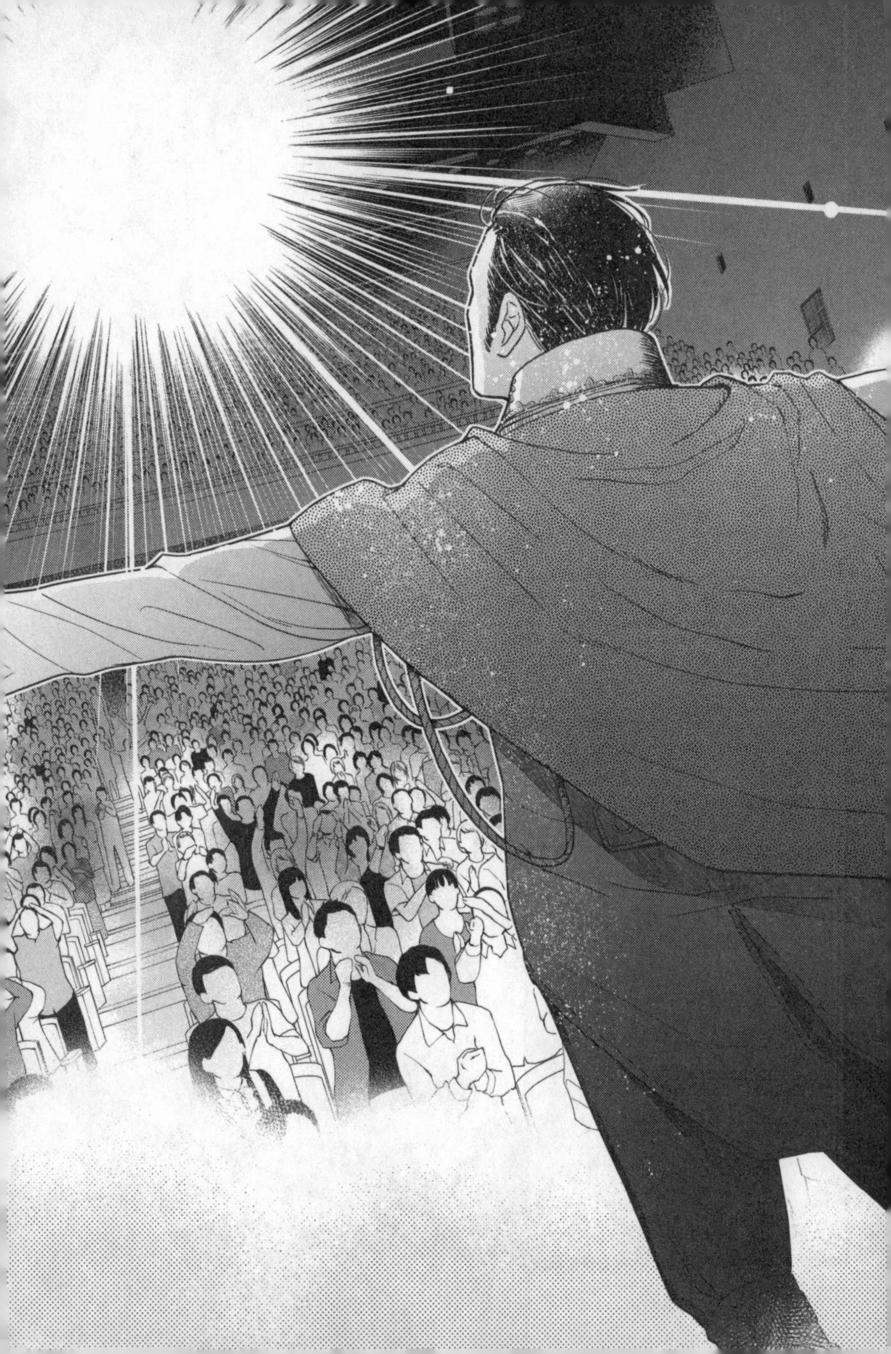

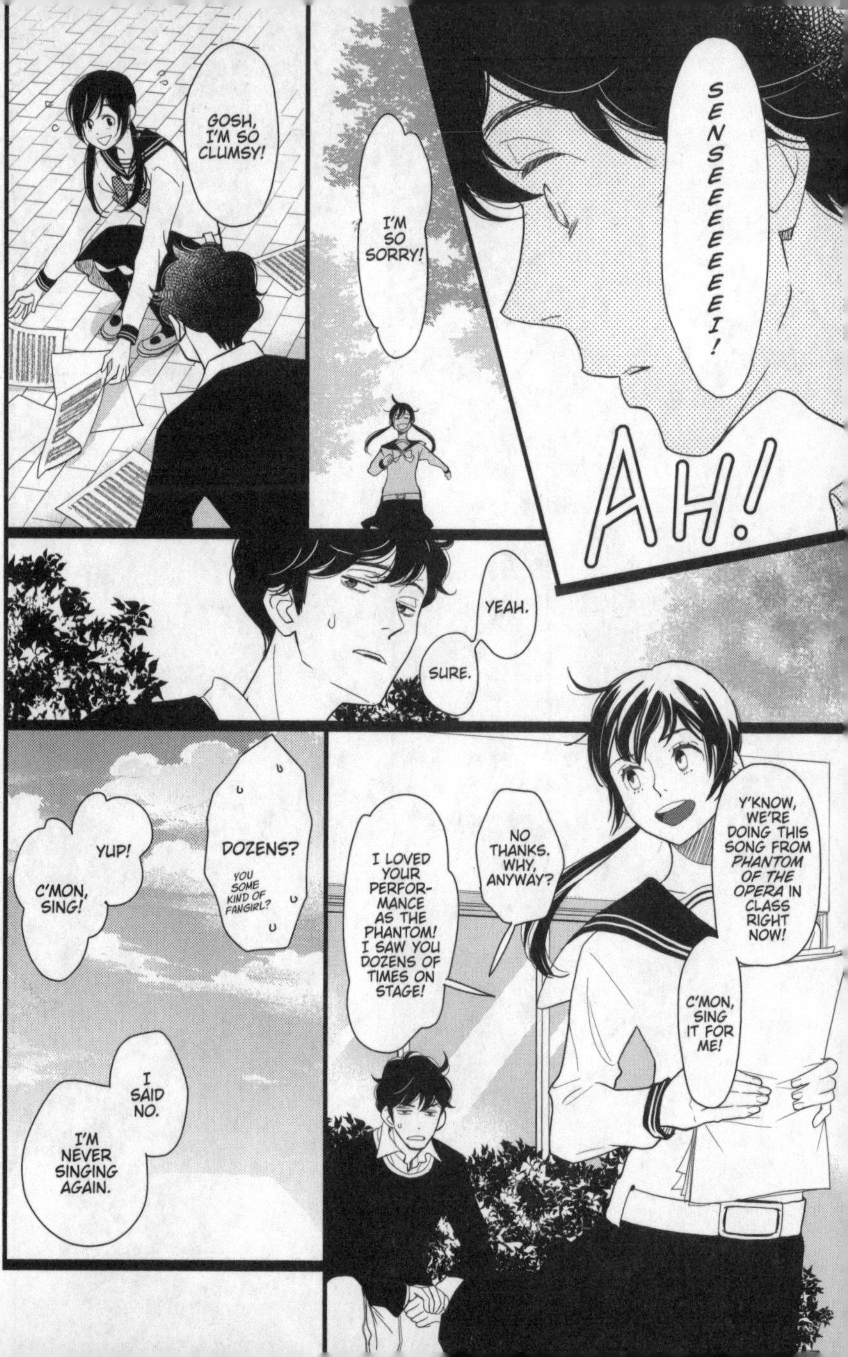
SENSEEEEEEEI!
AH!
I'M SO SORRY!
GOSH, I'M SO CLUMSY!
YEAH.
SURE.
Y'KNOW, WE'RE DOING THIS SONG FROM *PHANTOM OF THE OPERA* IN CLASS RIGHT NOW!
C'MON, SING IT FOR ME!
NO THANKS. WHY, ANYWAY?
I LOVED YOUR PERFORMANCE AS THE PHANTOM! I SAW YOU DOZENS OF TIMES ON STAGE!
DOZENS?
YOU SOME KIND OF FANGIRL?
YUP!
C'MON, SING!
I SAID NO.
I'M NEVER SINGING AGAIN.

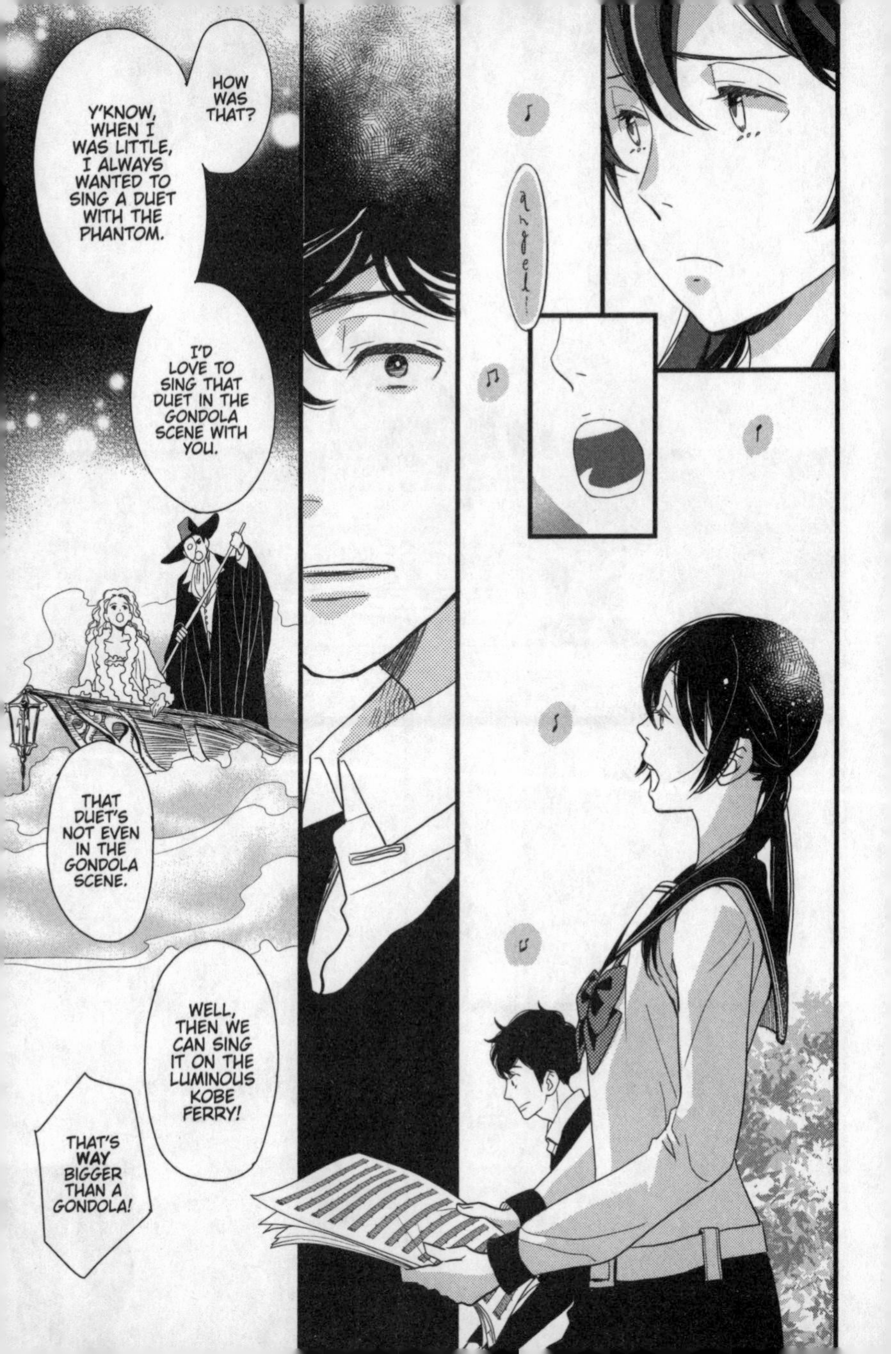
angel!
HOW WAS THAT?
Y'KNOW, WHEN I WAS LITTLE, I ALWAYS WANTED TO SING A DUET WITH THE PHANTOM.
I'D LOVE TO SING THAT DUET IN THE GONDOLA SCENE WITH YOU.
THAT DUET'S NOT EVEN IN THE GONDOLA SCENE.
WELL, THEN WE CAN SING IT ON THE LUMINOUS KOBE FERRY!
THAT'S WAY BIGGER THAN A GONDOLA!

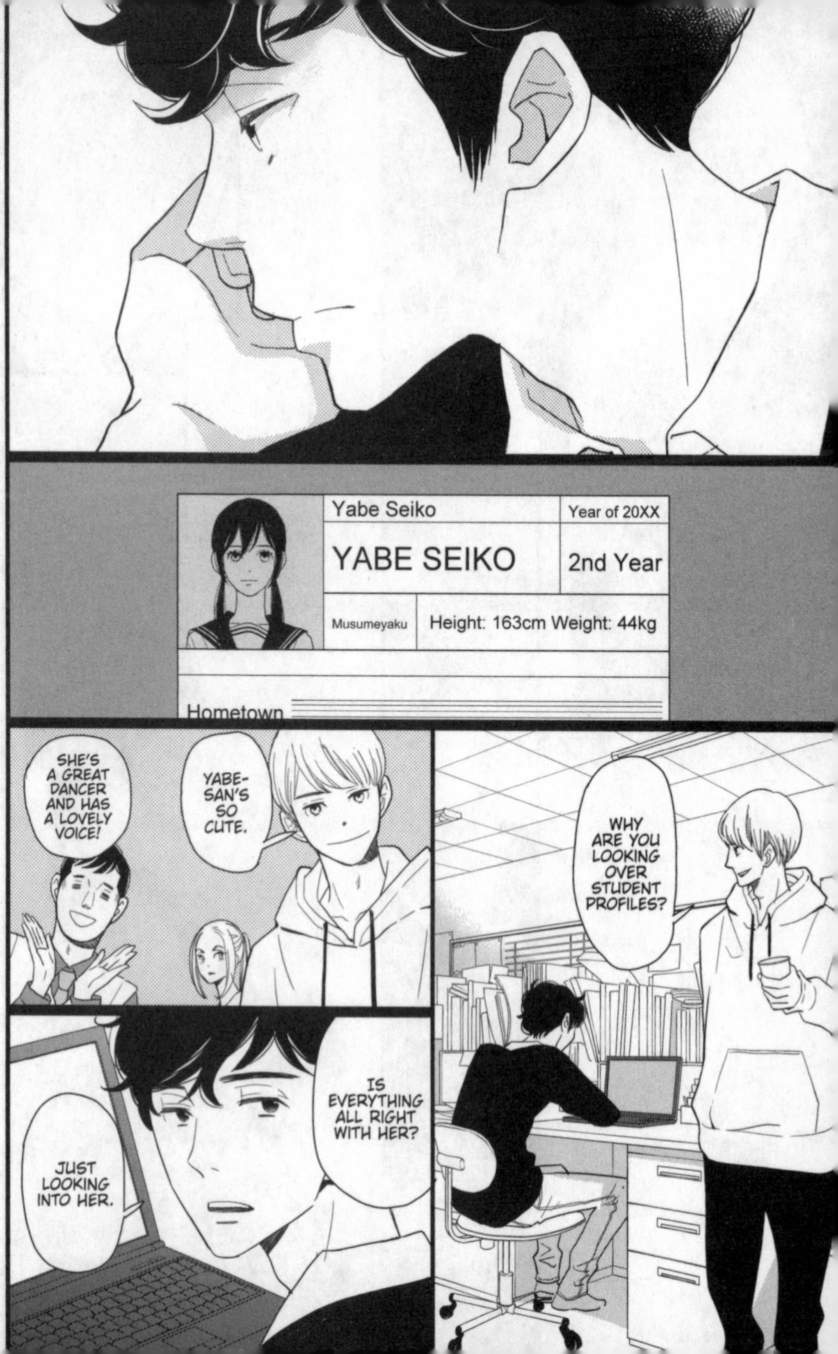
Yabe Seiko
Year of 20XX
YABE SEIKO
2nd Year
Musumeyaku
Height: 163cm Weight: 44kg
Hometown
WHY ARE YOU LOOKING OVER STUDENT PROFILES?
YABE-SAN'S SO CUTE.
SHE'S A GREAT DANCER AND HAS A LOVELY VOICE!
IS EVERYTHING ALL RIGHT WITH HER?
JUST LOOKING INTO HER.

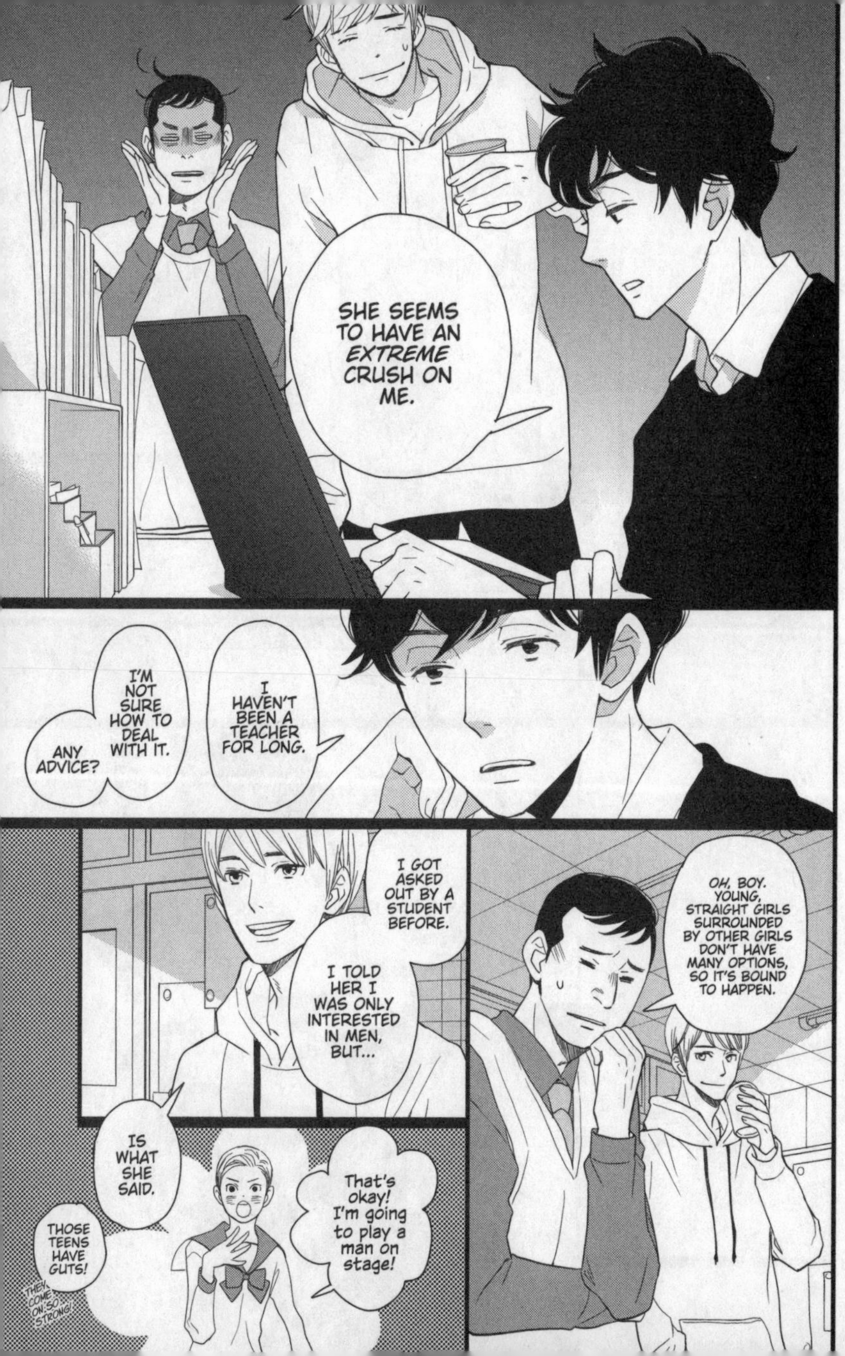
SHE SEEMS TO HAVE AN *EXTREME* CRUSH ON ME.
I HAVEN'T BEEN A TEACHER FOR LONG.
I'M NOT SURE HOW TO DEAL WITH IT.
ANY ADVICE?
OH, BOY. YOUNG, STRAIGHT GIRLS SURROUNDED BY OTHER GIRLS DON'T HAVE MANY OPTIONS, SO IT'S BOUND TO HAPPEN.
I GOT ASKED OUT BY A STUDENT BEFORE.
I TOLD HER I WAS ONLY INTERESTED IN MEN, BUT...
That's okay! I'm going to play a man on stage!
IS WHAT SHE SAID.
THOSE TEENS HAVE GUTS!
THEY COME ON SO STRONG!

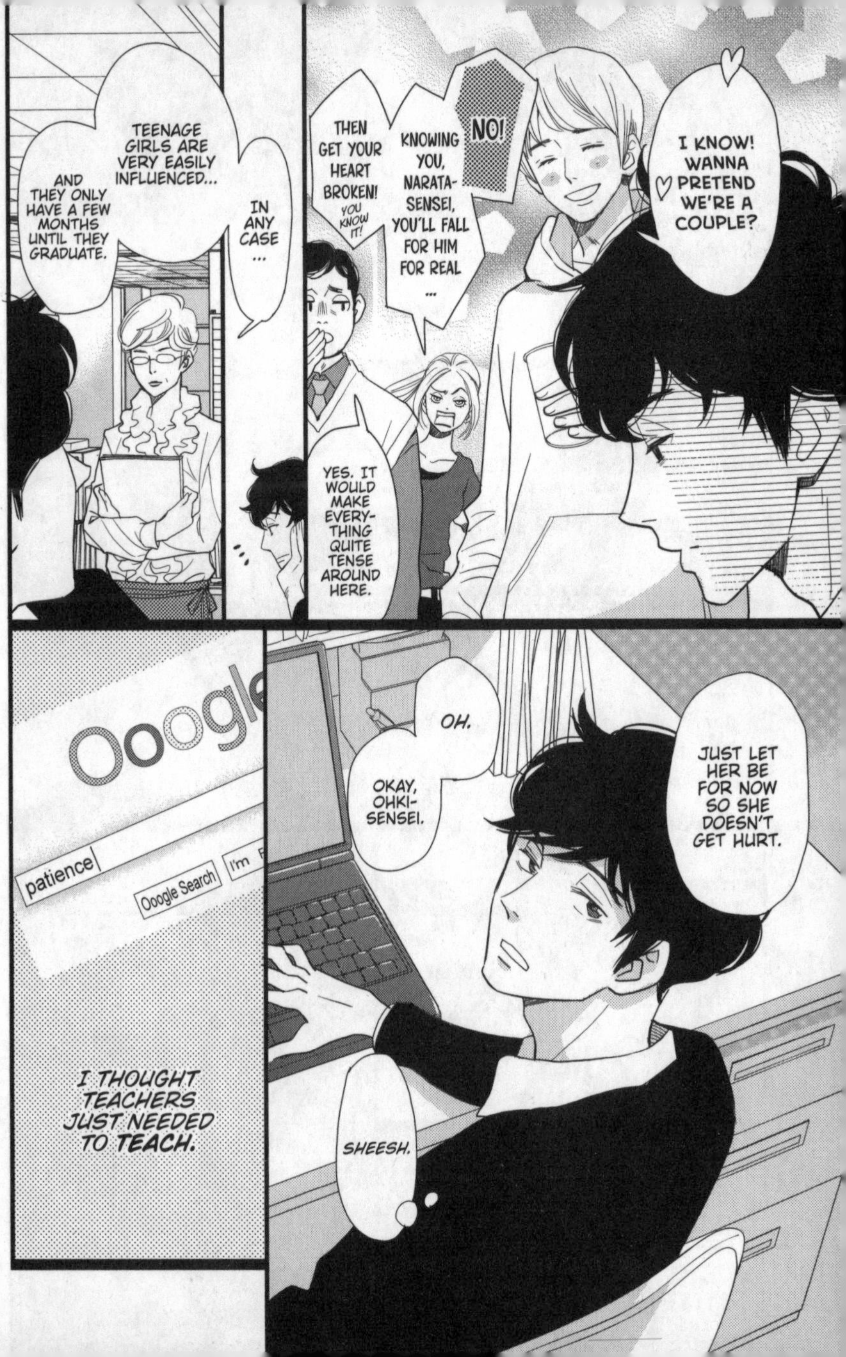

I KNOW! WANNA PRETEND WE'RE A COUPLE?
NO!
KNOWING YOU, NARATA-SENSEI, YOU'LL FALL FOR HIM FOR REAL ...
THEN GET YOUR HEART BROKEN!
YOU KNOW IT!
YES. IT WOULD MAKE EVERY-THING QUITE TENSE AROUND HERE.
...
IN ANY CASE ...
TEENAGE GIRLS ARE VERY EASILY INFLUENCED...
AND THEY ONLY HAVE A FEW MONTHS UNTIL THEY GRADUATE.
JUST LET HER BE FOR NOW SO SHE DOESN'T GET HURT.
OH.
OKAY, OHKI-SENSEI.
SHEESH.
Ooogle
patience
Ooogle Search
I THOUGHT TEACHERS JUST NEEDED TO TEACH.

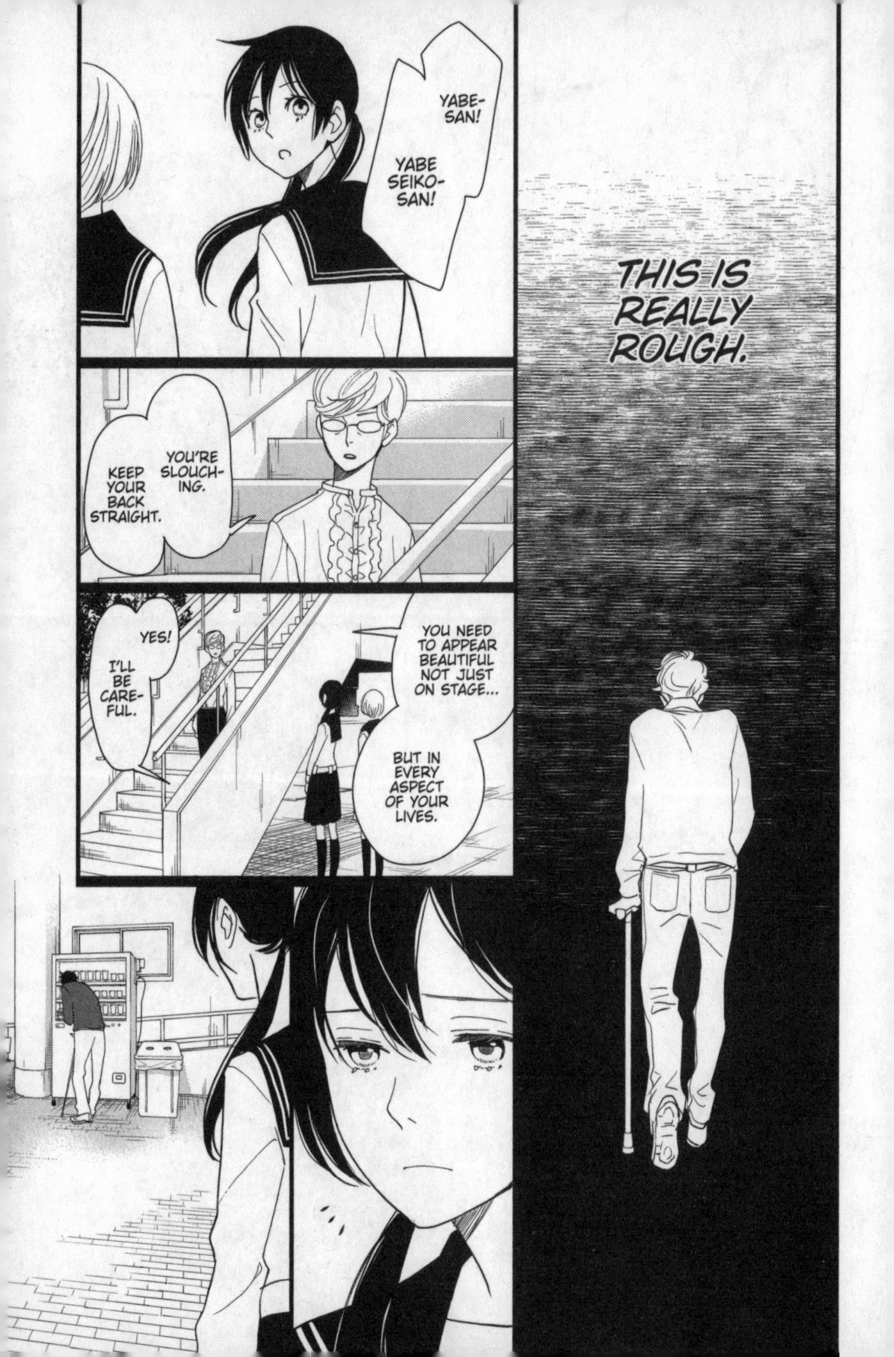

THIS IS REALLY ROUGH.
YABE-SAN!
YABE SEIKO-SAN!
YOU'RE SLOUCHING.
KEEP YOUR BACK STRAIGHT.
YOU NEED TO APPEAR BEAUTIFUL NOT JUST ON STAGE...
BUT IN EVERY ASPECT OF YOUR LIVES.
YES!
I'LL BE CAREFUL.

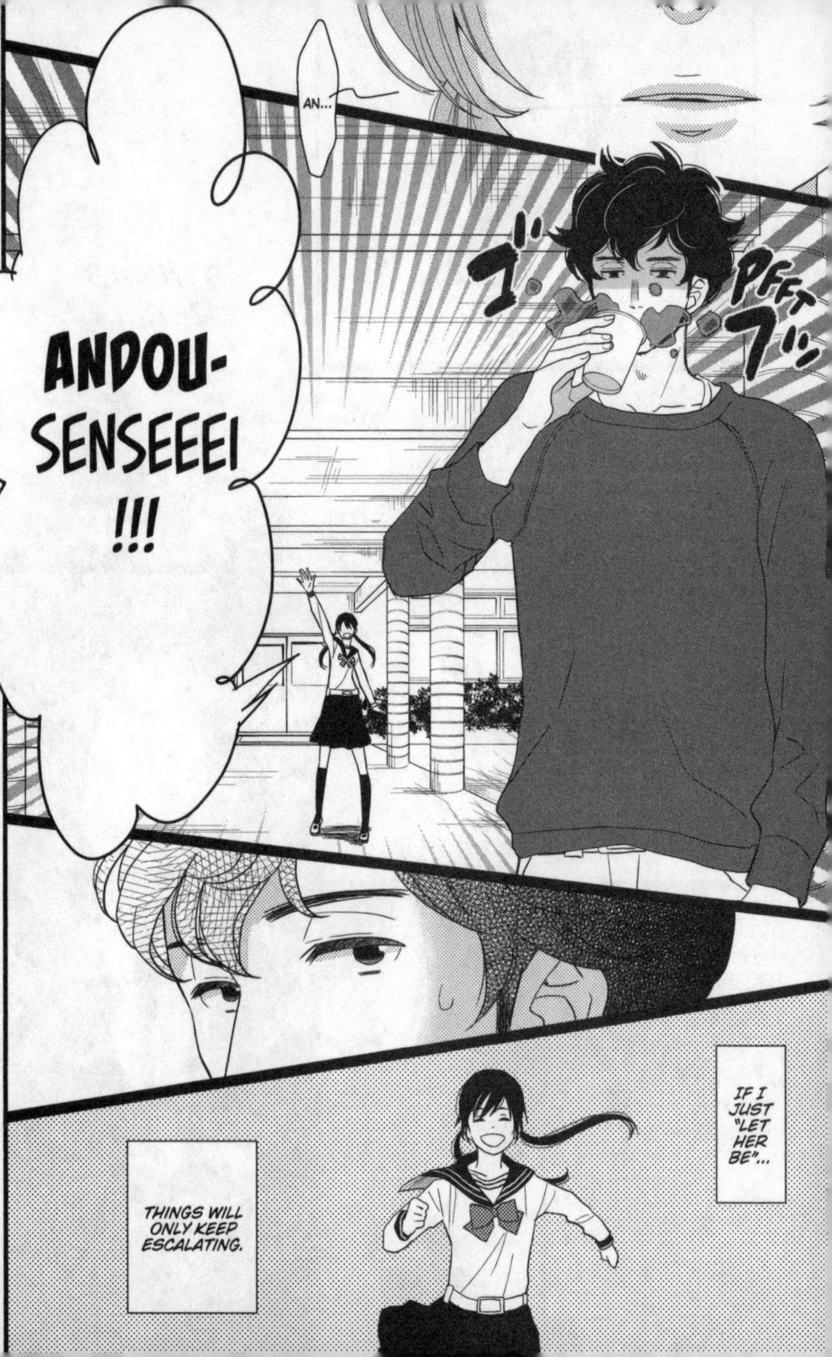
AN...
PFFT ブッ
ゴ
ANDOU-SENSEEEI!!!
IF I JUST "LET HER BE"...
THINGS WILL ONLY KEEP ESCALATING.

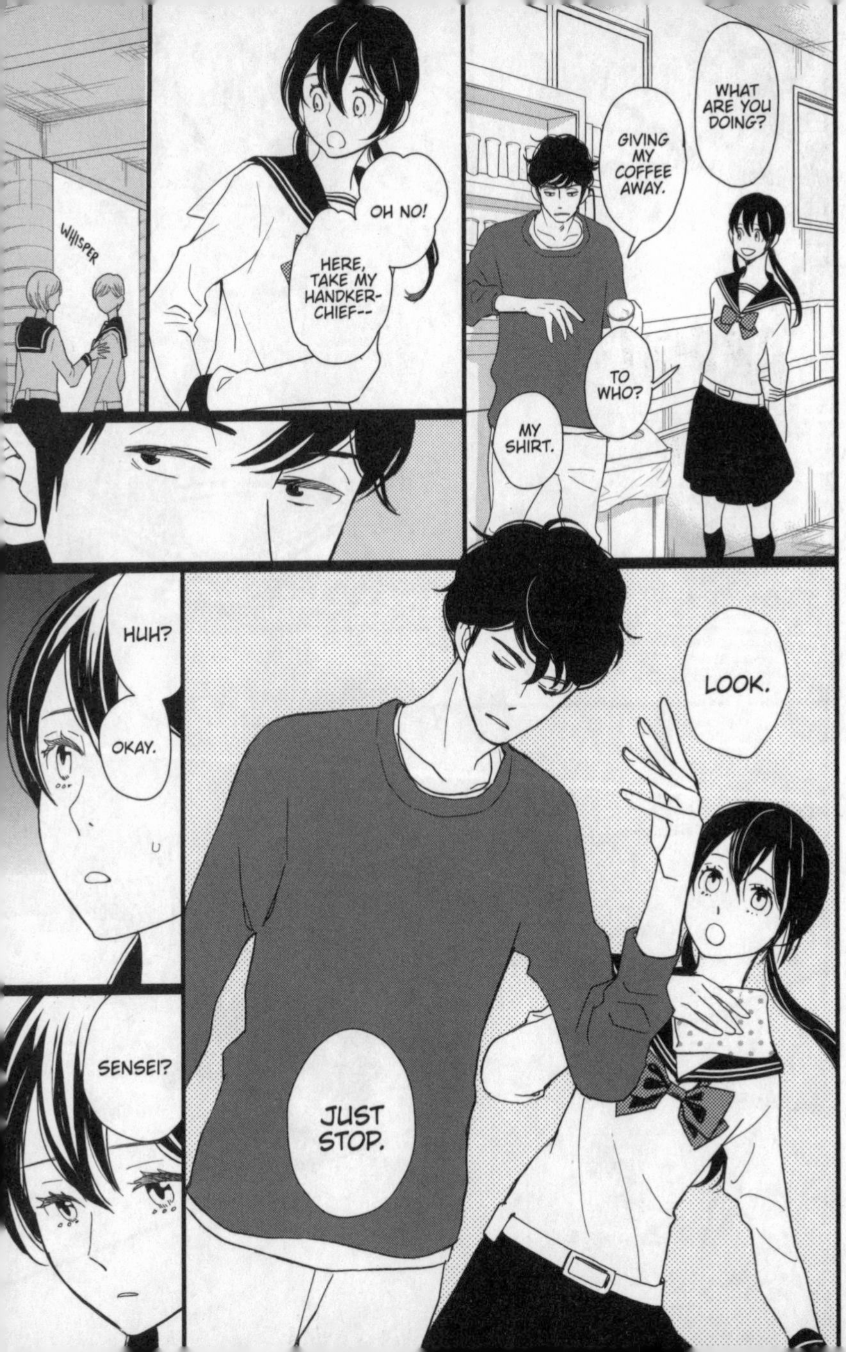
WHAT ARE YOU DOING?
GIVING MY COFFEE AWAY.
TO WHO?
MY SHIRT.
OH NO!
HERE, TAKE MY HANDKER-CHIEF--
WHISPER
LOOK.
JUST STOP.
HUH?
OKAY.
SENSEI?

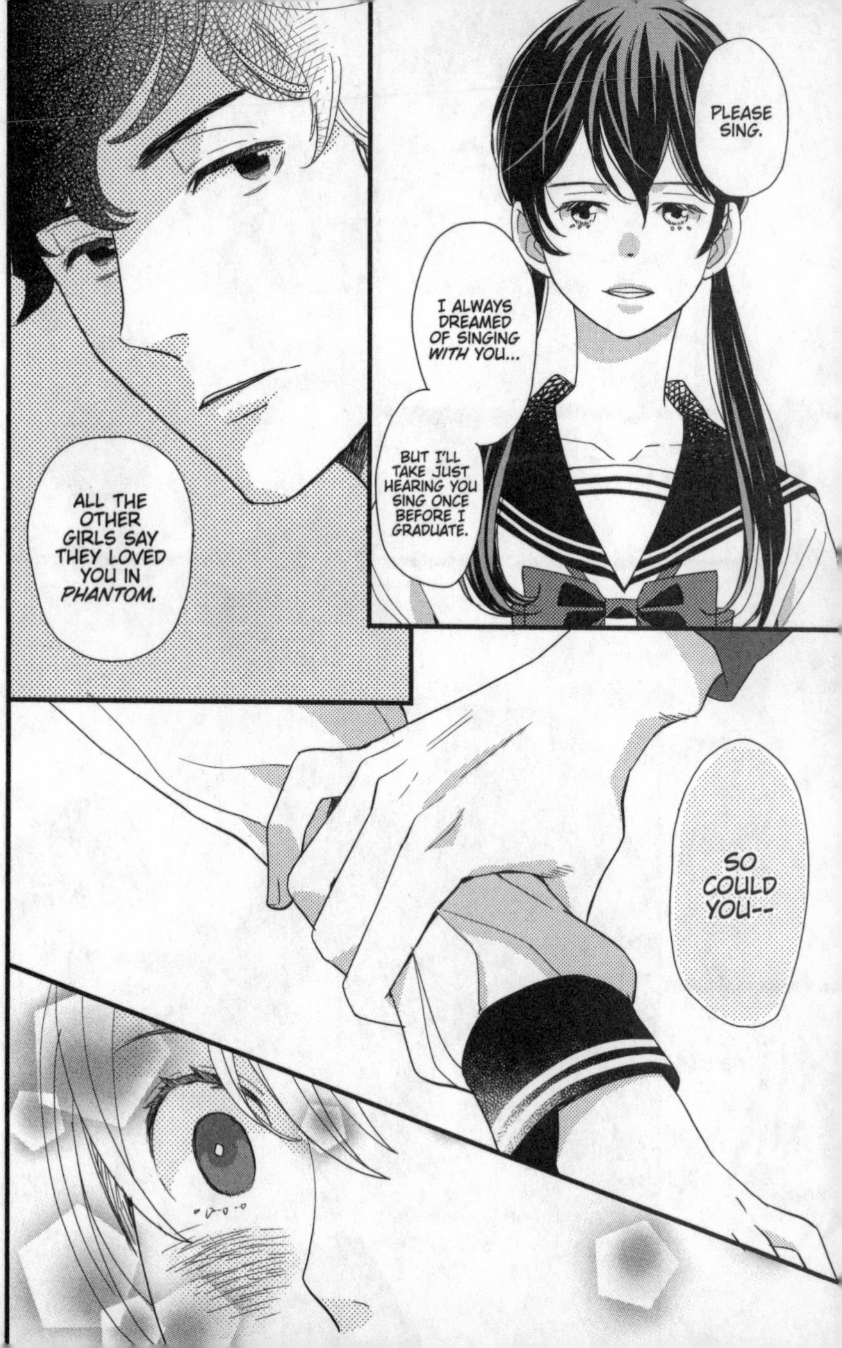
PLEASE SING.
I ALWAYS DREAMED OF SINGING *WITH* YOU...
BUT I'LL TAKE JUST HEARING YOU SING ONCE BEFORE I GRADUATE.
ALL THE OTHER GIRLS SAY THEY LOVED YOU IN *PHANTOM.*
SO COULD YOU--

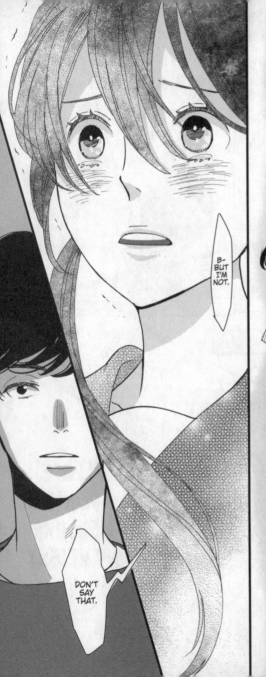

YOU'RE BOTHERING ME.

B-BUT I'M NOT.

YOU'RE JUST USING ME...

TO IGNORE REALITY.

DON'T SAY THAT.

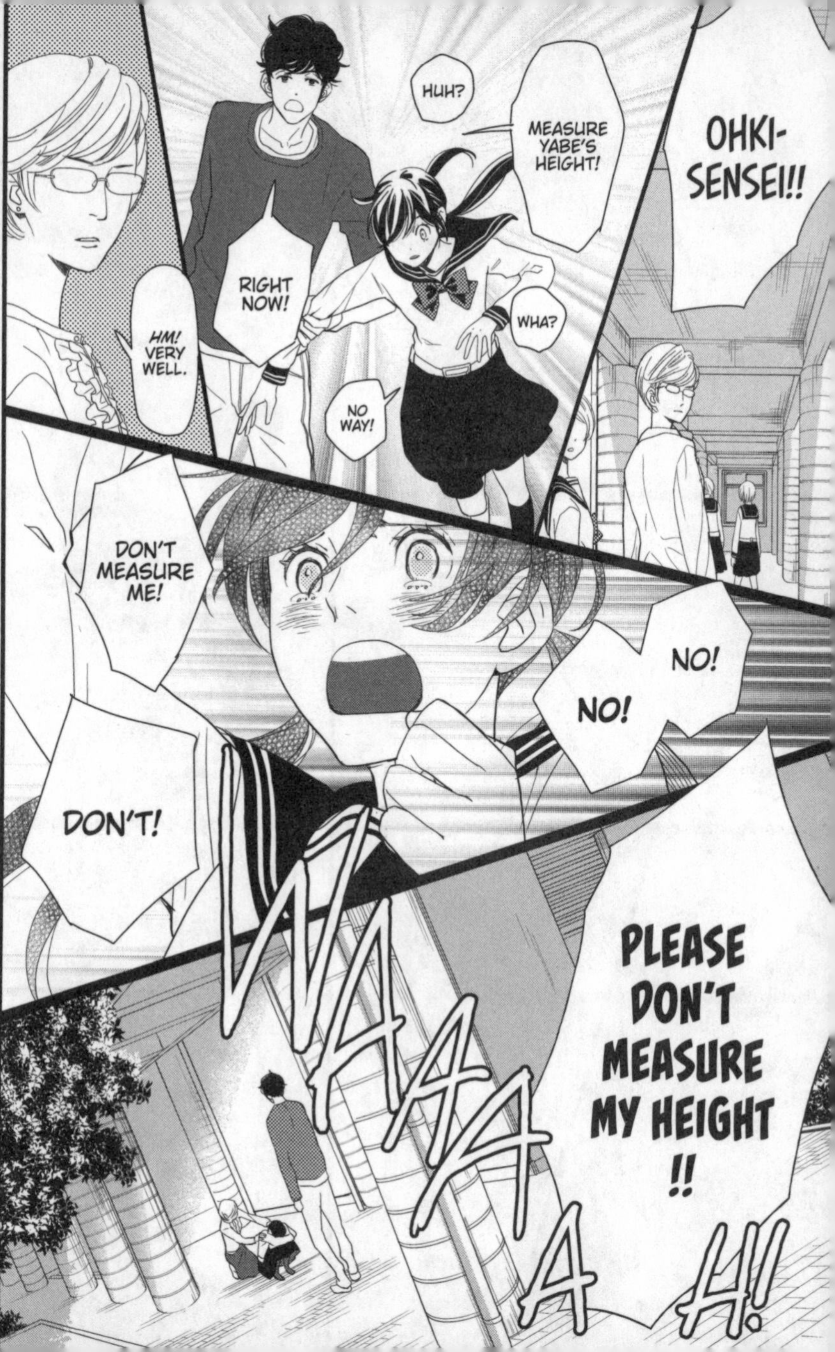
OHKI-SENSEI!!
MEASURE YABE'S HEIGHT!
HUH?
RIGHT NOW!
WHA?
NO WAY!
HM! VERY WELL.
NO!
NO!
DON'T MEASURE ME!
DON'T!
PLEASE DON'T MEASURE MY HEIGHT!!
WAAAAH!

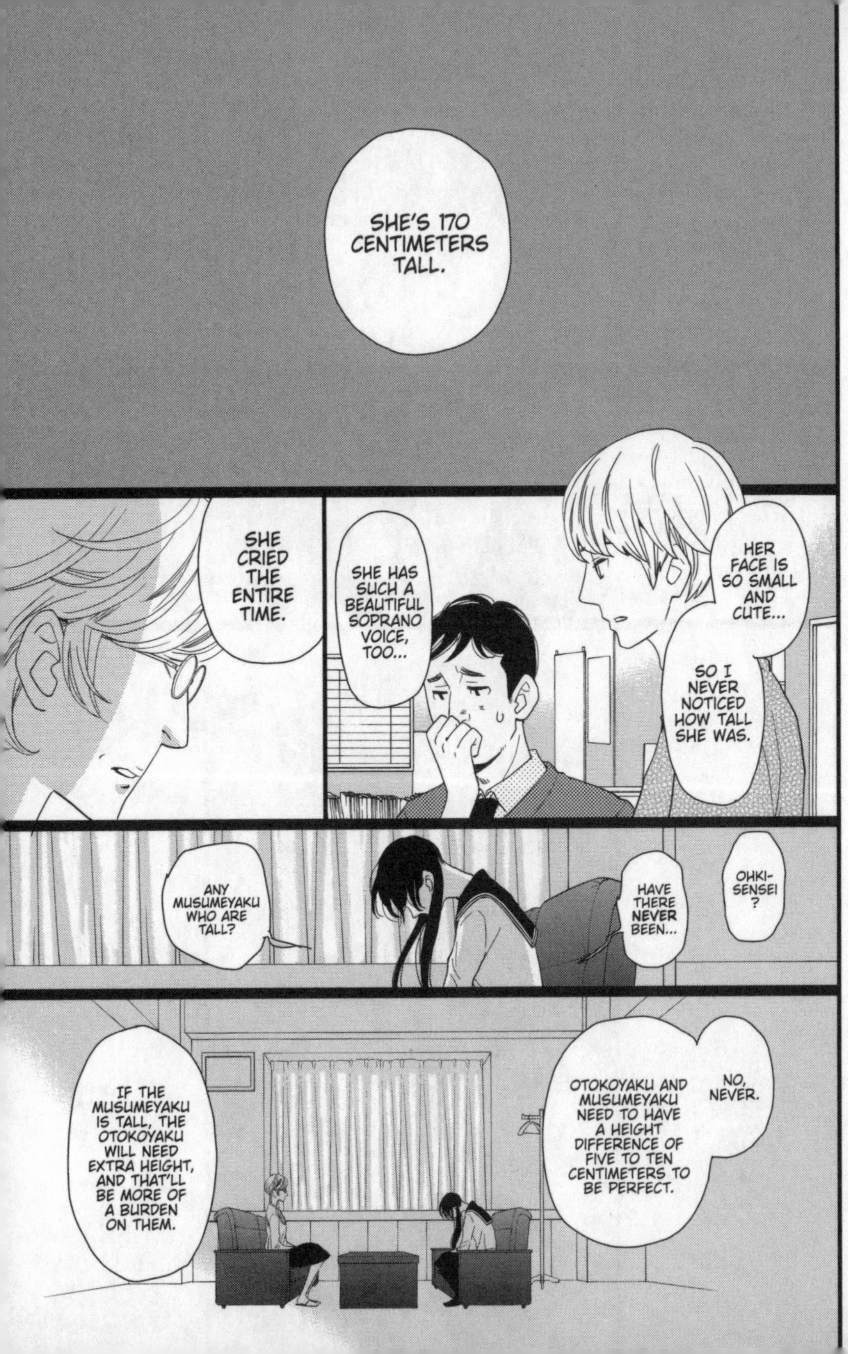
SHE'S 170 CENTIMETERS TALL.
HER FACE IS SO SMALL AND CUTE...
SO I NEVER NOTICED HOW TALL SHE WAS.
SHE HAS SUCH A BEAUTIFUL SOPRANO VOICE, TOO...
SHE CRIED THE ENTIRE TIME.
OHKI-SENSEI?
HAVE THERE NEVER BEEN...
ANY MUSUMEYAKU WHO ARE TALL?
NO, NEVER.
OTOKOYAKU AND MUSUMEYAKU NEED TO HAVE A HEIGHT DIFFERENCE OF FIVE TO TEN CENTIMETERS TO BE PERFECT.
IF THE MUSUMEYAKU IS TALL, THE OTOKOYAKU WILL NEED EXTRA HEIGHT, AND THAT'LL BE MORE OF A BURDEN ON THEM.

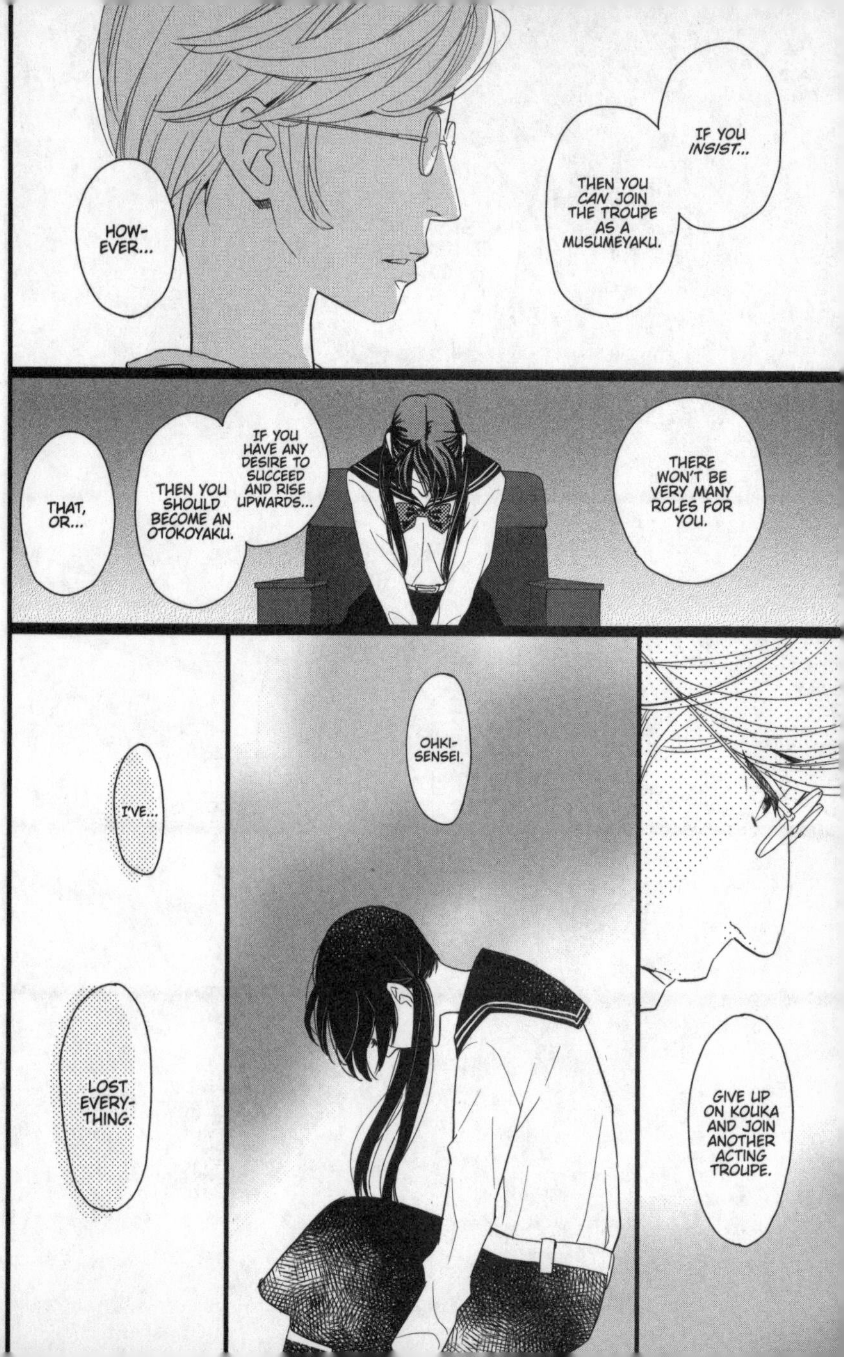
IF YOU *INSIST*...
THEN YOU *CAN* JOIN THE TROUPE AS A MUSUMEYAKU.
HOW-EVER...
THERE WON'T BE VERY MANY ROLES FOR YOU.
IF YOU HAVE ANY DESIRE TO SUCCEED AND RISE UPWARDS...
THEN YOU SHOULD BECOME AN OTOKOYAKU.
THAT, OR...
GIVE UP ON KOUKA AND JOIN ANOTHER ACTING TROUPE.
OHKI-SENSEI.
I'VE...
LOST EVERY-THING.

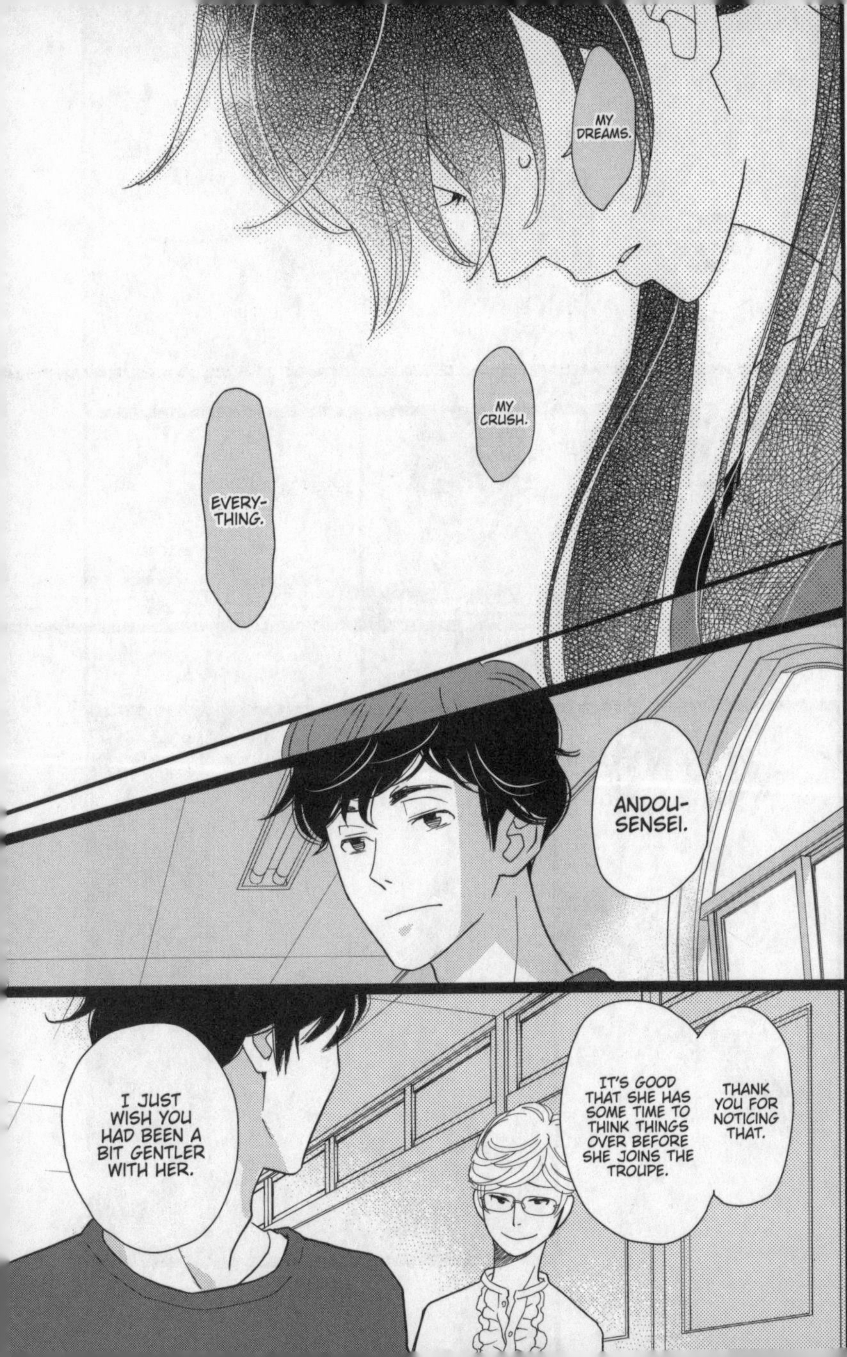
MY DREAMS.
MY CRUSH.
EVERY-THING.
ANDOU-SENSEI.
THANK YOU FOR NOTICING THAT.
IT'S GOOD THAT SHE HAS SOME TIME TO THINK THINGS OVER BEFORE SHE JOINS THE TROUPE.
I JUST WISH YOU HAD BEEN A BIT GENTLER WITH HER.

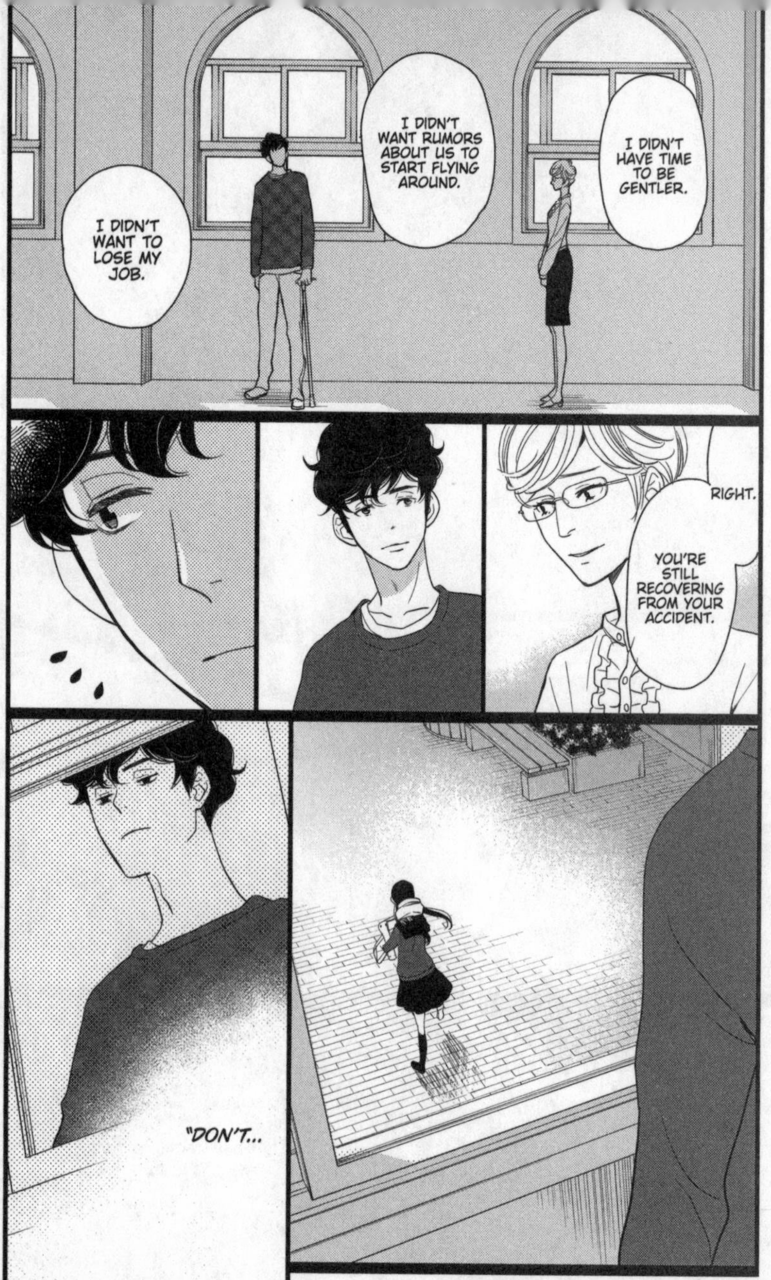
I DIDN'T HAVE TIME TO BE GENTLER.
I DIDN'T WANT RUMORS ABOUT US TO START FLYING AROUND.
I DIDN'T WANT TO LOSE MY JOB.
RIGHT.
YOU'RE STILL RECOVERING FROM YOUR ACCIDENT.
"DON'T...

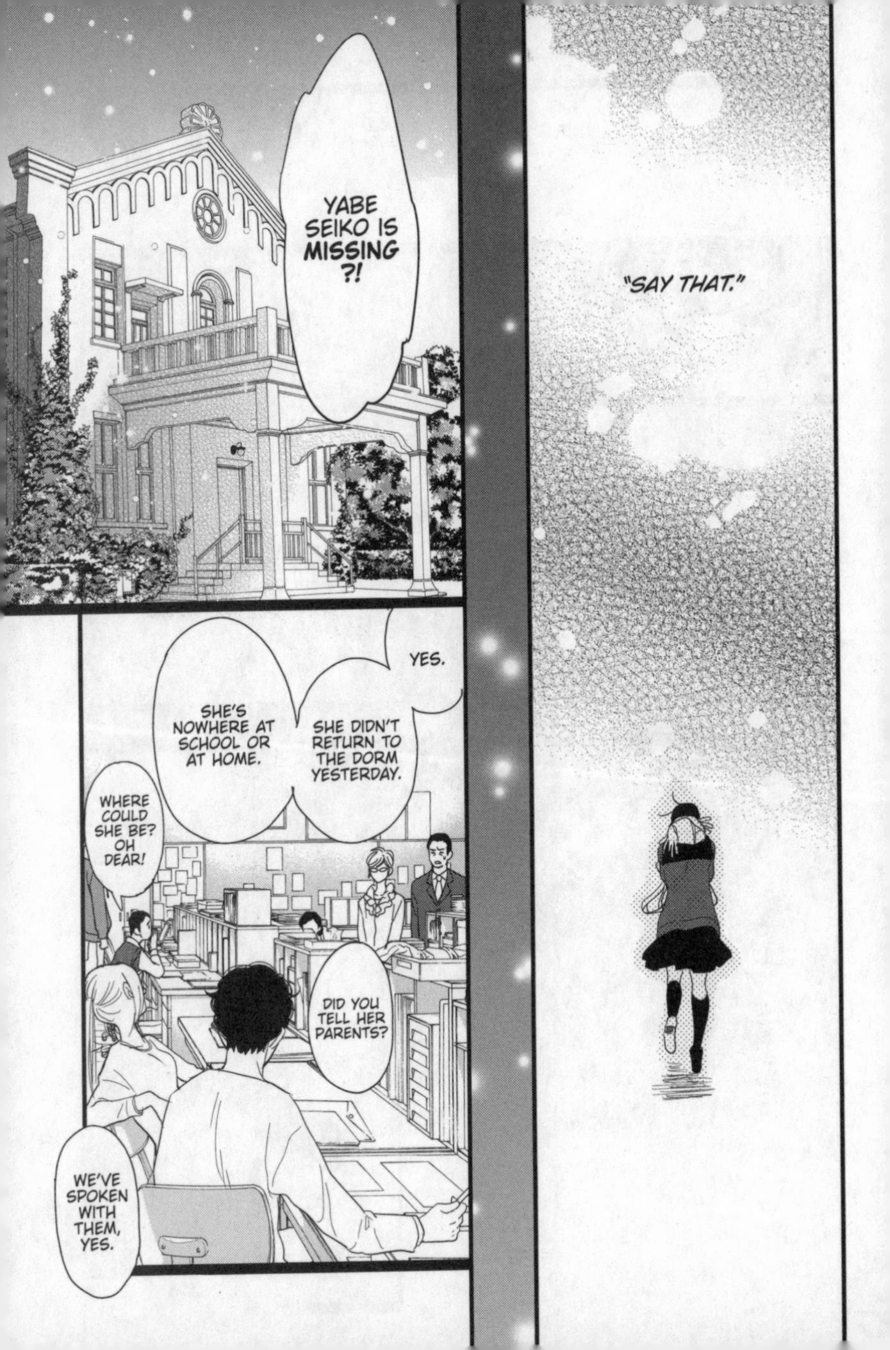
"SAY THAT."
YABE SEIKO IS MISSING?!
YES.
SHE DIDN'T RETURN TO THE DORM YESTERDAY.
SHE'S NOWHERE AT SCHOOL OR AT HOME.
WHERE COULD SHE BE? OH DEAR!
DID YOU TELL HER PARENTS?
WE'VE SPOKEN WITH THEM, YES.

DOES ANYONE KNOW WHERE SHE MIGHT BE?!
AH.
HUH ?!
WHAT IS IT, ANDOU-SENSEI?
DO YOU KNOW ?!
OH, NO, I DON'T.
NO WAY.
HAVE WE CALLED THE POLICE?
YES.
NO.
CAN'T BE.
THAT WOULD BE...

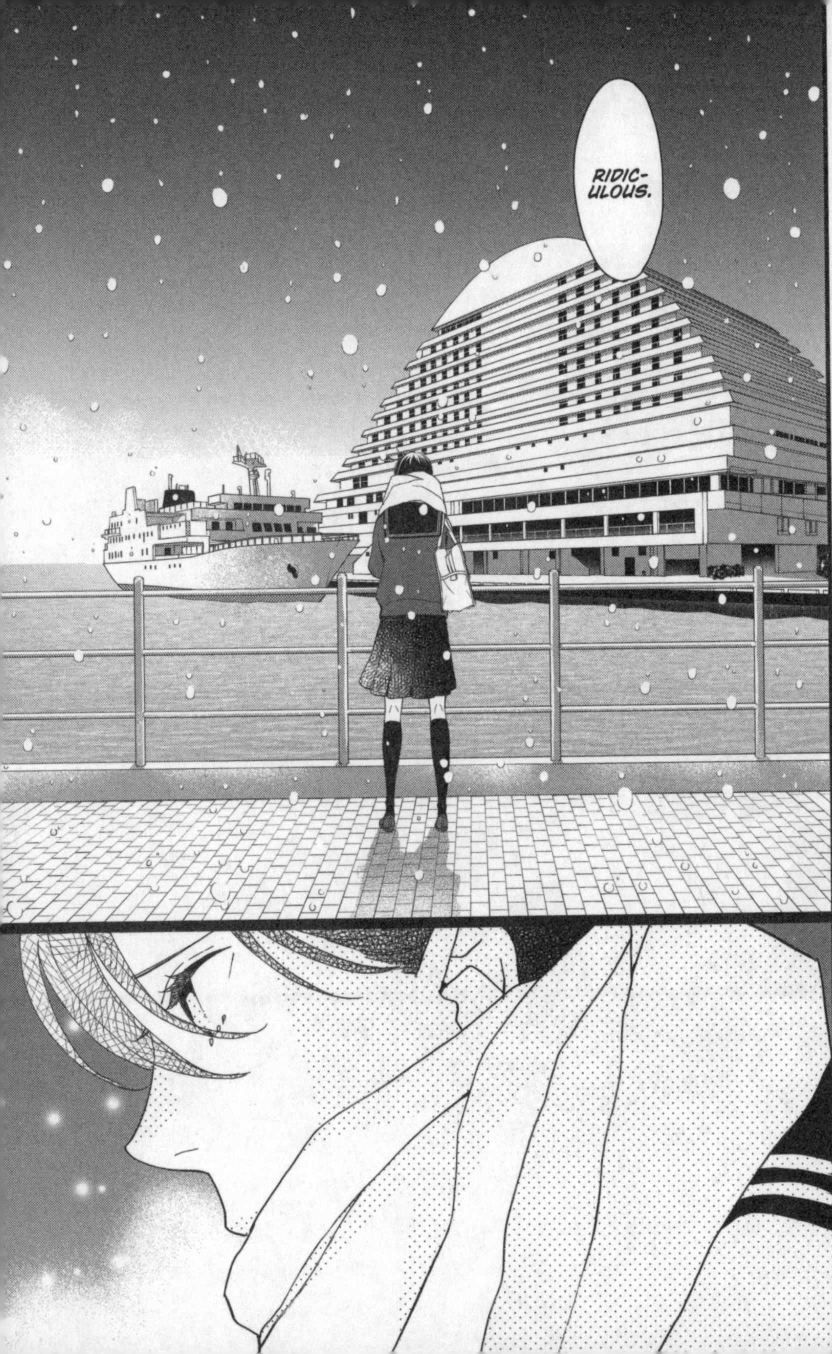
RIDIC-
ULOUS.

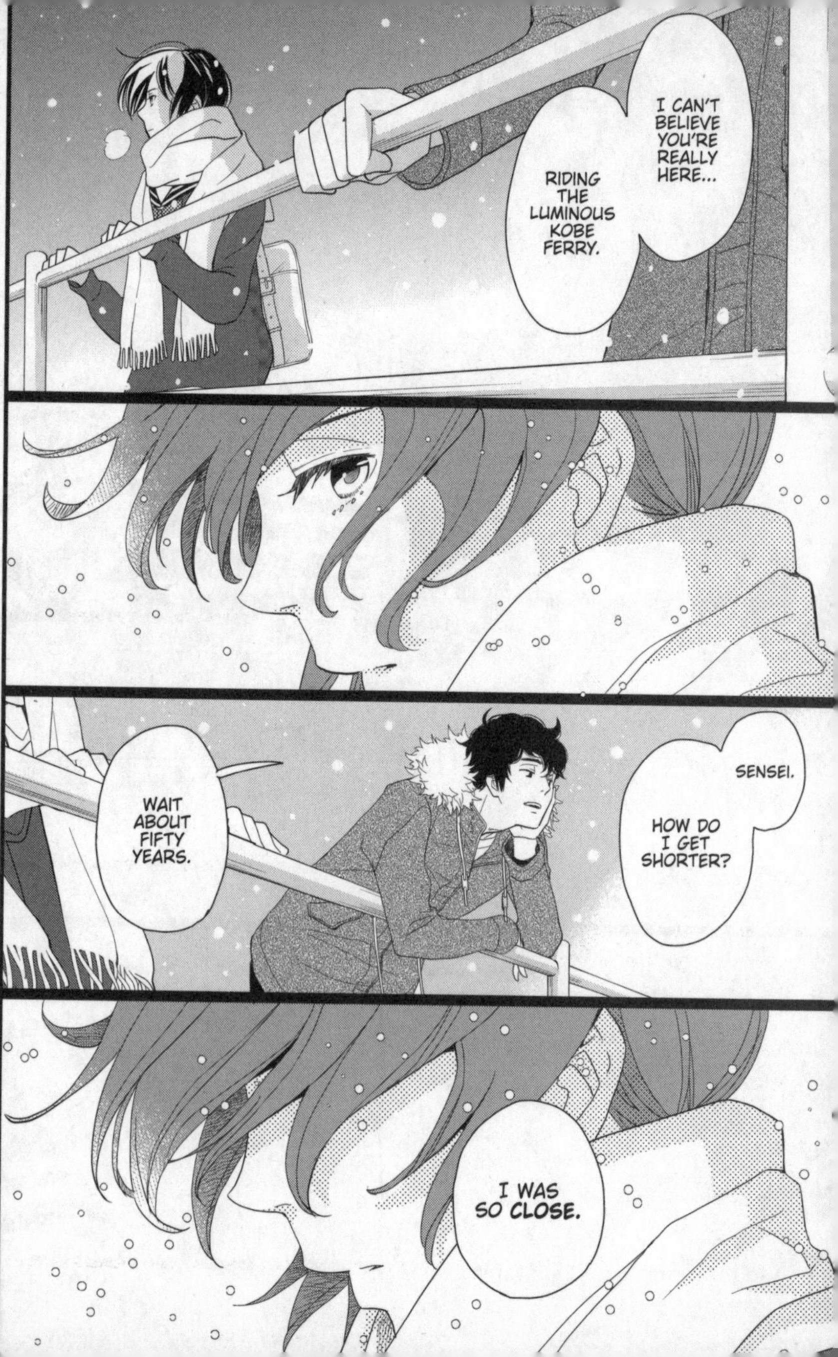
I CAN'T BELIEVE YOU'RE REALLY HERE...
RIDING THE LUMINOUS KOBE FERRY.
SENSEI.
HOW DO I GET SHORTER?
WAIT ABOUT FIFTY YEARS.
I WAS SO CLOSE.

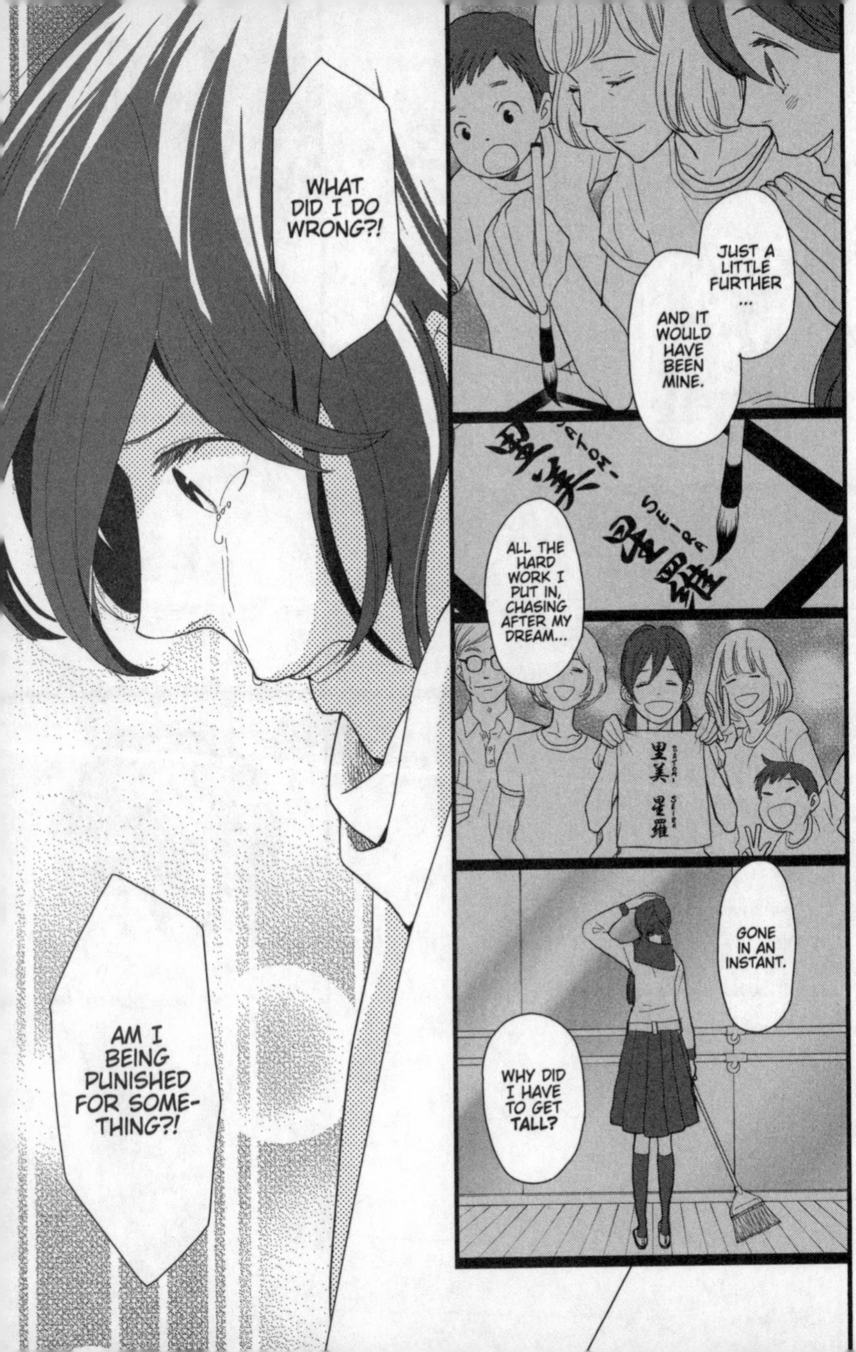
JUST A LITTLE FURTHER ...
AND IT WOULD HAVE BEEN MINE.
里美
星羅
SEI-RA
ALL THE HARD WORK I PUT IN, CHASING AFTER MY DREAM...
里美 星羅
GONE IN AN INSTANT.
WHY DID I HAVE TO GET TALL?
WHAT DID I DO WRONG?!
AM I BEING PUNISHED FOR SOME-THING?!

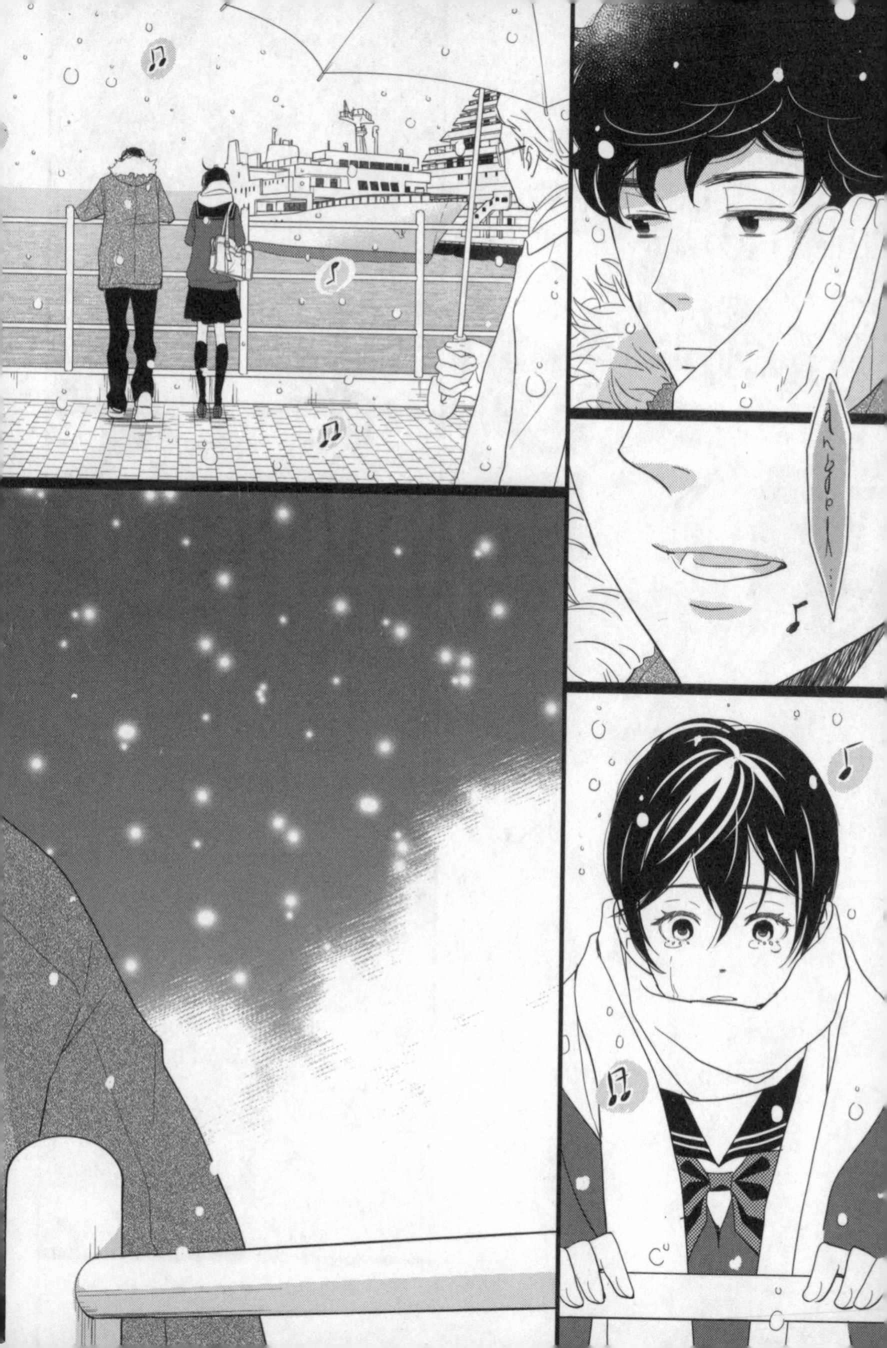
angel...

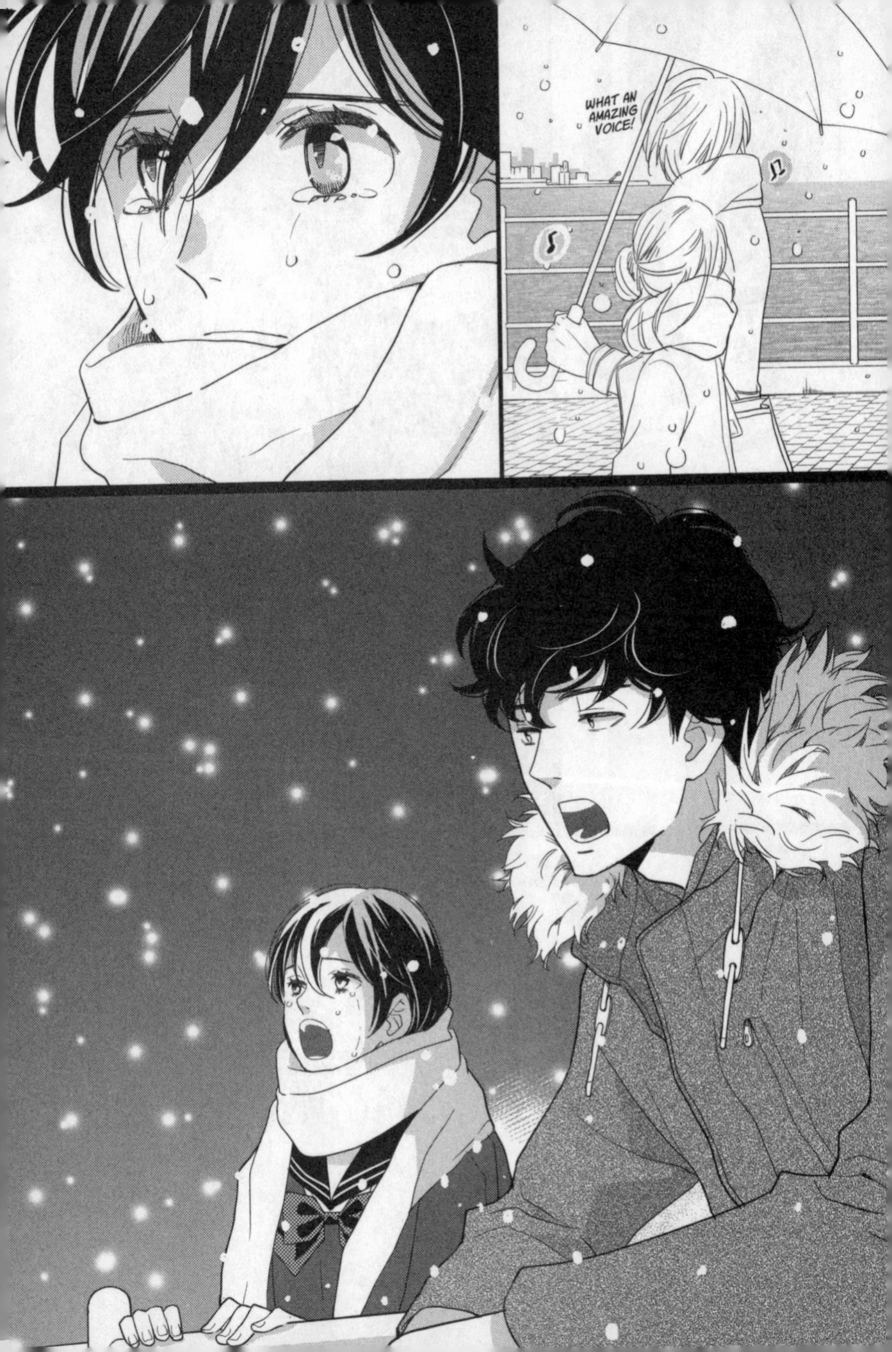
WHAT AN AMAZING VOICE!

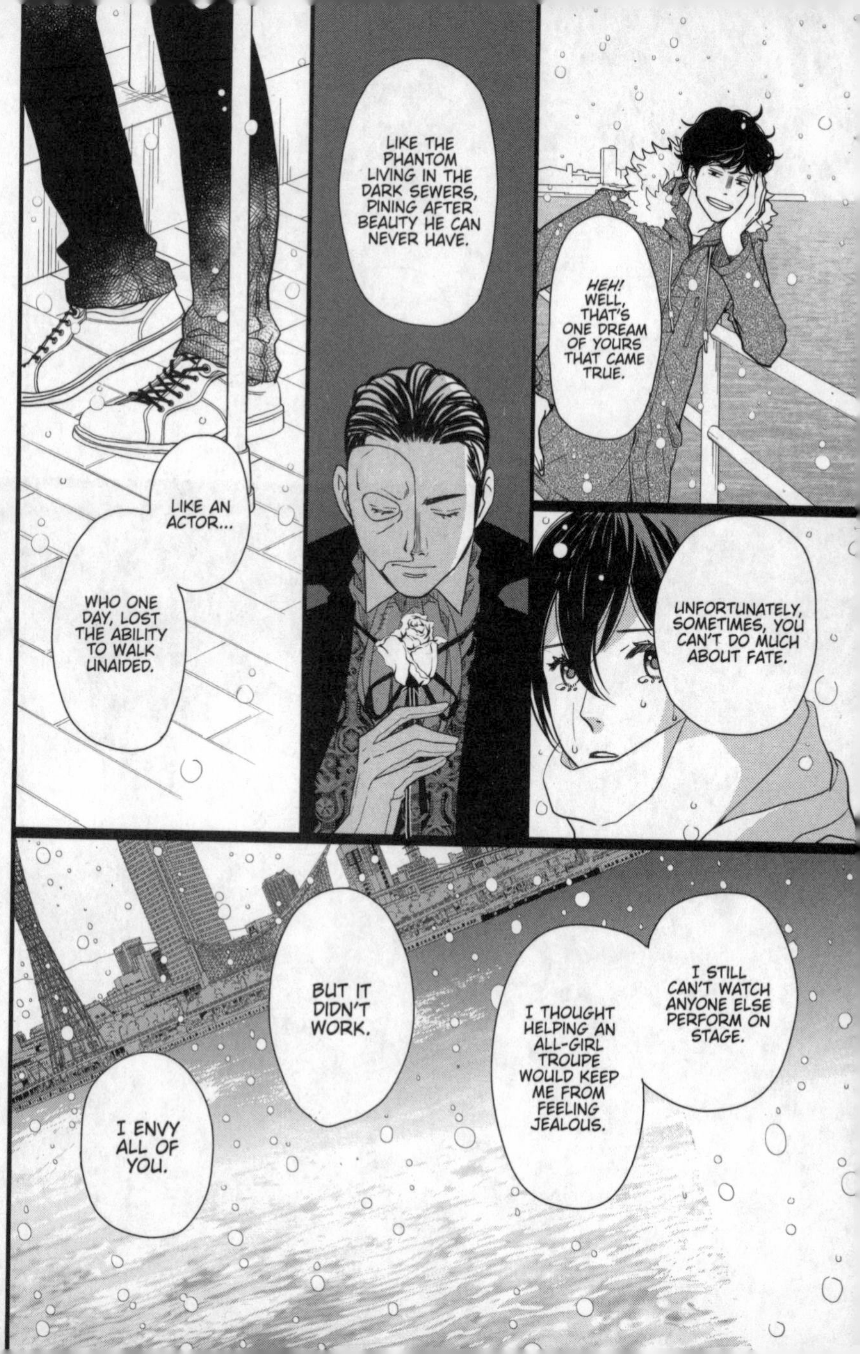
HEH! WELL, THAT'S ONE DREAM OF YOURS THAT CAME TRUE.
UNFORTUNATELY, SOMETIMES, YOU CAN'T DO MUCH ABOUT FATE.
LIKE THE PHANTOM LIVING IN THE DARK SEWERS, PINING AFTER BEAUTY HE CAN NEVER HAVE.
LIKE AN ACTOR...
WHO ONE DAY, LOST THE ABILITY TO WALK UNAIDED.
I STILL CAN'T WATCH ANYONE ELSE PERFORM ON STAGE.
I THOUGHT HELPING AN ALL-GIRL TROUPE WOULD KEEP ME FROM FEELING JEALOUS.
BUT IT DIDN'T WORK.
I ENVY ALL OF YOU.

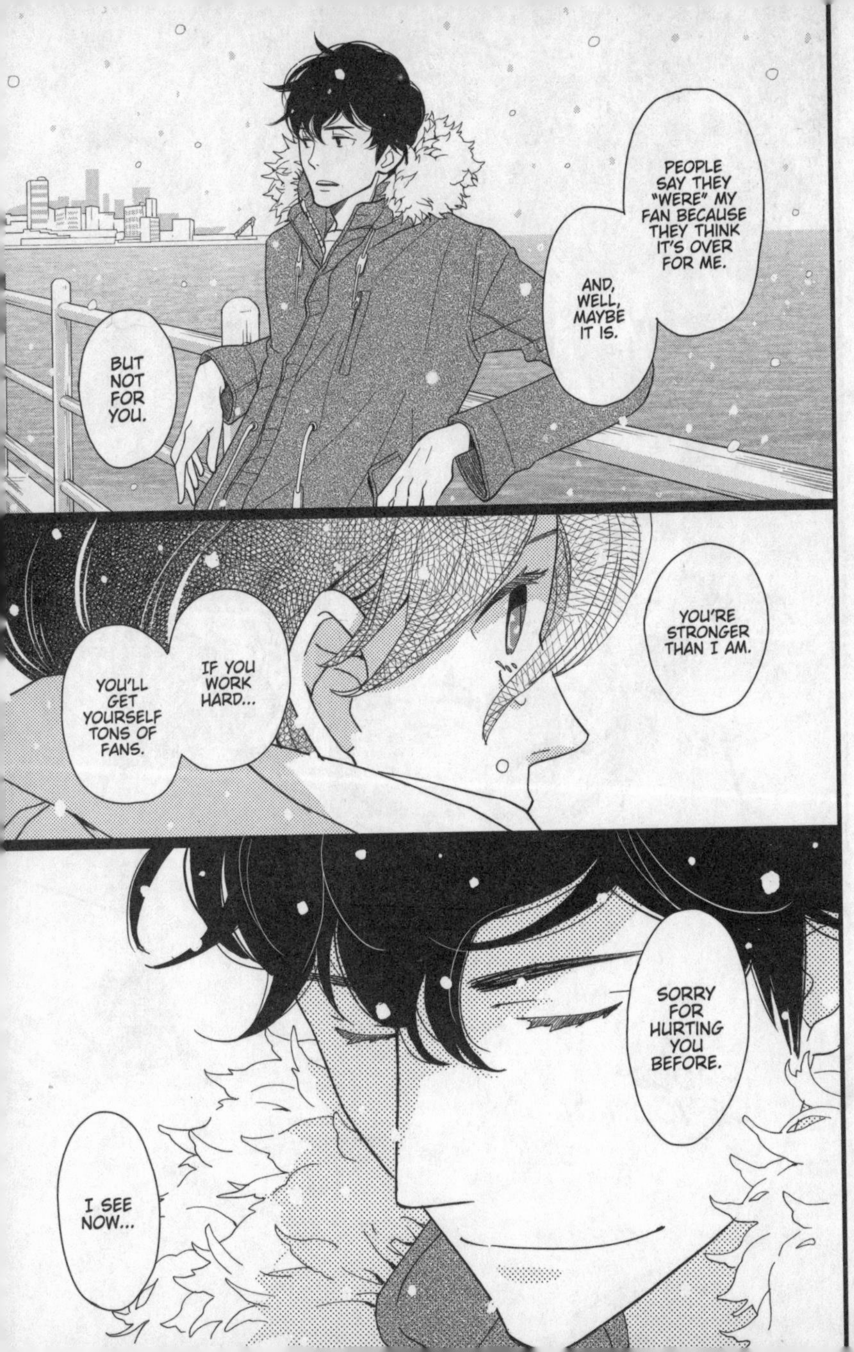
PEOPLE SAY THEY "WERE" MY FAN BECAUSE THEY THINK IT'S OVER FOR ME.
AND, WELL, MAYBE IT IS.
BUT NOT FOR YOU.
YOU'RE STRONGER THAN I AM.
IF YOU WORK HARD...
YOU'LL GET YOURSELF TONS OF FANS.
SORRY FOR HURTING YOU BEFORE.
I SEE NOW...

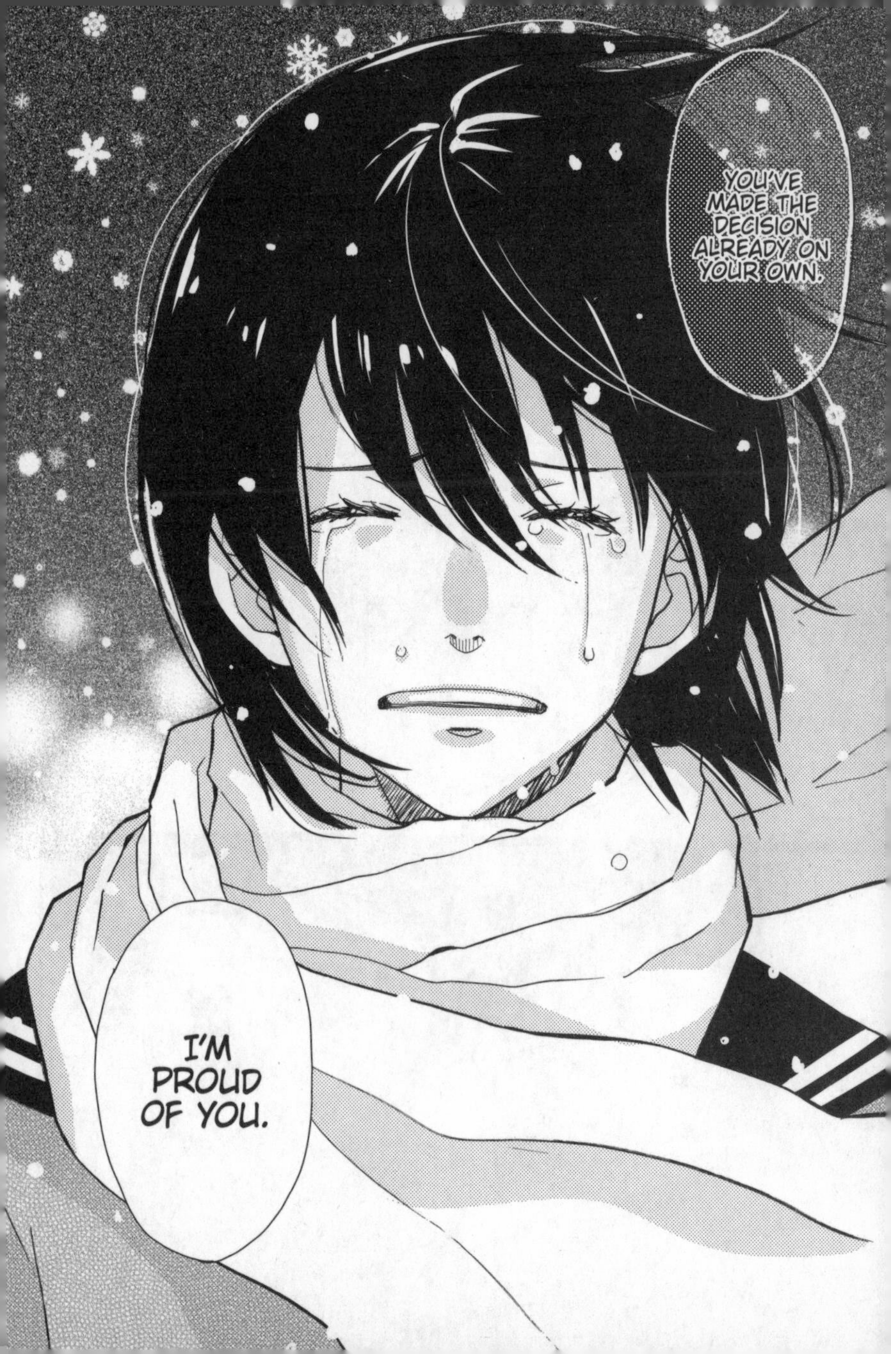
YOU'VE MADE THE DECISION ALREADY ON YOUR OWN.
I'M PROUD OF YOU.

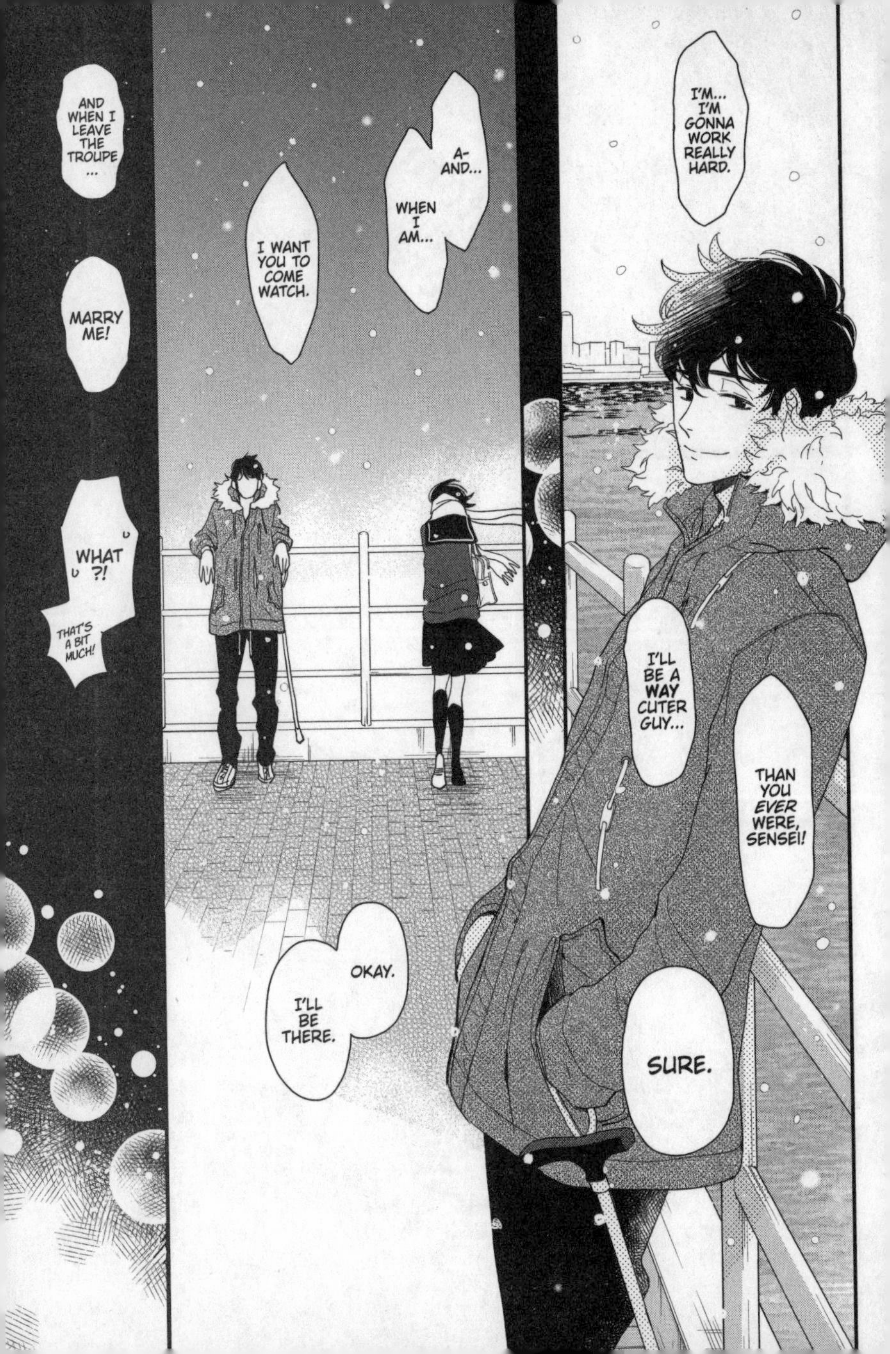
I'M... I'M GONNA WORK REALLY HARD.
I'LL BE A WAY CUTER GUY...
THAN YOU EVER WERE, SENSEI!
SURE.
A- AND... WHEN I AM...
I WANT YOU TO COME WATCH.
OKAY. I'LL BE THERE.
AND WHEN I LEAVE THE TROUPE...
MARRY ME!
WHAT?!
THAT'S A BIT MUCH!

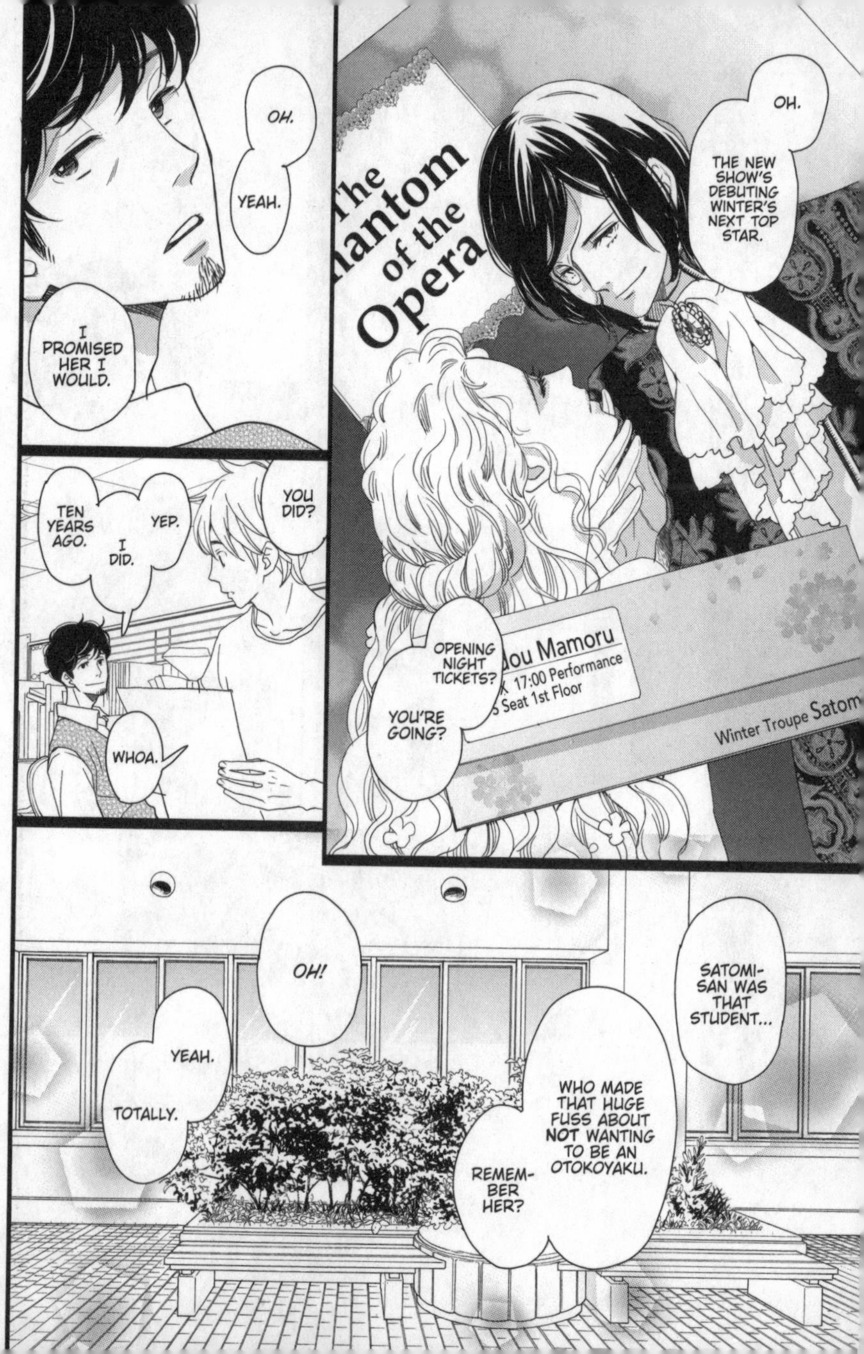
OH.
THE NEW SHOW'S DEBUTING WINTER'S NEXT TOP STAR.
of the Opera
Mamoru
17:00 Performance
Seat 1st Floor
Winter Troupe
OPENING NIGHT TICKETS?
YOU'RE GOING?
OH.
YEAH.
I PROMISED HER I WOULD.
YOU DID?
YEP.
I DID.
TEN YEARS AGO.
WHOA.
SATOMI-SAN WAS THAT STUDENT...
WHO MADE THAT HUGE FUSS ABOUT NOT WANTING TO BE AN OTOKOYAKU.
REMEMBER HER?
OH!
YEAH.
TOTALLY.

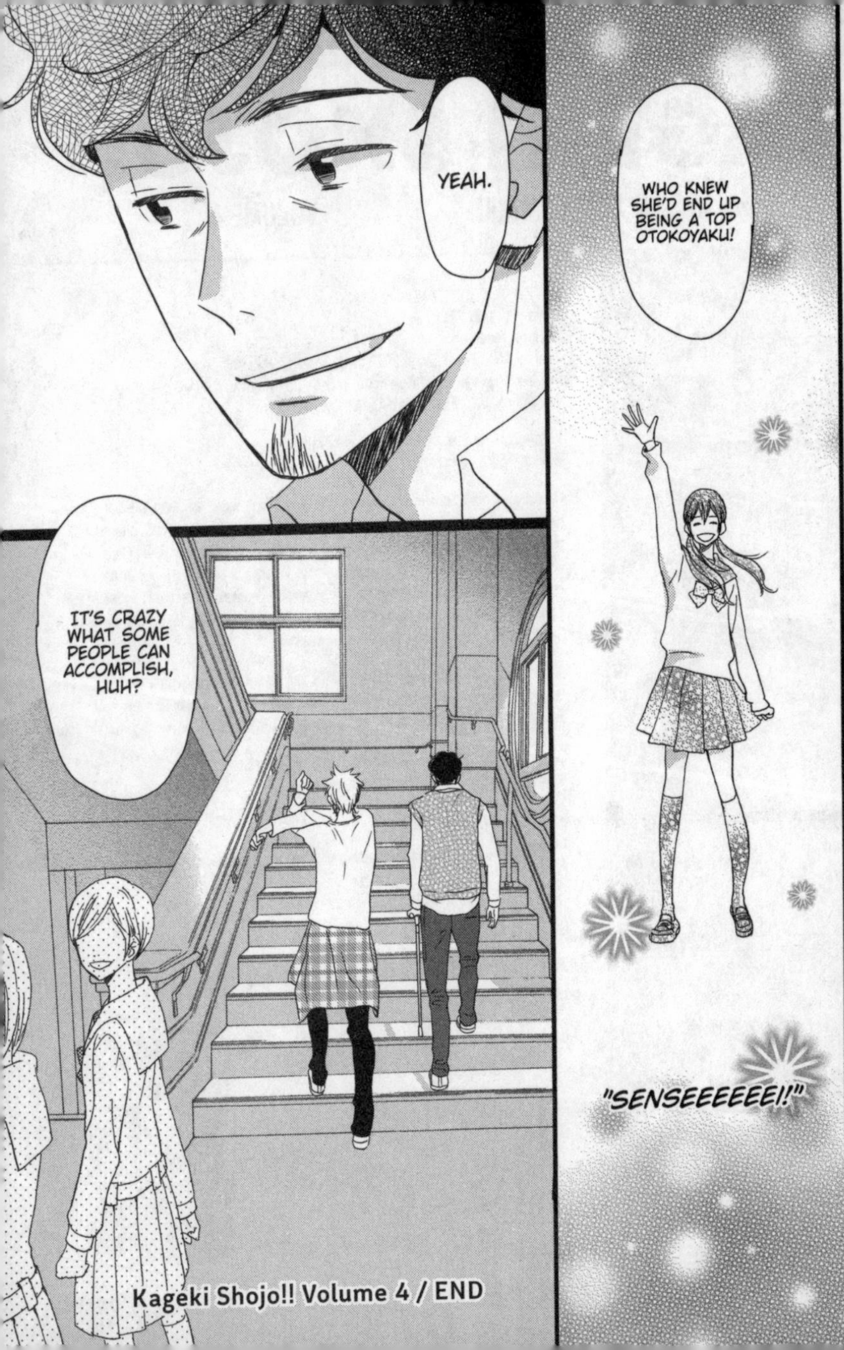
WHO KNEW SHE'D END UP BEING A TOP OTOKOYAKU!
"SENSEEEEEEEI!"
YEAH.
IT'S CRAZY WHAT SOME PEOPLE CAN ACCOMPLISH, HUH?
Kageki Shojo!! Volume 4 / END

SEVEN SEAS ENTERTAINMENT PRESENTS

KAGEKI SHOJO!!

story and art by KUMIKO SAIKI

VOLUME 4

TRANSLATION
Katrina Leonoudakis

LETTERING
Aila Nagamine

COVER DESIGN
Hanase Qi

LOGO DESIGN
Courtney Williams

PROOFREADER
Alyssa Honsowetz

EDITOR
Shannon Fay

PRODUCTION ASSOCIATE
Christina McKenzie

PRODUCTION MANAGER
Lissa Pattillo

PREPRESS TECHNICIAN
Melanie Ujimori

PRINT MANAGER
Rhiannon Rasmussen-Silverstein

MANAGING EDITOR
Julie Davis

ASSOCIATE PUBLISHER
Adam Arnold

PUBLISHER
Jason DeAngelis

First published in Japan in 2017 by HAKUSENSHA, INC., Tokyo.
English language translation rights in U.S.A. arranged with HAKUSENSHA, INC., Tokyo through TOHAN CORPORATION, Tokyo.

Seven Seas press and purchase enquiries can be sent to Marketing Manager Lianne Sentar at press@gomanga.com. Information regarding the distribution and purchase of digital editions is available from Digital Manager CK Russell at digital@gomanga.com.

ISBN: 978-1-63858-120-8
Printed in Canada
First Printing: February 2022
10 9 8 7 6 5 4 3 2 1

READING DIRECTIONS

This book reads from ***right to left***, Japanese style. If this is your first time reading manga, you start reading from the top right panel on each page and take it from there. If you get lost, just follow the numbered diagram here. It may seem backwards at first, but you'll get the hang of it! Have fun!!

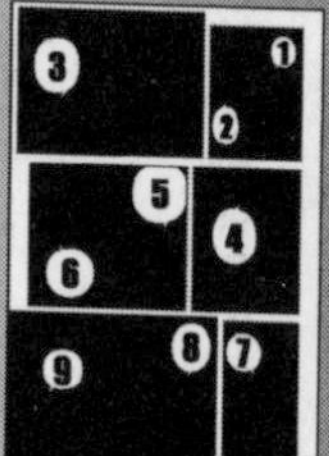
1
2
3
4
5
6
7
8
9

Follow us online: www.SevenSeasEntertainment.com